Endorsements

"We live in a pivotal moment in human history, when evidence from many sources reveals that physical death is not the end of consciousness. These sources range from near-death experiences, experienced by an estimated fifteen million Americans; to modern quantum physics, suggesting that consciousness is fundamental in shaping our world; to empirical evidence for the nonlocal nature of consciousness in research laboratories around the world. The resulting picture is that our consciousness is unbounded and unlimited in space and time, and therefore unitary, immortal, and eternal. *Dying to Die* is an important data point in this growing body of evidence, a human translation of these growing filaments of wisdom. It is an answer to the morbid message of materialism, that curse of the modern age which insists that death is the end of all we are. Janet Adkins' story is one of courage, pathos, and tenderness. It is an assertion that autonomy and privacy are a personal human right in *all* of life's phases. It expresses how the expanding vectors of human knowing point to transcendence. *Dying to Die* is hope in book form. It is a poignant reminder that human consciousness is not just precious but also unquenchable."

~ Larry Dossey, MD
Author, *One Mind: How Our Individual Mind Is
Part of a Greater Consciousness and
Why It Matters*

"*Dying to Die* is a powerful, reflective, story of love between Janet and Ron Adkins and their family. Dr. Kevorkian was a man who saw the inevitable, devastating, long suffering of Janet, as she was dying from Alzheimer's disease. Her final wish was to end her life, and Dr. Kevorkian used his *'suicide machine'* to make her wish, her reality. As a society, it's acceptable to euthanize our sick, beloved pets. When it comes to our family and loved ones, do we value and cherish them enough to consciously end their suffering and carry out their final wish? As I was dying in the hospital, due to AIDS complications, I was ready to die, and my family was devastated and heartbroken. All I needed, was to hold my precious daughter, Jeaneen, in my arms one more time, before I took my final breath of life. I had a profound near-death experience and chose to return to my daughter. The message I heard from Infinite Spirit guided me toward my new life purpose, 'Break the silence about death and dying and bring back the sacredness of life and death.'"

~ **Sharon Lund, DD** – Maui, HI
*Author, Sacred Living Sacred Dying: A Guide to Embracing
Life and Death and There Is More . . .
18 Near-Death Experiences*

"These chapters are amazing. Janet Adkins didn't only change the *right to die with dignity* movement. In her medical process of getting two physician opinions, having long-term therapy beforehand, and having to be conscious enough to push her own button, she has basically created what is now the law for assisted suicide. Very, very compelling. Love this love story."

~ **Jill Elsdon** – Retired Nurse Practitioner – Maui, HI

"What a great read. Thank you for sharing Janet and Ron's story. Sounds like they had quite the journey! What a special lady. I am grateful that she had the opportunity to die on her own terms. Shame on the press for harassing the family, it is hard enough to lose a loved one. You did a great job telling the story, it was easy to read and hard to put down! You are talented! The debate section was interesting because both sides were able to explain why they feel the way they do. I tend to lean toward personal choice, there is no need for people to suffer. It is interesting that we can stop food/water but we can't push a button. It's a sad subject; however, it needs to be talked about. Thank you for putting this out there."

~ **Cami Jones** – Nurse – San Diego, CA

∞

"OMG! I sat down to only read the introduction but was instantly spellbound, mainly because of the topic. But, what captured me most was hearing firsthand how the family reacted to the loss of Janet. This was such a publicized ordeal with most of the attention going to Dr. Kevorkian, I hadn't thought much on how the family felt. This book tells a lot of their side of the story, the actual events from their words and thoughts. The style, thought patterns, descriptive words flow . . . telling the story in a way that absolutely kept me reading. The love I feel for the family is incredible but not sappy. Their process of letting go and respecting her wishes, right or wrong, each one having to deal with all the emotion and loss; the process. My heart went out to each one of them. Knowing that this book was written in an unbiased manner, from actual events, actual interviews, helped me understand some of what they went through. It had to be so devastating to their hearts. I appreciated reading this true story about a very controversial subject! Well done!"

~ **Wendy Schell** – Retired Nurse – WA State

∞

"As a person in their mid-30's, with baby boomer parents who are in the veterinarian field, I grew up with death being a normal part of our family conversation. It was presented to me as a part of life, something to be sensitive about, but also to be responsible as a custodian to our pets in guiding them through their last transition into death. It's a gift, a responsibility, a humble obligation we go through with them. So, why wouldn't we want to help our parents with this transition, the people we love more than anything else in the world? I hope that one day my spouse and I will be able to choose this option for ourselves. If we can help our animals to leave in a quiet, peaceful manner, in their favorite bed with us surrounding them, why can't we have that for ourselves? My husband didn't grow up around this conversation; and when it came time to make the challenging decision to let our first pet go, he struggled, he let it drag on further than doctors recommended. This stirred up strong conversations between us. We, as a society, need to remove the fear of talking about death in our conversations."

~ **Virginia Bassetti** – Interior Designer – Seattle, WA

"Dying to Die brought up new thoughts about assisted suicide and stimulated conversation between me and my wife. I enjoyed the way you told Janet's story and then brought her and Ron's family and friends into the picture. Interesting how folks have different opinions on the path Janet took. I would think the book would spark a lot of conversation and thought for the general public as a whole."

~ **Tom Clevenger** – CFO, Small Business – Post Falls, ID

"OMG! I was just going to sample a bit of the writing, but once I started I couldn't stop. So very provocative! Made me think about the fact that while I was still caring for my mom, each night when I put her to bed she would ask me to kill her in her sleep, explaining that I could hold the pillow over her face. She longed to be released from life and to enter what she considered her next life, where she would be reunited with her beloved Albert. I would explain that I simply couldn't do that. In the morning when I would wake her, she would express her disappointment in me. Actually, during the final two years of her life when she did not speak or interact and lost weight down to 78 pounds, I had to admit to having had second thoughts."

~ **Beatrice Roy** – Devout Catholic
Living with Multiple Myeloma Cancer – Tacoma, WA

"Susan, Thank you for allowing me to read this. I have goosebumps, and I could not stop reading. This powerful information has been presented in such a way that I felt like I was close to Janet, the family and friends. Your detailed research shows how important human life is and how we all should have the right to *Die with Dignity*. I can't say enough about your fantastic writing!"

~ **Laura Williams** – Banker – Spokane Valley, WA

DYING TO DIE

THE JANET ADKINS STORY

A TRUE STORY OF DYING
WITH THE ASSISTANCE OF
DOCTOR KEVORKIAN

AS TOLD BY RON ADKINS
AND THE FAMILY AND FRIENDS
WHO WERE LEFT BEHIND

WRITTEN BY SUSAN CLEVENGER

DYING TO DIE: THE JANET ADKINS STORY

A True Story of Dying with the Assistance of Doctor Kevorkian

Copyright © 2019 by Susan Clevenger

ISBN: 978-1-7330393-2-1
ISBN: 1-7330393-2-5
Library of Congress Control Number: 2019906528

Concept for the Cover by: Virginia Bassetti
Cover design and text by: Crystal Green, KP Designs
Photo by Larry DeBord

Sacred Life Publishers™
SacredLife.com

Printed in the United States of America

Janet, an unknown woman from Portland, Oregon,
sent shock waves vibrating around the world
within hours of her death.

To Janet, thank you for pioneering the Right to Die
movement around the world.

To Ron, Neil, Norman, and Ronald,
thank you for having the courage to share
the intimate details of your life and personal
experiences regarding Janet's choice to die.

To family and friends, thank you for sharing your
heartfelt stories.

Contents

Introduction

This is the story about Janet Adkins, who made a choice to die after being diagnosed with early Alzheimer's disease. She was Dr. Jack Kevorkian's first patient and the only person to die by his *'suicide machine.'*

Janet was a beautiful human being who had a lust for life and a thirst to know more about the world. She hungered to know who had come before her—philosophers, poets, and musicians. More important, she was thrilled with each moment of each day and was excited to be alive. For many years, her belief had been that if a person had a terminal illness and his or her quality of life was diminishing, that person had the right to take action to exit when he or she decided. She was positive and happy right up until the end and was deliberate in choosing a way out that was truly her way. She was very pleased with the fact that she could make her own choice.

Diagnosed in 1989, Janet made the decision to end her life in 1990, which had a major and profound impact on the lives of her husband, Ron; their three sons; and their family and friends. Remembering things past has been an experience that Ron has tried to avoid but is one he has been unable to put behind him. Incomplete tasks, it is said, are remembered more than completed tasks.

It has taken Ron many years to make the decision to complete the painful task of sharing Janet's intimate life with the world. He does so with the intent that he and his family will be able to move forward with their lives and bring some empathy and understanding to the controversial subject of doctor-assisted dying.

The path that Janet chose is not the path for everyone. We as individuals with diverse backgrounds of social and religious beliefs will encounter many paths during our lifetimes. It is Ron's hope that this book will open the door to much needed conversations between family and friends to freely discuss life ending choices. If you were diagnosed with a terminal or debilitating illness would you like to have the freedom of choice to choose the path that rings true for you?

Janet's Journal—by Theodore Roethke

I learn by going where I have to go.

How This Book Came to Be . . .
A Synchronistic Encounter

The Author's Story

Why are you writing this book? I have been asked that question consistently since I first took on this project. It all started back in 1997 when I was living in Seattle, Washington. On one particular weekend, I sat down to scan the Seattle Times classified ads as I usually did every Sunday morning. My profession as an Executive Recruiter required diligence in knowing what was going on in the job market at any given moment. My eyes were drawn to an ad that read "Entrepreneurial Recruiter wanted to launch a company."

"Why not? What do I have to lose?" I thought as I dropped my resume in the mail.

Several weeks later, I found myself sitting in a reception area waiting to be called in for an interview. I was ushered into a small office with a picture window overlooking the elite city of Bellevue, Washington. That was the first time I met him. He was an attractive petite man, with distinguished gray hair and a well-trimmed mustache and goatee, dressed in a dark suit and bow tie. Sitting behind an enormous cherrywood desk much too large for the size of his body, he greeted me with a rich baritone voice and introduced himself as Ron Adkins. I was immediately put at ease by his gentle eyes and warm smile.

Perusing my resume, he glanced above the rim of his stylish black metal-framed glasses and stated matter-of-factly, "I'm the husband of Janet Adkins. Have you heard of her?" I shook my head no, and he said, "My wife received a diagnosis of early Alzheimer's and decided that she wanted to die with dignity. Janet was the first person to end her life with the help of Dr. Kevorkian's *'death machine.'* Today, June fourth, is the seventh anniversary of her death."

I admitted that I was familiar with Dr. Kevorkian, but I was not familiar with the case of Ron's wife. For the next two hours, Ron poured out the details of Janet's story. That she was still very much a part of his life was apparent to me. He talked about her as if she were right there in the room with us. I left the interview knowing much about Janet Adkins and little about the position for which I had applied.

Driving home, I knew that somehow my life had been changed with that encounter. I didn't know if I would ever see Ron again, but I felt honored that he had felt comfortable sharing the intimate details of his wife's death with a complete stranger.

The following week, I was surprised when I was invited back for a second interview. Ron explained that the position was actually working for his son, Neil, an entrepreneur. They were looking for someone to start a recruiting firm that would assist in expanding Neil's current company to other states. Because the idea of a recruiting firm was a new concept for their organization, defining the particulars of this new extension of their company would take some time before they were ready to make a commitment of a job offer.

The interview process continued over a three-month period. I eventually started my new position four months after my first meeting with Ron. When the position was presented, Neil informed me, "I'm offering you the job because my father likes you. You two will be working together as partners, and it's important that my father has a say in who will be working with him."

Like his father, Neil not only possessed charisma and charm, but he also carried an underlying sense of sadness and unrest that was visible on the surface. My experience with entrepreneurs was usually one of intense frustration. Imaginative and creative entrepreneurs were always one step ahead of their dreams, and it seemed like results never happened as fast as they should. Three months later, due to the lack of funding, my position was eliminated.

Ron and I remained friends, meeting for coffee on a regular basis. One day I pointed out that it had been eight years since the death of his wife, and I didn't understand why he had never written Janet's story. He told me that when the news first broke of Janet's death, he had been approached, on more than one occasion, to discuss publishing and movie rights. However, after careful consideration, the decision makers in the industry concluded that the financial risk was far too great for the controversial subject to appear on the big screen.

It was then that I heard the following words fall from my lips: "I'd like to write Janet's story. I think it is an important story for humanity and one that needs to be told. You're not getting any younger, and when you die the story goes with you." After thinking it over, Ron concluded that I would be the perfect person to write Janet's story. He felt that since I had very little knowledge on the subject, I would be open-minded prior to forming any conclusions. When I first started working on the project, Ron entrusted me with Janet's most precious possessions. He handed me a white foam cup containing Janet's wedding ring, a gold necklace, and a gold bracelet. Janet had gotten the cup from their motel room and had placed her jewelry in it just before she left for her engagement with Dr. Kevorkian. The jewelry had remained in that cup for eight long years, and it held all the emotions that were attached to Janet and the last days of her life.

Gradually, Ron released the remainder of Janet's treasures into my care. I received boxes of videotapes, newspaper articles, magazine articles, family photos, and Janet's journals from the early sixties and seventies. Nearly everything had sat in those boxes, untouched, for the past eight years. I was mesmerized by their contents and brought to tears when I realized that Ron had very little knowledge as to the contents of the journals because it had been too painful for him to read them and to be reminded of his previous life with Janet and the family.

I interviewed the participants, transcribed more than forty cassette tapes, viewed more than twenty television shows that carried Janet's story, researched countless books, and sifted through the contents of the boxes. I thought it odd that she had left nothing of her later years. To me, that she had been intuitive enough to know what lay ahead was remarkable. She had accepted death many, many years before and had left everything needed to write her story.

Completing the interviews with Janet's family and friends, had a chilling effect on me. There appeared to be a commonality among them. Everyone was still grieving the loss of Janet. They talked about her as if she were still there with them, as Ron had on the day I met him. Tears flowed freely as each person humbly shared his or her most intimate moments with Janet. Eight years later, they were still raw from their experience.

As their stories unraveled, I began to see the threads that were so delicately woven throughout their lives. These individuals had been drawn together to interact with one another and to live out their happiness and their sorrow.

In May 1999, my husband, Bill, and I moved to the San Diego area to escape the wetness of Seattle. In the silence of our spacious home, I received the solitude I needed to begin the writing of Janet's story. In that solitude, I gained my insights. There was much more to the story of Janet Adkins than I first realized. Before the book was complete, I would come to know Janet on an intimate level through her journals, friends, and family. And so was the beginning of Janet's story.

Upon completing the manuscript, in 2000, I excitedly sent out queries to locate an agent to represent the book to publishers. Because of the controversial nature of the subject matter, I received many rejections in the months and years that followed. After a gallant effort, the manuscript was put into the storage cellar where it would age like a fine wine for nearly twenty years. Ron continued accepting speaking engagements and fighting for Janet's cause by bringing awareness to the subject of doctor-assisted dying.

While vacationing in Maui in March 2019, I met with my friend, Sharon, who owns Sacred Life Publishing. Her area of publishing represents subjects on death and dying, which prompted me to bring up Janet's story. In our discussion, Sharon informed me that the Death with Dignity Act had recently been passed in Hawaii. To me, obviously the timing for this book had finally arrived.

PART I

Janet's Diagnosis and Choice to Die

1

Face-to-Face with the Enemy

It had been more than a decade since she left him, his sweet, sweet Janet or Jannie as he called her. Some say he was responsible for his wife's death. Some say he conspired to murder her. Others stand in judgment of his willingness to go along with what she wanted. He has been blamed for her death. Yes, he's guilty. He's guilty of loving her too much and of supporting her deliberate choice to die.

The radiance of her spirit is with him every moment of his existence. He still grieves her loss, and in his mind, he replays memories of their life together.

"You must stay for the boys," Janet told Ron. "They will need you after I'm gone."

Had it not been her wish that he stay for the boys, he would have surely joined her in her exit. He was not afraid of death, but he was terrified of losing the woman he loved.

She proceeded to pack her overnight bag with a few clothes and toiletries. "There is cold chicken in the refrigerator, and I've stocked the freezer," she said. "Your laundry is folded, and your shirts are ironed," she announced matter-of-factly.

That was just like Janet, making sure that everything was under control.

"You will be okay for the first week," she insisted.

"But what about the week after that and the months that will follow? I'll be utterly alone. How will I possibly cope without you?" Ron asked.

His mind screamed with unanswered questions. She was leaving her family and friends to embark on a new journey. For the past year, she had been at war with her darkest enemy. She had schemed and connived, determined to beat the enemy at its game. She intended to win the war because winning meant that she would at last be free. And to be free meant that she must be willing to sacrifice her life. She must die.

Early Life Together

Janet, his partner of thirty-four years, was a devoted wife and mother. She was a highly intelligent woman who taught English as a second language at Portland Community College. She had a passion for literature and philosophy and kept a journal of quotes and paragraphs from the writings of her favorite authors. She possessed a quick mind and was captivated by the challenge of winning at chess and other games. Janet loved adventure, exploring the outdoors, mountain climbing, and tennis. She climbed Mount Hood, the 11,239-foot mountain in the Cascades, and she made a special trip to Nepal to trek the Himalayas. She was also an accomplished musician, playing the piano and French horn and sang in the choir.

They were a perfect pair. Ron was also an accomplished musician, playing the French horn, string bass, flute, and guitar. He had performed professionally for more than twenty years while maintaining a successful career as a stockbroker.

The early years of their marriage had been devoted to nurturing their three sons, Neil, Norman, and Ronald. Now empty nesters, unchained from the restrictions that come with raising a young family, they were free to enjoy the remainder of their years in ways that satisfied their individual needs for expression. Most evenings were spent together sharing their love of music. After dinner, they usually poured themselves a glass of fine wine and adjourned to the loft, where Janet played the grand piano while Ron played the flute. Janet had a special gift for sight-reading music. She looked forward to her weekly trips to the library to select the piano music that she would play for the week. Because she never saw the notes for the music prior to sitting at the piano, her ability to sight-read required a sharp mind, intense concentration, and a keen awareness of her every move. Like a thief in the night, her proficiency in reading music began to diminish, subtly at first and then a little at a time until it became obvious to her that she needed new glasses. However, she found that the new glasses did nothing to correct the problem, so Janet and Ron passed off this red flag as a sign of aging even though she was a relatively young fifty-three years old.

The early signs of Janet's illness were insignificant, but as time went on, to Ron, something was obviously wrong. Janet began forgetting things on a frequent basis. She had always taken care of the bank account and was proficient at handling the bills. When she got a call from Albertson's grocery store, informing her that she had bounced a check, she was humiliated because that had never happened before. As a teacher of English as a second language, Janet had never asked for Ron's help in scoring tests or grading papers, but now she required his regular assistance. Friends and family had begun noticing things as well, but all the signs were passed off as forgetfulness or as symptoms of menopause.

Janet and Ron had been recognized, among their friends, for their intriguing dinner parties. Janet made it her specialty to invite selected people that she felt would bring a unique and interesting perspective to the conversation. She entertained herself by arranging the seating in such a way as to ignite a spark between the people sitting next to one another. The guests always lingered into the wee hours of the morning until they were finally ushered to the door. The wine flowed, the food was delicious, but the conversation was the highlight of the evening. Each guest played his or her part in creating an evening to remember. Janet always started the conversation by bringing up a subject of interest, and then she went around the table asking for everyone's opinion. Many new and interesting ideas were put out for discussion. Although most people felt comfortable voicing their point of view, others remained silent, listening intently to the conversation at hand.

On one particular evening, years before Janet's diagnosis, the dinner conversation had centered on the subject of death and dying. Janet's lifelong friend Peggy, who was Janet's elder, became uneasy about the issue and asked Janet to stop talking about death at the dinner table. This idea of death was not new to Janet. On numerous occasions over the years, both Janet and Ron had discussed the issues surrounding death among their friends. They both agreed that if they were ever to become terminally ill, it was their right to exit if their quality of life was diminished and their dignity compromised. They believed that they had the right to choose to die a *'good death.'*

Signals indicating that something might be wrong continued to present themselves on a frequent basis. Janet continually forgot where she left the car, and Ron repeatedly had to explain things to her in more detail. He was worried but wasn't sure how to approach the problem. He didn't want to alarm Janet unnecessarily by talking with her about his concerns because he thought her actions might be consistent with her age.

To Ron, that he needed to seek help eventually became evident. He called the Alzheimer's Society for information and read all the materials it provided. To his dismay, he discovered that Janet was showing multiple symptoms, which prompted him to consult with a doctor. Because Janet was already scheduled for her annual physical, Ron took the initiative and called her personal physician, who was a friend and neighbor. He advised the doctor that he had some concerns about Janet and requested he check out her mental acuity. Janet's appointment was in November, but due to a conflict in her schedule, she postponed it until after the first of the year. When Janet finally followed up with her appointment, she was very excited to report to Ron that she had received a clean bill of health. With the lapse between Ron's first call and the rescheduled appointment, the doctor evidently had forgotten about his concerns.

Upon learning that Portland's Providence Hospital had an Alzheimer's Division, Ron scheduled an appointment for Janet to meet with a specialist. The day before the appointment, he was a bundle of nerves as he mustered the courage to approach her with the subject. "Honey," he said, "you know, and I know that something is going on with your health. I've set up an appointment for you to see a doctor for medical testing."

At no time did he share his concerns about Alzheimer's. Having this conversation with Janet was extremely difficult for him because doing so meant admitting something was seriously wrong with her health. Janet agreed to see the doctor because she thought she might have a brain tumor.

The following day, prior to her appointment, they spent lunchtime at the Rose Festival Fun Center along the Willamette River. They wandered through the carnival enjoying the festivities and sampling the carnival cuisine. While eating chocolate ice cream, they were approached by two friends who were stockbrokers. They chitchatted and commented on what a wonderful day it was. Although Ron pretended to be light-hearted, he was uncomfortable with what lay ahead in the next few hours.

After arriving at the clinic, Janet was interviewed by the doctor and scheduled for diagnostic testing. She believed that she was being tested for a brain tumor. She had no idea that they were also testing for Alzheimer's disease, which is classified as a neurological condition that impairs the brain's functioning. In the early stages of the disease, symptoms can manifest as various forms of forgetfulness, much in the same way that Ron had been frequently noticing with Janet. Because Alzheimer's disease produces symptoms similar to dementia, ruling out other conditions was important. Diagnosing Alzheimer's is difficult and is a process of elimination through various methods of testing. The psychological area of testing involved puzzles and projects to determine Janet's thought processes. In her case, the testing was humiliating to her because of the numerous mistakes she made. Try as she might, she struggled to get it right because she had no idea what right was. A follow-up appointment for Janet to receive the results of her testing was scheduled for June 12, 1989.

Ron was filled with a sense of anxiety and uncertainty in anticipation of Janet's diagnosis. The preceding months had been a daily upheaval in their lives, a roller coaster of emotions mixed with fear of the unknown. He wondered if their lives would ever be the same. He would soon discover that there was no turning back the clock. Time was moving forward, and time had its own agenda, one to which they were not privy.

Beads of sweat trickled from his brow while shivers of panic traversed his spine. He hoped that Janet wouldn't notice the obvious change in his breathing pattern as they impatiently awaited the news. His guilty conscience for not having warned her about his suspicions played havoc with his mind. With clammy hands clutched together, they sat before the executioner, the one who would deliver the blow that would change their lives forever.

"Your wife has Alzheimer's," the doctor blurted out.

Those words struck like a bolt of lightning unleashed from an angry God.

"But that can't be true. I'm only fifty-three years old," Janet cried out in disbelief. "How can that be possible? Alzheimer's is for old people, and I'm in the prime of my life! There must be some mistake!"

"There is no mistake," the doctor replied in a cold flat tone. The doctor was talking to Ron as if Janet were not present in the room. "Your wife will lose her mind; she will not recognize you or anyone else, for that matter. Her bodily functions will cease to work; you will have to feed her, dress her, and change her diapers."

The delivery was so cruel, so sadistic, as if the devil himself had been sent to gouge out their hearts with a searing iron. Janet turned and looked at Ron, the partner she had trusted for so many years. The reflection in her eyes was one of sheer horror as if she had caught a glimpse of a hideous monster lurking in the night's shadows.

The long drive back to Portland was spent in awkward silence as they held back their tears. Ron felt as though he had been given a death sentence along with his wife. As their lives flashed before him, he was stricken with the realization that all their dreams of growing old together, enjoying their grandchildren, and traveling around the world had just been shattered. In one moment, their lives as they knew them had just been wiped out from under them by a vicious hurricane, which appeared to show no mercy.

Ron pulled the car off the road alongside the Columbia River. They held each other tight while they cried torrents of tears. Their shock and immediate grief were like a devastating earthquake. Their foundation had been cracked, and their structure was on the brink of collapse. There would be the aftershocks to deal with, which could go on and on with unlimited fury. From that moment on, they remained on guard in fearful anticipation of the next event, and they forever wondered if something had been lost in the rubble. Janet felt that God had played a bad joke on her. She could not imagine this tragedy was happening to her. She always held the opinion that if she had a problem, all she had to do was make up her mind to solve it, and she could overcome the challenge. Ultimately, this theory worked, but how was she to put this theory to practice when she was losing her greatest asset, her mind? She reread the book *On Death and Dying* by Elizabeth Kübler-Ross, MD, that she had read some years earlier. The book explored the five stages of death: denial, anger, bargaining, depression, and acceptance. After they discussed the book, Janet was more accepting of her fate.

∞

Janet's Journal—Sylvia Plath

*What I fear most is
the death of the imagination.*

In the eighties, they had taken some personal development courses through EST (Erhard Seminars Training), which was organized, in the early seventies, by Werner Erhard. The two weekends and one weekday-evening sessions helped them to see new possibilities for effective action in everyday matters. They were able to achieve higher standards of excellence and to think and act beyond existing limits or paradigms. One of the basic goals was to break old patterns and enable them to confront issues in their lives in a new way. Another valuable, often-stressed goal was reminding them about their mortality, asking what they would stop putting off until later if they knew that today was the last day of their life.

As a result of those teachings, Janet realized that she needed to let go of controlling anyone but herself. That included their marriage, their family, and most everything else in their lives. Once Janet's attitude changed, life became easier and much more enjoyable for everyone. But now, with death at her doorstep, controlling the remainder of her life became paramount. She was driven and determined to find a way out before the enemy beat her at her own game.

∞

Janet's Journal—*The Forest Calls Back,*
by Jack Mendelsohn

*Happiness makes me the better person,
not misery. There are people who say
that by suffering you grow best.*

I don't believe that.
Personal suffering makes me quite the opposite.
I become quite bitter and I believe
that if I suffered too much;
I would end my life.
I see no merit in excess suffering.[1]

Seeking support, Ron contacted the Hemlock Society crisis intervention line. Founded in 1980 by Derek Humphry, the Hemlock Society is the oldest and largest right-to-die organization in the United States. The Hemlock Society believes that people who wish to retain their dignity and choice at the end of life have the option of a peaceful, gentle, certain, and swift death in the company of their loved ones.

Myriam Coppens, a volunteer and family therapist, accepted the call. She carried excellent credentials. She was a marriage counselor, a family therapist, and a nurse practitioner with the Student and House Staff Health Service at the Oregon Health Sciences University in Portland, Oregon, since 1975. In March 1989, just three months prior to taking Ron's call, she founded the Portland chapter of the Hemlock Society. Her personal log reveals much about the Adkins family's concern and sadness about Janet's fate.

Notes from Myriam Coppens, Family Therapist

June 15, 1989—First call on the Hemlock Society phone recorder. (This line comes into my home). The call was from Mr. Adkins. His wife, Janet, has been diagnosed with Alzheimer's (verified by two physicians). She is in her early 50s and wants death with dignity. Can I help? After listening to him, I trusted that what I was hearing was a thought-out request from the patient (Mrs. Adkins) and I gave him the names of two

---

[1] Jack Mendelsohn, *The Forest Calls Back* (New York: Little, Brown, 1965).

doctors, who at least, would be able to actually help, as aid in dying is presently still illegal.

July 11, 1989—Son Ronald is having trouble with mom's decision. I offered family mediation. Date is set for July 15th.

July 15, 1989—Home mediation to help everyone hear about mom's decision, and for everyone a chance to talk to mom about their reactions to her wishes to find a way to die before Alzheimer's takes her mind away. She was competent and bright, yet sad about her disease. Son Norman found a recipe card for death in mom's recipe box when he was younger. It was a long-standing decision she had made in case she became terminally ill or was faced with the possibility of a degenerative disease like Alzheimer's. Mrs. Adkins, Mr. Adkins and two of their sons, Ronald and Norman, were present at that meeting. For the family I suggest they read *Last Wish* by Betty Rollin.

I have not kept track of all the phone calls I have made to say hello and see how this family was doing, but I would call (as I do with other people facing a difficult situation), now and then. Mrs. Adkins would sound fine on the phone. It was her husband who was struggling with the losses coming ahead; either through Alzheimer's or through her wish to find a way to die before Alzheimer's took over.

Myriam Coppens would later testify on April 30, 1991, before the Oregon State Health Insurance and Bioethics Committee in Salem, Oregon. She spoke to the Senate Committee with passion in support of Oregon State Senate Bill 1141 about physician aid-in-dying:

Patients with legitimate requests for physician aid-in-dying are able to lengthen their lives and regain some control over their medical situation once they know they have support in dying. Just knowing that they have a way out, seems to bring about peacefulness and a chance for deep connectedness to significant others. It gives them a chance to communicate, work through unfinished business with loved ones, say their goodbyes and their final I love you(s) while living to the fullest until the time of their death.

For family members, it takes a tremendous amount of courage to let go of their loved ones. But there is consolation in knowing that they put aside their own needs to hear those of the patient. Some health care providers, and others, fear that the patient may be subtly influenced to request physician aid-in-dying by his/her family and/or society at large. One way to rule this out would be through an immediate home visit, following the first phone request for physician aid-in-dying, as is done in Holland. This is not possible here, as physician aid-in- dying is illegal. My clinical experience with these cases, however limited, tells me that family members or loved ones generally tend to do all they can to keep the patient going, to keep him/her alive. Instead, patients tend to be influenced toward trying to hang on to life for the sake of the family.

We live in a pluralistic society. People address the issue of death and dying, the meaning of suffering, notions about dignity, love and courage in many different ways. That makes for the richness of our society and its complexity. What is right for one individual may not be right for another. For some families and patients, doing all that can be done medically is very important. But for others, that may not be true.

These differences need to be respected. There is no doubt that each situation needs individual attention, compassion and care, as would any other medical intervention.

Although Myriam made some excellent points, the bill did not pass.

2

Deliver Me from Evil

Because Janet was determined in her decision to end her life, she and Ron spent the time they had left together discussing all possibilities of her death. Her first inclination was to go to Holland. They had viewed a television program in support of doctor-assisted dying, which was quasi-legal in the Netherlands. It showed examples that honored the individual's choice to exit with a doctor's help. Ron did some research and found it was only available to citizens and residents of the Netherlands, so that option was quickly eliminated.

Janet considered many other possible options: jumping from the tenth floor of their apartment building, walking into the ocean, driving her car off a cliff, taking an overdose of pills in a hotel room, and even shooting herself. It was definitely a dilemma, and none of those methods appealed to her. The methods were too messy for those remaining, and the choices weren't foolproof. There was always a chance that things might not go as planned, and if she didn't die, she might end up in a worse condition.

Janet was obsessed with locating a doctor who might have sympathy for her situation, one who would be willing to prescribe the preferred drug, Seconal, to end her life. That was not her first choice, by any means, but at the time, it was the only method she was willing to consider. Finally, a doctor was located in the Willamette Valley, and an appointment was scheduled to meet with him. Medical records in hand, they arrived at his office on a Saturday afternoon. To Janet's immediate relief, the doctor was in complete sympathy with her decision. He stated that he would need time to think it over, but after careful consideration, the doctor declined his assistance. He said he wanted to help, but the risk was too great. He was an emergency room doctor and felt he would draw attention to himself if he prescribed a drug not normally prescribed in the emergency room.

Any hope that remained for Janet was shattered on hearing the doctor's decision. Overcome with sadness and disappointment, she felt deserted and desperate once again. She believed that the government having the authority to set rules that could restrict a doctor from helping her terminate her life was unjust. She couldn't understand how doctors could bring souls into this world, walk with them through life, and then abandon them when they reached the doorstep of death. The doctor held the key to open the door and allow the person to die with dignity, yet the door remained locked. She was passing through the dark night of the soul and had only a dim lantern to light the way. The territory was unfamiliar, and walking through her fears required a tremendous amount of courage. And so, the quest continued for Janet to find a way out while Ron carried the lantern down the dark, narrow corridor.

When friends and family learned that Janet had Alzheimer's, several sent letters expressing their condolences. Some were privy to her intent to take her life while others knew nothing about her intended demise.

To Kati, Janet's niece, she was a hero and a woman to be admired.

∞

Letter from Kati to Janet, August 14, 1989

I don't want this to be true! It's not right or fair. Why does this have to happen to you? My hero— my heroine! You're too young. You give so much to everyone around you. My heart aches. I feel guilty because I haven't seen you in years. I always figured I'd move back to the area and then we'd see each other more regularly.

I've had some time to let this sink in. I've been remembering all that I've learned from you

as a result of spending time with you and your family. My most specific memories include things like french pancakes and fighting with your sons.

But more significantly are piano, *Jonathan Livingston Seagull*, *Our Bodies Ourselves* and the guitar you all gave me. I still have that guitar and I still know how to play exactly what I knew how to play then, not much more. Tennis, challenging conversations and on and on.

Janet, I wanted you to be my mom. I remember that. I felt that way for many years. Without your influence I wonder if I would have discovered so many talents in myself. I wonder if the philosopher in me would have been so encouraged. Whenever I left your house, I felt so potent—like anything was possible.

One of my favorite interview questions was "Who is your hero?" I explained that I had two, my Aunt Alice and my Aunt Janet. You are pioneers I would say. Women willing to take risks, take control, and take responsibility for your lives.

I remember reading *Our Bodies Ourselves* in your bedroom and you and mom coming in to talk about things. You wanted me to be aware and to have access to information and to know about choices. We always had these amazing and challenging conversations. I felt like a grown up. I loved having the support of you and your family, at plays especially. I guess music and theater were a big part of what we all shared. Remember all of our plays and *Carol Burnett Shows?* Everything was a stage for us.

Janet, so much of my favorite parts of myself is a direct result of your influence. I, of course, have always known this. Have I been any good at telling you? I'm so mad it takes you facing illness for me to write you, to tell you the truth about the effect you've had on my life. I just hope I can be an 'Aunt Janet' to someone. You've had the effect of another parent.

There's more I want to say. I want to hug you and I want you to meet Bill. He's my life's mate in a big way. Is there a good weekend anytime in the next month when we can see you? Just for lunch, dinner, tennis, or whatever? We have other friends in Portland we can stay with. Mom said she'd come when we were in town and we could all spend some time together. If this doesn't sound good, I'll understand. But, if you need to hear my loving words in person as much as I'd like to share them, let me know! I love you Janet. And Ron, a big hug to you too. I can't wait to speak with you. Bill and I are planning to start a family soon. We'd love to hear your thoughts on that.

Janet quietly accepted the thoughts of others, but she didn't waiver from the path to her chosen destination. Together, she and Ron continued to search for an acceptable way to escape from the totally undignified life that was creeping closer every day.

The next opportunity presented itself; a trip to Hong Kong that came as a result of Ron's business dealings. Knowing their time together was short, they decided to take their last overseas trip together and travel first class. Ron knew that he could legally obtain drugs in Hong Kong without a prescription, so he went to a drug store in the city and asked the pharmacist for Seconal, stating that he was having trouble sleeping. The pharmacist filled the order, giving him a much stronger drug than the one he requested. Ron informed his business associate about the drugs he had obtained and learned that customs authorities had been cracking down on drugs. When it came time to board their next flight to Hawaii, he became concerned that the drugs might create a problem as he didn't have a prescription. Because of his anxiety, he decided it wasn't worth the risk and flushed the drugs down the toilet. As it so happened, when they arrived in

Hawaii, they were detained while their luggage and personal belongings were searched with a fine-toothed comb. Every item was literally dumped from their luggage and laid out for all to see. When the authorities came across a gold necklace that Ron had given Janet many years before, they were insistent that he admit to having purchased it in Hong Kong. Paranoid as he was, to him, the authorities seemed to have been tipped off and were searching for drugs in order to detain them on an illegal offense.

Once home, they resumed their quest to locate a doctor. They believed their search was complete when they were finally referred to a doctor who agreed with the idea of assisting terminally ill patients. Janet's medical records from the two previous doctors who had diagnosed her were passed on to the new doctor for his review. They met with him for an initial visit, and Janet's hopes were again deflated when the doctor advised them that he needed to think it over. The waiting was unbearable; the torture, so inhumane. The anxiety was building like an active volcano ready to spew its ash without warning. Janet wondered if she would be successful in planning her exit or if she would reach a point of exhaustion and give in to any conceivable method to take her life.

Janet's fears were put to rest when the second visit proved successful, and the doctor agreed that he would assist her by prescribing the necessary dose of drugs. The process took many visits because the drug had to be prescribed over time to accumulate the necessary quantity to cause death. With Janet's knowing that she now had a way out, her anxiety turned to relief.

Able to finally relax, Janet began enjoying life again. Taking time to spend with friends and family was important, and for Janet, time was of the essence. To her, whether everyone knew about her plan to end her life wasn't necessary, but in her own mind, it was time for her to say her goodbyes. She was able to do this in a subtle way by just getting together with a friend or family member for an afternoon or evening outing.

∞

Letter to Janet and Ron from their dear friend Susan, August 16, 1989

Last week's events were filled with so many moments to treasure. There were times of tension, excitement, sadness, laughter, elation, frustration, poignancy, and a real combination of so many feelings in such a short time frame. There is so much I want to share with you after seeing you both. We are all overwhelmed by the prognosis you have been forced to deal with. This Alzheimer's disease must be one of life's greatest challenges to confront. It's impossible to understand what both of you have gone through these last few months.

Knowing how supportive you both have been of each other as long as I have known you made me realize how involved you are, Ron, in Janet's illness. It affects you deeply to the core, but what a help and support. I know you will continue to be there for her.

Carroll shared with me some information that helped me understand what's happening with you, Janet. Did you know that after Carroll heard about you, Janet, she immediately called Virginia Mason Hospital to have them send information about Alzheimer's? She also talked to her pastor, which was a great source of strength for her. We have talked and talked. What a special friendship you folks have shared for so many years. It spans decades and countries and kids.

My, oh my, what memories. I too recall with fondness the times spent together. What I appreciate so much about you both is your curiosity and love of life. Janet, some of your experiences in life are so unique, like climbing mountains in Nepal, your trips to France and other parts of the world, your interest in learning and taking classes, your involvement with tennis. You have embraced life so richly. That kind of spirit will always be one of the things I have so admired about you, Janet. And you too, Ron, an endless search in living life fully.

After being with you for that lovely lunch I have seen another side of you that I will cherish. Your ability to still laugh and be involved with other's lives on top of what you are dealing with gives you a grace that perhaps transcends understanding. You are both very special people and I'm so glad we had a chance to spend precious time together. Know that you are in our thoughts daily. I will send you the book *Love, Medicine and Miracles*, which we talked about.

The next step in Janet's death plan was to select a motel and devise a scheme. Together, Ron and Janet decided that he would go with her to the motel room and exit the premise after she had taken the pills. It seemed like a good idea at the time, but Janet became concerned that the authorities might arrest Ron if anyone saw him there. She was also concerned about being left alone after taking the pills in the event she might vomit them up and was not successful in her attempt to end her life. To Janet, that would have been worse than anything she could imagine. She now had a way out, but she was still very uneasy with the idea that something might go wrong.

Notes from Myriam Coppens, Family Therapist

October 12, 1989—Phone call from Mr. Adkins. Needs to talk. We (Hemlock Chapter Coordinators) had received notice by the central Hemlock office in Eugene, not to see any potential aid-in-dying persons in their homes.

We set up an appointment for an informal talk to meet at the Carnival Restaurant on Saturday, October 14, 1989.

October 14, 1989—Ron speaks of being scared. Never been alone. How will he do this? He does not want to lose Janet, but he feels he has no option other than to follow the path she has chosen; to respect her wishes. November 1, 1989, was the first date Janet had set to die, but it was postponed by request of the children who wanted her to at least try to find treatment for her Alzheimer's.

October 29, 1989—Janet read about Dr. Jack Kevorkian in a magazine. She is very excited by it.

3

An Ideal Candidate

While reading *Newsweek Magazine*, Janet happened to notice a very small article about Dr. Jack Kevorkian, a pathologist in Michigan who was interested in assisting the terminally ill in ending their lives. Janet became ecstatic after reading the article about Dr. Kevorkian's *'death machine'* and asked Ron to get in touch with him.

> **Plug it into a wall socket, punch it into your arm, press a button and five minutes later, you're dead. It's painless, portable and legal. Kevorkian is certain it would work, if only someone would give it a whirl. Applications are being accepted.**
>
> **Oppressed by a fatal disease, a severe handicap, a crippling deformity? Show him proper, compelling medical evidence that you should die, and Dr. Jack Kevorkian will help you kill yourself, free of charge.[1]**

Little was known about Dr. Kevorkian at that time, but his obsession with relieving pain and suffering would soon make worldwide headlines. Born on May 28, 1928, in Pontiac, Michigan, to parents of Armenian descent, Dr. Kevorkian was one of three children. He was brilliant in school and obtained both his bachelor's and medical degrees from the University of Michigan in just seven years. A man of high intelligence, Dr. Kevorkian had been the top medical student at the University of Michigan in the early fifties.

---

[1] "In Royal Oak: The Death Machine," Detroit Free Press Magazine, March 18, 1990, 24.

After graduation, he took a position at Pontiac General Hospital before moving on to Saratoga General Hospital, in Detroit, as the chief of pathology. An internationally accredited medical scholar, Dr. Kevorkian had published numerous papers in indexed journals on diverse topics including the ethics and practice of euthanasia. Unlike his conventional parents, Dr. Kevorkian was a crusader for causes, and he had always challenged conventional thinking and philosophical viewpoints. He was not afraid to go where other men feared to tread. He was often the center of heated debates, exhibiting a fearless courage in his quick defense of outlandish taboos.

Dr. Kevorkian's father died from a heart attack when Dr. Kevorkian was thirty-three years old, and his mother died a painful death from bone cancer several years later. By the time Dr. Kevorkian became interested in assisted suicide, his two sisters had secretly asked their mother's doctor to help her die. The doctor had refused, which explains why the two sisters would later agree to assist Dr. Kevorkian with Janet's death.

As a medical intern, Dr. Kevorkian was exposed to explicit suffering that branded an impression on his soul that would surely pass with him to the next dimension. His description of a dying patient paints a vivid picture of Dr. Kevorkian's reality:

> **The patient was a helplessly immobile woman of middle age, her entire body jaundiced to an intense yellow-brown, skin stretched paper-thin over a fluid-filled abdomen swollen to four or five times normal size. The rest of her was an emaciated skeleton: sagging, discolored skin covered her bones like a cheap, wrinkled frock. The poor wretch stared up at me with yellow eyeballs sunken in their withering sockets. Her yellow teeth were ringed by chapping and parched lips to form an involuntary, almost sardonic smile of death. It seemed as though she was pleading for help and death at the same time. Out of sheer empathy alone I could have helped her die with satisfaction. From that moment on, I was sure that doctor-assisted**

euthanasia and suicide are and always were ethical, no matter what anyone says or thinks.[2]

Dr. Kevorkian was committed to his cause. At the age of sixty-two, he invented a device that propelled him to national and international notoriety. The invention, which he dubbed *'The Mercitron,'* was a simple device that cost him less than $30 to build. It was constructed from various odds and ends that Dr. Kevorkian had scavenged from local flea markets. *The Mercitron'* was rigged to hold three bottles of solution that would be injected into the patient's arm via an intravenous (IV) drip. With the *'suicide machine,'* it was a simple process that would end life quickly and painlessly at the flick of a switch. Dr. Kevorkian would insert a needle into the patient's arm to start the IV saline drip from the first bottle. When ready to exit, the patient was instructed to push a button that would activate a mechanism that would infuse a large dose of thiopental from the second bottle. Sixty seconds later, the timer would release a rapid infusion of concentrated potassium chloride solution from the third bottle that would flow concurrently with the thiopental through the same IV needle. Within twenty to thirty seconds, the patient would be suspended in a deep coma, followed by a painless heart attack. If all went as planned, the patient would be dead within three to six minutes after activating the machine.

Dr. Kevorkian had wanted to test his machine on an animal scheduled to be put down at a local animal shelter; however, he was unsuccessful in obtaining clearance to perform this type of experiment. Although Janet had explicitly made it known to her family that she didn't want to be anyone's experiment, just ten months later, she would be the first and only person to ever test his machine. Always at the forefront of new ideas and quick to challenge philosophical thinking, Janet would turn out to be an ideal candidate in more ways than one.

At Janet's request, Ron promptly located Dr. Kevorkian, who later reported that "Ron Adkins's rich, baritone, matter-of-fact voice was tinged with a bit of expectant anxiety as he calmly explained the

---

[2] Jack Kevorkian, Prescription Medicide: The Goodness of Planned Death (Amherst, NY: Prometheus Books, 1991), 188.

tragic situation of his beloved wife."[3] Excited by the possibility of an immediate candidate, Dr. Kevorkian requested more information before making his final decision. Once again, Ron gathered all of Janet's medical records from all the doctors she had consulted with and shipped them off to Dr. Kevorkian.

Upon complete review of Janet's medical records, and after further discussion with Janet, Dr. Kevorkian determined that she was of sound mind. Janet had been successful in convincing Dr. Kevorkian that she was determined to end her life; he, in turn, committed himself to assist with her exit. Janet was elated with the outcome of the conversation and felt confident that Dr. Kevorkian would be there to take care of any problems that might arise.

∞

Janet's Journal—*The Long Lavender Look*, by John MacDonald

I am a grown-up making choices,
And sufficiently grown up to live
with the choices I make.

Therapy sessions with Myriam Coppens continued for the entire year, until the time that Janet ended her life. These sessions were meant to help their family understand Janet's choice, deal with their feelings about doctor-assisted dying, and bring closure on the personal issues between the family members. Ron supported Janet's decision, as did their middle son, Norman, who was twenty-nine. Ronald Jr., their youngest son, who was twenty-six, needed time to process the information whereas their oldest son, Neil, who was thirty-two, was extremely uncomfortable with his mother's decision because of his strong Christian beliefs.

In support of Neil's position, a family member attempted to influence Janet's decision by sharing her strong Christian belief and

---

[3] Kevorkian, Prescription Medicide, 221.

26

the affect that Janet's decision would have on the lives of her son Neil; his wife, Heidi; and her grandson, Justin.

Letter from a friend, October 24, 1989

Dear Janet,

My heart has been burdened for you, and so I thought I would write you a letter. You are such an important person in the lives of my family, and me. But of course, you will always be important to the Lord.

He loves you so much more than I could even describe. I'm sure this could be difficult to understand in the face of a disease like Alzheimer's. But Jesus is the source of life for everyone. He is our comfort and our hope. I remember this summer when I was struggling for air with my pneumonia. He was my hope and he can be your hope, too. His love can give you the courage to face this disease instead of running away by taking your life.

"By this the love of God was manifested in us that God sent his only begotten son into the world so that we might live through him." (I John 4:9).

We can live with Jesus inside us, giving us his wisdom and love and courage by just asking him into our heart. I don't know where you are in relationship to Jesus, but I just want to encourage you to trust him.

In revelations it says, "Behold I stand at the door and knock; if any one hears my voice and opens the door I will come in to him and will dine with him and he with me."

I really like knowing that God wants the kind of intimacy with me that I find with good friends around the dinner table. And I like knowing he is always available. I also appreciate the fact that he wants to know all of my feelings. I can pour out my heart to him and know he really cares.

Peter says, "Humble yourselves, therefore under the mighty hand of God, that he may exalt you at the proper time, casting all your anxiety upon him because he cares for you."

In the Psalms it says, "God keeps track of every tear from my eye." It's so good to be able to call upon him as his child.

"Before I go, I want to give you my prayers for you that the God of our Lord Jesus Christ, the Father of glory, may give to you a spirit of wisdom and of revelation in the knowledge of him. I pray that the eyes of your heart may be enlightened so that you may know the hope of his calling, the riches of the glory of his inheritance in the saints, the surpassing greatness of his power toward us who believe." (Ephesians).

P.S. Many people are praying for you. Also, if you have any questions, please feel free to call me.

When Janet was diagnosed with Alzheimer's, the doctor had made mention of an Alzheimer's research program. The research was focused on developing a method to slow down the disease. When this was brought to Janet's attention, she objected to being in the program. Meanwhile, Neil heard an advertisement on the radio for a study being done at the University of Washington Medical School on Alzheimer's disease. He placed a call to a doctor heading up the program and discussed Janet's condition. The doctor believed Janet would qualify for the program, so he granted an invitation.

Once again, the medical records were shipped to yet another doctor. The program involved the testing of a drug called Tacrine, or THA. This drug would not cure the disease, nor would it stop the disease, but it had been known to slow the disease down in certain individuals. Janet had been adamant that she did not want to be a guinea pig in someone's research study. Neil and Ronald, Jr. became upset with their mother because she had taught them that there wasn't anything they could not accomplish if they put their minds to it. Ironically, however, she was losing her mind, so she didn't have a mind to put to it. To Ronald Jr. and Neil, Janet appeared to be copping out by not giving it a try. The debate went on for two weeks while Ron implored Janet to enroll in the program for the boys.

Note from Myriam Coppens, Family Therapist

December 20, 1989—Janet to go through experimental treatments in Seattle.

Janet finally agreed to take part in the program and enrolled as a participant in the study in January of 1990. Ron drove Janet back and forth from Portland to Seattle every Thursday for three months. Her drug therapy consisted of a daily dose of THA, which carried a restriction from taking any other medications during the program.

Dr. Kevorkian was put on notice that Janet was participating in an experimental drug program and concurred: "Janet should enroll in the program because any candidate for 'The Mercitron' must have exhausted every potentially beneficial medical intervention, no matter how remotely promising."[4]

As time went on, there was not the slightest noticeable improvement, and Janet's condition continued to worsen.

In March, they received a call from the doctor heading up the program advising the family to schedule an appointment to meet with him in his office. Janet and Ron, along with their three sons, huddled together to receive the results of the program. The doctor was sympathetic as he informed the family that the drug was not working. Although Ron already had his suspicions, having that fact confirmed by the medical professional was a dreadful event for their family. The death sentence had been delivered for the second time, and whatever hope they had left quickly diminished as they faced the reality that

---

[4] Kevorkian, Prescription Medicide, 222.

Janet intended to deliver herself from the evil enemy. During their drive back home, Ron's mind was bombarded with thoughts of his own death. He thought about driving the car off the road into the pillar that rested between the two lanes. He had no idea how he could go on without his beloved Janet and decided that he would most likely join her in her exit. They had shared so much life together, and he was certain that he was willing to share death with her as well.

Their lives as they once knew them had disappeared into the abyss, replaced with darkness and horror. He felt helpless in the struggle to save his wife from this disease. He had no idea how to battle against this unfamiliar, invasive enemy. How was he to defend the woman he loved and adored for more than thirty years against a disease that had no cure? Janet was slipping away a little bit each day, and he was defenseless against this evil demon courting his beloved wife. The demon was cunning and conniving and would stop at nothing until he had gained complete control of Janet's body and mind.

Ron always believed that he would be the first one to exit, but now with the inevitable dread on their doorstep, he was unable to imagine life without Janet. As the man of the house, his duty and responsibility had been to provide financially for his family. The exciting world of finance was something he knew and understood. But he was helpless when it came to his daily needs as he had become dependent on Janet.

Although she was never elaborate in the kitchen, Janet always made sure that her family was fed a well-balanced diet. She planned their social calendar well in advance and was careful to include both dinner parties and cultural events with family, relatives, and friends. She took great pleasure in performing her daily ritual of selecting Ron's suit, shirt, and tie, which was always laid out neatly on the bed. Dressing for his stock market clientele, he was viewed as a fashionable dresser whose closet was filled from end to end with the most exquisite attire. He had expensive tastes and purchased only the highest-quality clothes. On the contrary, Janet's closet contained a very modest wardrobe that was simple and ordinary. She had never been interested in fashion and had no desire to purchase stylish clothes for herself. She was content to wear the same outfits, day after day, until they were worn and in need of replacement.

To an outsider, this pair might be considered a mismatch. But intellectually, Janet was an excellent match for Ron, and he found her exciting, stimulating, and intriguing. As the year passed, their relationship which Ron had come to take for granted was fading as was the woman he worshiped and had placed on a pedestal.

When their daughter-in-law Heidi learned that Ron was considering exiting with Janet, she became extremely upset. She was adamant that it would be a very bad choice. Ron had his children and grandchildren to think about. The thought of losing Janet was bad enough, but to lose both of them was inconceivable. Janet also expressed her dissatisfaction as well. As far as she was concerned, Ron needed to stay for the grandchildren and build a new life for himself. The more Ron thought about it, the more he knew that Heidi and Janet were right. Even though he loved Janet and would have liked to exit with her, he knew he had to stay for the ones that would be left behind.

Note from Myriam Coppens, Family Therapist

March 17, 1990—Treatments in Seattle stopped. Janet wants to work with Doctor Kevorkian. Physician told her she had to be rational for him to help her with her request.

Immediately after Janet was released from the Alzheimer's study, in April 1990, she was back in contact with Dr. Kevorkian to set the stage for her final exit. This was the second-most significant event in her existence. She had made a contract with death, and she intended to keep the ceremony simple and to the point. She would say her goodbyes and plan her memorial service, a simple wake, and that would be the end of it. It never occurred to the family that Janet, an unknown woman from Portland, was about to send out a shock wave vibrating around the world within hours of her death.

"I was obliged to scrutinize Janet's clinical records and to consult with her personal doctor," Dr. Kevorkian reported.[5]

---

[5] Kevorkian, Prescription Medicide, 225.

When Dr. Kevorkian contacted the attending physician, he was met with opposition to Janet's decision to end her life. "It is totally inappropriate of you, Dr. Kevorkian, to assist in Janet's suicide because she has several more years of an enjoyable life."[6]

The doctor's believed that Janet would remain mentally competent for at least another year with time to enjoy her family. That may well have been the case, but Janet was not about to risk losing her mind in that year.

"She dreaded what would have come. I would too," said Dr. Kevorkian. "I don't want to die of Alzheimer's, smeared with my own urine and feces, not knowing who I am. Come on!"[7]

Based on Ron's description of Janet's condition, Dr. Kevorkian concluded that her doctor's opinion was wrong and that time was of the essence. Because Janet's condition was deteriorating and nothing else would arrest it, he decided to accept her as his first candidate: "She is a qualified candidate, justifiable candidate if not 'ideal' . . . ."[8]

Note from Myriam Coppens, Family Therapist

March 26, 1990—Office visit by request of Mr. Adkins. Planning to go to Michigan, and get assistance with aid-in-dying from Doctor Kevorkian. Mr. Adkins is very sad, experiencing anticipatory grief; also sad about her deterioration. Mrs. Adkins, over the phone, appears as determined as ever, always sounding up. This does not appear unusual to me, as it had been reported that people going through this process and having found the help they will need to die, actually feel tremendous relief and joy.

To Dr. Kevorkian, that he was Janet's only hope for deliverance from the deadly disease that was invading her brain was evident. Dr. Kevorkian made a vow to assist Janet in taking her life, and he

---

[6] Interview with Ron Adkins.

[7] Interview with Ron Adkins.

[8] Kevorkian, *Prescription Medicide*, 222.

immediately went about the task of locating a facility where he could enact the ceremonial exit. It turned out to be a major obstacle once he explained that he intended to assist in a suicide for an out-of-state guest. He diligently approached family, friends, motels, funeral homes, churches, rental offices, buildings, clinics, and doctors' offices. He even considered renting an emergency ambulance. He was met with sympathy for his cause, but no one was willing to risk the negative publicity or the damage it might do to his or her business. Finally, a friend of Dr. Kevorkian came forward and offered his home.

The first choice of dates was Memorial Day. However, Dr. Kevorkian was concerned that the police would be short-handed that day, and he wanted to be certain that there would be someone sent out to investigate what he was sure would be termed a crime. Everyone agreed that Monday, June 4, 1990, was the date of choice. It was agreed that Janet and Ron would travel the two thousand miles from Portland, Oregon, to Detroit, Michigan, for the purpose of ending Janet's life. Ron purchased the plane tickets and bought Janet a round-trip ticket giving her the option to change her mind at any time.

Notes from Myriam Coppens, Family Therapist

April, 25, 1990—Office visit. Mr. Adkins is depressed. The actual date has been set up. It will be the first Monday in June 1990. Carroll (an old family friend) will accompany them to Michigan. Talked again with Janet. Feeling very fine. My concern is with Mr. Adkins.

April 27, 1990—Reading materials sent to Mr. Adkins on grieving. Suggested he also get a book called *The Grieving Time*.[9]

[9] Anne M. Brooks, *The Grieving Time: A Year's Account of Recovering from Loss* (New York: Harmony Books, 1982).

Two weeks prior to the event, Ron received a call from Dr. Kevorkian advising him that a problem had arose. The friend who had offered the house had now declined his offer after being advised, by a medical friend, that the risk was too great. All possibilities had been exhausted. As Dr. Kevorkian later reported on national television, *"There was no room at the Inn."*[10] He called back and advised Janet that he had only one alternative left; to use his old 1968 Volkswagen van. It was old and run-down, not a pretty sight, but he was willing to set up a little bed and make it comfortable for Janet. The plan was to reserve a spot at a public camping ground where he could hook up to electricity, which he needed to run the machine and the electrocardiogram to monitor the heart. Because this was the only option available, he would understand if Janet didn't want to do it. She didn't hesitate in her decision. Her mind had already been made up, and she was adamant at keeping her appointment with death. Janet didn't care where it took place; she only cared how it was carried out. She always had a love affair with Volkswagens, so using Dr. Kevorkian's van seemed like the perfect solution under the circumstances.

Notes from Myriam Coppens, Family Therapist

May 23, 1990—Office visit. Mr. Adkins states June 4th will be the actual date. June 10th will be her memorial service. Everything seems unreal.

May 29, 1990—Office visit with Ronald. Then jointly with Mr. and Mrs. Adkins. The session is mostly between mom and son. Janet is very appropriate and clearly competent.

Same day, phone call from Mr. Adkins. Norman, another son, would like to come in with mom.

Two-hour office visit with Norman and Janet. Very moving, very appropriate. This will

---

[10] Jack Kevorkian, repeated statement to media.

be my last visit with Janet. I leave for vacation May 30th till June 20th to go to Europe.

I felt very fortunate to have known her and her family. So courageous to let her go as she wished.

Prior to departing for Michigan, Janet and Ron met for two hours with the Unitarian minister, making final arrangements for Janet's memorial service. The Unitarian Church supported Janet's decision in making her personal choice.

"Do you have any regrets, Janet?" the minister inquired.

With an expressed feeling of contentment, she responded, "No. I've lived my life to the fullest."

And she had. She was honest with herself, and she made decisions that were in tune with her beliefs. She was thirsty for life and always found new things to be excited about. She didn't wait and put things off until retirement. Janet was in the now, and she really was resolute with her decision. The only disappointments she had were not seeing her grandchildren grow up and not having a granddaughter whom she could take to Europe and introduce to the European culture.

The immediate family spent their last days together over Memorial Day weekend. Janet invited the boys to the apartment where they each took a turn at the piano playing their favorite tunes. Together, they watched family slides of their special moments over the years. Ironically, several years prior, Janet had taken the time to organize and label several hundred slides. This had been a huge undertaking for her, but one she was dedicated to completing. At that time, Ron had been puzzled by this project because this was out of character for Janet. Perhaps, on an unconscious level, she knew what lay ahead. As the family reminisced over days gone by, they laughed and they cried as memories continued to bubble to the surface knowing full well that those slides summed up their previous years as the Adkins family. Their family, as they knew it, would never be the same again. They videotaped Janet as she addressed all three of her grandsons, expressing her love and best wishes for their future.

The following day, they gathered as a family for their last supper at Norman's house. Tami Jo, Norman's girlfriend at that time who later became his wife, prepared the meal while everyone tried to make light conversation. When it came time for Neil to leave, everyone stood in the parking lot crying and hugging and saying his or her last goodbyes. It was difficult for everyone, but especially for Neil because he was adamantly opposed to his mother's decision. As the evening came to a close, Ron's mind was bombarded with thoughts of Janet and the role that she had chosen with Dr. Kevorkian as the *'ideal candidate.'*

4

That's What Friends Are For

A unique and special bond is created through trust that comes naturally to women. That bond carries the responsibility of keeping each other's deepest secrets. Women tend to share their thoughts and feelings when they feel safe—safe in knowing that they will receive understanding rather than judgment. It takes time to build a deep and trusting relationship, but once the trust has been proved, the friendship will endure and withstand the test of time.

Carroll and Janet had a friendship like this that lasted more than thirty years. Having met in France during their early married life, they continued corresponding by mail and getting together on occasion for holidays and birthdays. The letters Carroll received from Janet were always written from the depths of Janet's heart and soul. Speaking of the death of one of her favorite people, Janet wrote, "Oh Carroll, why do beautiful souls have to die? We have such need of them here."

As close as they had been over the years, Janet withheld the information concerning her illness until put on the spot. When Janet failed to appear for Carroll's daughter's wedding, Carroll became concerned and called her on July 30, 1989.

Realizing that she had missed a very special event in Carroll's life, Janet apologized. "I'm sorry I didn't call, but I've been dealing with some personal difficulties. I don't know how to tell you this, but I have Alzheimer's."

Carroll reacted as though someone had punched her in the stomach. Holding the phone in one hand and clutching her stomach with the other hand, she fought to hold back the tears. "That can't be true," she blurted out.

"It's all right, Carroll; I'm going to get out," Janet exclaimed.

That came as a double shock to Carroll. She had always known that Janet believed that if she became terminally ill, dying was okay. She knew in no uncertain terms that Janet meant what she said. Janet had always been very determined in all areas of her life. Once she formed an opinion, she wanted everyone to see her point of view. Not only see it but believe it as well.

Carroll was stunned and dazed as she tried to grasp what Janet had just revealed to her. It didn't make any sense. It couldn't possibly be true, she thought in disbelief as she hung up the phone. Stumbling down the stairs, she stood outside her husband's office trying to regain her composure. Shaking uncontrollably, with tears streaming down her cheeks, she staggered into her husband's home office.

"The children are okay," she assured her spouse, not wanting him to think that something tragic had befallen one of their own. Forcing the words from her lips, she painted the picture of her best friend's demise.

The following day, she contacted several close friends from her church and called them together for support. She discussed the situation not only with her friends but also with the pastor of her church. One of her friends stated that he could not imagine losing his dignity. If he had gotten the same diagnosis, he would have taken his wife to the beach for a picnic, said his goodbyes, and walked out into the ocean.

The next week Carroll and her husband, Dick, made the three-hour drive from Seattle to Portland to spend time with Janet and Ron. She expected to spend the week comforting her grieving friend but was shocked to see that Janet had her emotions in check. That she had accepted her situation and was at peace with her decision was obvious. She was determined not to go on living to the end of her disease, and she was not going to let it take her. Carroll observed that Janet had pasted the phone number to Ron's office up on the wall in the kitchen and that she had trouble following recipes. She frequently looked to Ron to finish her sentences. But, overall, Janet seemed to be enjoying every minute she had left and showed no signs of depression or distress.

During their drive to the restaurant to have lunch, Carroll noticed that Janet didn't wear a seatbelt, nor did she lock the car door when she got out. When Carroll questioned her about it, Janet responded, "Why?" It was apparent that Janet had let go of what she considered to be trivial concerns.

Janet shared with Carroll the details of her plan to exit. It was way out of Carroll's comfort zone, and her belief system, to think that Janet would actually want to go through with it. Carroll asked a lot of questions to try to understand Janet's thinking.

"Don't you trust us to take care of you? Don't you trust that there might be a cure?" she asked.

Janet was adamant that she didn't want to burden her family and friends, and there was no time to wait around for a cure that might never come. She felt that she was running out of time, and she was determined to go ahead with her plans.

Later, Janet and Ron went to visit Carroll and Dick in Seattle. It was decided that they would take a ferryboat ride and eat lunch in Poulsbo, a town founded by a Norwegian, on the Olympic Peninsula. On the return trip while waiting in line for the ferry, Janet fell asleep in the car while Dick was reading the paper. Carroll and Ron decided it would be a good time to exit the car and discuss Janet's situation over a beer.

"We need to meet with Dr. Kevorkian soon before Janet loses her ability to make a clear-headed decision. Janet doesn't want me to go with her alone to meet with Dr. Kevorkian, and she doesn't want any of the boys to go," Ron explained to Carroll.

Without thinking, Carroll heard the words spilling from her lips. She described it as an out-of-body experience where she was looking down on the situation and watching herself speak. "I'll go with you," she told Ron reassuringly.

She was startled by her own commitment, as this was not something about which she had given any prior thought. The words had just exploded from somewhere deep within her. On the long drive home, she became concerned about her commitment.

The next week, Carroll received a card from Janet expressing her happiness that she would be joining them on their trip to Michigan:

Janet's Letter to Carroll and Dick
March 27, 1990

It was so great being with you both, and what lovely weather. And it's still here this morning. You are both great cooks and we enjoyed being pampered. I can't tell you how much it means to me, knowing that you will come with me to Michigan. I think it would be too hard for the boys.

I'm loving you, Janet.

Feeling locked in, Carroll was certain she'd have a way out when she discussed the plan with Dick. She expected Dick to tell her she couldn't go and that he wasn't about to put up with it. Her fears were intensified when Dick responded, "That's good. I think you should go. If you don't go, I probably will have to go myself."

"I don't want to do this. Let this cup pass from me," Carroll prayed to God.

Worried sick, she made an appointment to talk with her church pastor about her concerns. She was surprised to find that he offered her comfort and complete understanding of the situation. The entire session was focused on her and never on Janet's death. He told her that she could only go so far. She could walk with her friend, and then she had to let her friend go. After the meeting, she felt a sense of release and acceptance of Janet's journey.

Once she put her fears to rest, she discovered a personal conflict. Her daughter was due to have her first child in early May. Janet offered to postpone her death to the first part of June so that Carroll could be present at the birth of her grandchild. It was just like Janet, always considering other people first and making sure that everyone was happy. She wanted Carroll to be with her daughter, but she still wanted Carroll to accompany her to Detroit. It was to be an eventful year for Carroll. She had received invitations from two of the most special women in her life: an invitation to a birth and an invitation to a death, back to back. The irony of it all played havoc on her mind.

Who would believe it? How could she explain it? Her mind could not make sense of it all. Holding her precious grandbaby in her arms, she cried tears of joy. But the tears of joy were overshadowed with tears of grief as she contemplated the next scene that was about to play out in her life.

5

Interview with Doctor Death

Prior to Janet's death, she and Ron had discussed his living arrangements. He was adamant that he wanted to find another apartment immediately. While their current apartment was listed for rent, a prospective renter came to view it. During the course of the conversation, they discovered that the man was a tennis player. Feeling comfortable in their presence, the man asked if he could share a couple of jokes. Ron was an avid fan of good jokes and was always open to hearing new ones.

"The good thing about Alzheimer's is that you can hide your own Easter eggs," the man chuckled.

Janet and Ron both looked at each other and burst out laughing. That sent a signal to the man that he was safe to deliver the second joke.

"A good thing about Alzheimer's is that you can buy your own Christmas presents," the man roared.

By now, Janet and Ron were laughing hysterically with tears streaming down their cheeks. They thought it ironic that the stranger had come up with two Alzheimer's jokes. They were certain he wouldn't think it was so funny if he knew what Janet was facing.

The man had no way of knowing that Janet had Alzheimer's, and to him, the jokes were perfectly appropriate. It certainly cheered them up that day. Janet's ability to face her disease with humor helped Ron make the decision to stay in their current apartment for the time being.

When it came time to leave for Michigan, Norman arrived at the apartment and took Janet's bag. The apartment was on the tenth floor of a classic apartment complex in Portland. Each floor had long stretching halls that were set up similar to a cross. Ron used to make a joke that they were living in that place for *'the long haul.'* Ironically, Ron was closing the door on his life with Janet, and nothing about it was funny. As he walked down that long hall, he watched Janet and Norman walking ahead of him, two people whom he loved dearly and the same two people who he would never see walking together down that hall again. That scene embedded itself in his memory and is one that he has never forgotten.

Norman drove Janet to the airport, and Ron rode with Ronald. He thought it was ironic that this, in a sense, was preparation for his return home when he would no longer have Janet at his side. When they arrived at the airport, Carroll and her husband, Dick, joined them for breakfast. They all knew the seriousness of the situation. Dick took the initiative to ask Janet if she really wanted to go through with her plan. He, in a sense, tried to talk her out of it, but she was not about to back down.

When it finally came time to board the plane, Janet kissed and hugged Norman, Ronald, and Dick for the last time. Carroll, Janet, and Ron boarded the plane and took their seats together in the front compartment behind the bulkhead. The seating arrangement was perfect in providing them the privacy that was so needed during their time of grief. Not a word was spoken as they each sat with their thoughts, which brought torrents of tears. As the plane taxied to the runway and ascended into the morning sky, Janet turned to Carroll and tearfully stated, "It is really hard to say goodbye to my city, to a city that I really love," as she looked down on Portland for her final time.

Taking their seats, the flight attendant noticed their obvious distress, which had nothing to do with a fear of flying.

"It doesn't look like you are having a very good day. The drinks are on us," the flight attendant stated as she served them Bloody Marys to calm their spirits.

Carroll later wrote in her journal referring to the flight attendant as their angel. She wondered if the flight attendant might later have recognized the story of Janet on television and felt good about her act of kindness.

As they each sipped their drinks, their emotions settled, and their moods shifted. They laughed and shared stories of their lives together, which lightened the atmosphere and temporarily deflected their thoughts of what was ahead. If Janet was fearful, she didn't show any outward signs of anxiety.

Their plane landed in Minneapolis with a short layover, which gave them time to visit the lounge. Janet's only disappointment came when the bartender failed to fill her order. She had been looking forward to having a specialized beer from the Midwest and was forced to settle for a Heineken.

When it came time to board the next plane, it suddenly dawned on Janet that she had left her purse in the lounge. As trivial as it might seem to anyone who was about to die, for Janet, her purse contained identification and personal belongings needed to identify her body after her departure into the next dimension. Ron exited the plane, made a mad dash to the lounge, and retrieved the purse just as they were closing the doors to the gate.

Once the plane landed in Detroit, they picked up a rental car and headed directly to the Red Top Inn, a modest motel, in Romulus, Michigan. They checked in about 10:00 p.m. and went out for a Mexican dinner at a nearby restaurant. As they drank their drinks, they talked about their life together as married couples. In the course of their conversation, they discovered a strange coincidence. While Carroll was living in Columbus, Ohio, a close friend of hers was diagnosed with terminal cancer. During the illness, her friend wore a religious oblong silver medal that had the imprint of a dove. Carroll had the medal duplicated and wore it during difficult periods in her life. On one particular holiday, she had the same medal made for Janet. Janet had not worn the medal for a number of years, but for some strange reason, when they were getting ready to leave, Ron picked up the medal and put it around his neck. During their conversation, Carroll was startled when she noticed that both she and Ron were wearing their medals of the Holy Spirit.

While in Michigan, they wrote Janet's obituary. It was hard for Carroll to believe that she was having that conversation with her best friend. But by then, they had gone beyond the place of mourning.

"I don't want anyone to know I have Alzheimer's, especially the people in Portland," Janet informed her.

"You don't have to list what you died of. All they need to know is that you died," Carroll assured her.

Saying their final goodbyes, Janet handed Carroll the following letter:

∞

Janet's Letter to Carroll—June 4, 1990

Thank you so much for coming to Michigan with Ron and me. Especially for helping Ron get back home. You have been a wonderful friend to us for many great years. This gesture of being with us at this time means so much to me. We love you, and love you, and love you ... and I couldn't be more thankful. Janet.

The following day, Dr. Kevorkian arrived at the motel with his two sisters, Margo Janus and Flora Holzheimer. Flora had made the trip from Frankfurt, Germany, to assist her brother in this monumental event. The group sat in the motel for about an hour getting acquainted. To their surprise, they discovered that Dr. Kevorkian had a personality similar to Ron's. He was witty, with a great sense of humor and liked limericks, puns, and good jokes. Similar to Janet and Ron, he was also a musician. He played the flute and organ and loved to play Bach. Janet also loved Bach but disliked organs, which was the main reason she had chosen a string quartet for her memorial service. She politely shared her thoughts with Dr. Kevorkian regarding her distaste for organs. The similarities in their personalities and their common interest in music allowed Janet to relax and feel comfortable in the presence of Dr. Kevorkian.

Meeting with the group for dinner, the conversation centered on the *'right to die'* and the events that were scheduled to take place. Janet was sitting at the table with her head down. Carroll, feeling her anger rising over the insensitive topic of dinner conversation, grabbed Janet and ushered her into the bar for a drink. They sat drinking brandy and sharing intimate details of their lives together. That was the last personal sharing they had. The two friends made a pact, and Carroll vowed never to reveal their final conversation to anyone for any reason.

The next day was spent with Dr. Kevorkian talking and discussing life in general. He asked a number of questions to determine if Janet was of sound mind. After he had completed the line of questioning, a video camera was set up on a tripod while Flora spent the next hour videotaping the interview. Janet sat in the middle with Dr. Kevorkian on her right and Ron on her left. They knew that the tape was an important part of the equation. If Dr. Kevorkian were accused of murder and perhaps Carroll and Ron as well, the tape would be their only proof that Janet was of sound mind when she made the decision to end her life.

The following is the transcript of this tape.

Kevorkian: Where do you live?

Janet: Portland, Oregon.

Kevorkian: Where is that?

Janet: It's on the West Coast.

Kevorkian: What country is that?

Janet: [Unable to answer, Janet looks to Ron.]

Kevorkian: What other states are on the West Coast?

Janet: California, Washington.

Kevorkian: How old are you?

Janet: Fifty-four.

Kevorkian: When did you first start having problems?

Janet: One year ago.

Kevorkian: What did you first notice?

Janet: Ron noticed more than I did.

Kevorkian: Ron, what did you notice?

Ron: We are musicians and we used to play a lot. We would play page after page at night. Janet could no longer read the music and we thought she needed new glasses. Little things like that made me wonder if she had a brain tumor or was entering menopause.

Kevorkian: Were you alarmed?

Ron: I was suspicious. She had trouble writing checks.

Kevorkian: Was it the writing or the numbers?

Ron: She had trouble writing the numbers and writing out the numbers long hand.

Janet: I knew what it should be, but it wouldn't come out that way.

Kevorkian: With the physical act of writing the mind didn't coordinate.

Janet: I taught English as a second language and I began to notice things.

Kevorkian: How long were you teaching?

Janet: Twelve years. I loved it.

Ron: It was at the community college. On the last term we were virtually working together. She was the teacher, but I had to correct her. We would kid about it. I was worried and concerned. In November 1988 I contacted a doctor and asked him to check things out. The doctor forgot I had called him, so I made an appointment for Janet to be checked out by a specialist. On June 12, 1989, she was diagnosed. I was suspicious for a year prior to her diagnosis and so I started reading about Alzheimer's.

Kevorkian: Janet, when did you first find out?

Janet: Not until the bomb was dropped. It was just awful the way it was presented to us.

Kevorkian: How?

Janet: Ron, you need to be the spokesman.

Ron: He just coldly blurted out that Janet has Alzheimer's. There was no warming up.

Janet: It was so awful. It just devastated me right on the spot.

Kevorkian: What treatment did they give you?

Ron: The doctor recommended she participate in a program. Janet did not want to be a guinea pig. The Hemlock Society supported the concept of self-deliverance. Janet set a date to deliver herself, but our sons were upset because Janet is such a powerful person who always believes you can overcome anything in life. Our son found a study at the University of Washington and influenced Janet to enroll in the program. She took a dose of THA on a weekly basis, had blood tests and psychological testing but the program was not working.

Kevorkian: Did the doctor offer any proposal for treatment or care?

Ron: He suggested an Alzheimer's group, a test program and a support group. Janet was not interested since she had already decided she didn't want to go that route.

Kevorkian: Janet, what bothers you most about this affliction? Why do you feel the way you do about it? How was your life before, and how is it different now?

Janet: My life before was wonderful. I could play the piano and read. I can't do any of those things now. It is too taxing.

Kevorkian: When you see a musical slate with notes, can you identify those notes?

Janet: No. I don't even try anymore.

Kevorkian: If you saw a note that was a G-natural would you know it was a G-natural?

Janet: Yes, but I couldn't put it together. It doesn't register.

Kevorkian: You couldn't put it in a series?

Janet: No.

Kevorkian: It doesn't register between what you see and what your hand plays?

Janet: No. Norman tried. He said let's play "Rule, Britannica!" which is something that we used to always play together. We did a wonderful job and even played it in a concert.

Kevorkian: What is the most complicated musical piece that you could play before?

Janet: A Brahms piece. I love Brahms.

Kevorkian: Something that was a concerto?

Janet: I can't come up with a name now.

Kevorkian: What did you do that you can't do now? Were you active in physical things?

Janet: Absolutely. I'm a tennis player.

Kevorkian: How good were you?

Janet: Fantastic! [A great smile and enthusiasm]

Ron: She was seventh in the club on the doubles ladder and still to this day is a very good player.

Kevorkian: Really? Physically you are not too impaired. When you see the tennis ball coming do you know where to hit it?

Janet: Yes. No problem.

Ron: The score is the problem.

Kevorkian: Or anything you are reading that has an abstract to its meaning?

Janet: Yes.

Kevorkian: Do you find this so incapacitating that it distorts the balance of life on the negative side so you can't put up with it at all?

Janet: Absolutely. It is not the way I want it at all.

Kevorkian: Ron, how do you feel about it?

Ron: I know through our thirty-four years of marriage that Janet has loved ideas. For all of our friends and myself included, Janet has been the light in our lives as she was always coming up with new ideas and always abreast of philosophical thoughts. She enlarged our lives because of her interests and mental curiosity. To see the things she loved the most taken away from her, especially the music, is just devastating. Tennis is about the only thing she has left.

Kevorkian: Janet, you don't want to go on?

Janet: No, I don't.

Kevorkian: It is your decision?

Janet: Yes, it is my decision.

Kevorkian: Ron, how do you feel about her decision?

Ron: I think it is important that she does what she wants to do. I think it is her decision.

Kevorkian: How do you feel about it?

Ron: I think that if I were in a similar situation with a terminal disease, and Alzheimer's is a terminal disease, it is the fourth-leading killer of people today, I would not want to be around to see it run its course.

Kevorkian: Are you for or against what she wants to do?

Ron: I am for it.

Kevorkian: Are you for it because of the way you feel or because that is what she wants?

Ron: Both. I am for it because I love her and I want her to have what she wants, and also philosophically if I were in her position this is what I would want.

Kevorkian: Is that what you mean when we are talking about autonomy and self-determination?

Ron: That's right. The right to not have to suffer and to have a humane way to exit if you have a terminal situation.

Kevorkian: You do realize that she is not terminal at this moment?

Ron: Not in a physical sense, but mentally.

Kevorkian: How would you characterize her mental state?

Ron: I think she is rational and able to make decisions on her own and exercise her own free will.

Kevorkian: Janet are you aware of the implications of your decision?

Janet: Yes.

Kevorkian: What does it mean?

Janet: That I can get out with dignity.

Kevorkian: What are you asking for? Can you put it in plain words?

Janet: I don't know.

Kevorkian: What is it that you want? Put it in simple English.

Janet: Self-deliverance?

Kevorkian: No. Simpler than that. Do you want to go on?

Janet: No, I don't want to go on.

Kevorkian: You don't want to go on living? Do you know what that means?

Janet: Yes, I do.

Kevorkian: What does that mean?

Janet: That it is the end of my life.

Kevorkian: What is the word for that?

Janet: Euthanasia?

Kevorkian: No. What is the word for the end of life? What happens when you stop living? What is it called?

Janet: You are dead.

Kevorkian: Is that what you wish?

Janet: Yes.

Kevorkian: That is the word I want. Do you understand the implications of what that means?

Janet: Yes.

Kevorkian: Do you know what the word death means? Does it mean the end of life?

Janet: Yes.

Kevorkian: How do your sons feel about it? How many sons do you have?

Janet: Three sons.

Kevorkian: How old are they?

Janet: [No answer; looks to Ron for the answer.]

Kevorkian: Are they small or grown?

Janet: They are adults. They said, "Go with peace, Mom." They understand.

Kevorkian: The whole time you have had support from the family?

Janet: [No answer; tears have begun to flow.]

Kevorkian: You understand that I have to ask these questions?

Janet: I know.

Kevorkian: Why do you want your life to end? In other words, do you feel it is better than going on the way you are now?

Janet: Right.

Kevorkian: I don't want to put words in your mouth but what's facing you is worse than death?

Janet: I've had enough. I've had enough. [Sigh]

Kevorkian: What does that mean? That you've lived enough? That you have had a full life?

Janet: Yes, very. [Smiling now.]

Kevorkian: Are you in agreement with everything she is saying, Ron?

Ron: Yes, I am.

Kevorkian: How has the process been going recently? Is it stabilized? Is it getting worse?

Ron: It is progressing. She is getting worse.

Kevorkian: Since January, how would you say?

Ron: When she goes to play tennis in the morning, I have to call her up. I have to tell her when it is time to go play tennis, or she has to call me to find out if it is time. That is something she never used to have to do. The other night we went out with some friends to dinner, and when we got home, we got a call that Janet had left her purse there. This is just another little thing. When we changed planes on our flight to Minneapolis, we stopped for a snack at a restaurant in the airport terminal. After we boarded our plane, we discovered that Janet had left her purse in the airport. I had to get off the plane and retrieve her purse before the plane took off. This happened again last night at the restaurant. These are things that are slipping away, and she knows they are slipping away.

Kevorkian: Janet, did you go to college?

Janet: Yes.

Kevorkian: Was it out west?

Janet: Yes.

Kevorkian: Did you graduate?

Janet: Yes.

Kevorkian: Do you remember what degree you got?

Janet: [Looks to Ron.] Was it a BS?

Ron: Yes.

Kevorkian: Ron, did you go to college?

Ron: Yes.

Kevorkian: Janet, you know what you are asking me to do? You realize that?

Janet: Yes.

Kevorkian: You want help from me?

Janet: I do.

Kevorkian: You realize that I can make arrangements for everything, but you have to do it, you have to push the button? You realize that you can stop at any time and you don't have to go on? You realize that you can change your mind at any time, now or anytime without any time frame?

Janet: I understand.

Kevorkian: It is planned for the day after tomorrow. Do you understand that?

Janet: Yes.

Kevorkian: At any time, you can change your mind. Ron, do you have any questions or points that you want to bring up?

Ron: One thing that I want to say is that when a person in your family has a tragedy and it is so difficult to find a way to handle it in a humane way, a way that is fitting a human being, I think it is a tragedy. I think that mankind has come a long way, but I think in certain areas they are still in the dark ages. With all of our advancements, we as a society have to address this problem and find a way to make it legal so it can be accomplished in a humane way so that people can die with dignity and die in a very peaceful way. It is very difficult to find any good solution to this.

Kevorkian: You realize that Janet's decision is going to be harshly criticized by many people. Janet, do you realize that?

Janet: Yes.

Kevorkian: Have I encouraged you in any way to do this?

Janet: No.

Kevorkian: In any way?

Janet: No. No.

Kevorkian: Have I encouraged you to keep going, to go on living?

Janet: [Looks to Ron, not sure how to answer.]

Ron: You have encouraged her decision in whatever she wants to do, right?

Kevorkian: But I have not encouraged you in any way to take this action?

Janet: No.

Kevorkian: You understand of course that I prefer that she change her mind and go on living? You do understand this?

Ron: Yes.

Kevorkian: It is a tragic event at best and the end of human life is never desirable under reasonable circumstances. What we are doing here is pondering whether the circumstances are unreasonable. You have come to the conclusion that the circumstances are unreasonable. The circumstances are such that the decision is rational. Is that what you are saying?

Ron: That is what I am saying.

Kevorkian: The termination of Janet's life now becomes a rational decision.

Ron: In that regard, she was going to do it in November and did have a means to do it then.

Kevorkian: What were the means?

Ron: She had drugs available, but she preferred this option because it is a more humane way.

Kevorkian: Why do you say it is more humane?

Ron: Everything I have read about the subject, doctors have concluded that the most humane way would be the use of sodium pentothal. With drugs, there can be problems with the dosage and the body's way of accepting those drugs.

Kevorkian: Just to repeat to you, I have not suggested to you that this is the best way to go? I did not solicit you.

Ron: Your name came up in an article in *Newsweek Magazine*. We talked about it and decided to get a hold of you.

Kevorkian: I am helping you for one reason. The highest ethical principle to me is one of self-determination. That is what I let guide me on my feelings and reason on this. It has to be a combination of the principle of self-determination on the one hand and the medical circumstances on the other. You and Janet may be in a position to determine and analyze the medical circumstances, but most people will say that the doctor has that authority. Therefore, the benefit I can bring to you is the expertise on the medical side. With the principle of self-determination, I can come to a decision to do something no matter how I personally feel about it. The physician's personal feeling, in my opinion, should never enter into the physician–patient relationship. In other words, what is most important is the well-being of the patient who is in front of the doctor. Even if I find it repellant or distasteful to help you do this, it becomes of secondary importance to the main principle. Is the physician doing what is best for the patient in front of him? It is a tough decision and I think that more doctors should make it because they are in a position to do so. Therefore, in doing this, even though it is a disagreeable action on my part, because it is rationally correct, I take the principle of self-determination and look at the medical circumstances involved. The solution that comes out is "yes," the action is justified. That is why I am doing this. Not because I like to see people die. Do you understand that?

Ron: Yes.

Janet: Yes.

Kevorkian: Well, any other closing comments by you, Janet or you, Ron? Anything you would like to say? People will look at this. Some will say you are right, and some will say that you are wrong. What will you tell them?

Janet: That I want to get out.

Kevorkian: What would you say to them if they say you are doing the wrong thing?

Janet: I'm sorry, I still want to get out.

Kevorkian: Ron, what would you say to them if they say Janet is taking the wrong course?

Ron: I would say that it is her decision. She has made it, and she has the right to make her own decision. It is her life and her dignity.

Kevorkian: In closing, I would say that these tough decisions have got to be made and who is in a better position than the physicians, because life and death are in their domain and they are abrogating their responsibility by dodging issues. If this is going to be kept incorruptible, which everyone is going to bring up, the corruptibility, it calls for the deepest and most serious and hardest thinking on the part of doctors. The hardest decision is not whether to operate or not but whether this person's life should continue or not. It is their responsibility to do so. They have got to do this no matter how distasteful it is. That is one of the points to be brought out. That is what I would say to those who look and say it is wrong. Janet, I will go along with you because I see that you are a very intelligent woman from a very intelligent background from a good and loving and intelligent family. I can empathize with you and what is facing you with this diagnosis. The day may come when what you have can be cured. Unfortunately for you and your family, I don't think it will come quick enough. I therefore agree to help you in the spirit of Hippocrates. Disregarding my personal feelings and all the emotionalism that is going to swirl around what you want, in the name of human rationality, which you are beginning to lose, I have decided to help you on two days hence on the morning of June fourth.

Ron: We thank you.

Kevorkian: Don't thank me. I think the world will one day thank you, Janet and you, Ron because what you are doing is a historic move. I don't think it has ever been done officially since the days of classical Greece. I think the world will thank you one day.

Once the tape was complete, they signed legal documents indicating Janet was of sound mind and that she gave Kevorkian permission to assist in her death. Attesting to Janet's mental competence, both Carroll and Ron signed the documents as well.

They had to be sure that the tape was in working order, as finding out later that it hadn't recorded properly would be devastating. In desperation, they made a bold move and took the tape to the video department at a local department store and brazenly inserted the tape into a VCR. They were alarmed to see Janet's interview come up on all the TVs in the video department for anyone to see. Fortunately, the tape went unnoticed by the store personnel and the customers, as they most likely would have called the authorities if they had understood what was happening.

In the hotel room, they packed up the tripod and agreed to meet at a nearby restaurant for dinner later that evening. The entire group was present at dinner including Ron, Janet, Carroll, Dr. Kevorkian, and his two sisters. Dr. Kevorkian was seated at the head of the table as they exchanged interesting conversation, laughing and enjoying the evening. Dr. Kevorkian would later report, "I constantly observed Janet's behavior and assessed her moods as well as the content and quality of her thoughts. There was absolutely no doubt that her mentality was intact and that she was not the least depressed over her impending death."

During the conversation, Dr. Kevorkian asked Janet if she wanted Carroll or Ron to accompany her to the van. She was adamant that she didn't want either of them present. She feared that if Dr. Kevorkian got arrested and taken to jail, the authorities might consider Carroll and Ron as accomplices.

After dinner, Dr. Kevorkian departed with his two sisters. Carroll, Janet, and Ron adjourned to the bar for an after-dinner drink to sum up the day's events. Janet was content in knowing that she has passed her interview with Doctor Death and that her mission would soon be complete.

6

Goodbye, My Love

Filled with the excitement and anticipation of two lovers on vacation, their last day together was likened to a honeymoon. Their feelings and emotions were running high, and they were greatly influenced by the new, unfamiliar surroundings. The waitress who had served their early-morning breakfast mentioned the obvious love that was exchanged between them. "You must be celebrating an anniversary or a very special occasion," she commented.

Earlier that morning, Janet gave Ron the following love letter:

My Dearest Ron,
How I love you and how hard it is to leave you.
The tears must flow and flow and flow. The loss
is overwhelming! I have enjoyed Chamber Music
Northwest so much this season with you by my
side.

Please remember to live with all your heart
and love again. You have been the dearest
husband and the most caring lover. Go to
England or someplace you wish. Maybe you'd
like to take a son.

All other things, to their destruction draw, only
our love hath no decay; This, no tomorrow hath,
nor yesterday, running it never runs from us away,
but truly keeps his first, last everlasting day.

Love, love and more love, Jannie.

Who could have possibly imagined what lay in store? To the hotel clerk, they sounded like any other weekend tourists who wanted information on what the city had to offer. Janet wanted to see a concert, but no group playing interested her. Carroll decided to join them in a scenic drive up to Lake Huron to visit a place called Port Huron. They stopped at a spectacular community on the lake that had a waterway and took a stroll along the railroad tracks. They visited the Edison Convention Center and then stopped at a lounge. The television in the lounge was tuned to a station that was playing the NBA game between Detroit and Chicago. When Detroit beat Chicago, putting them in the playoffs against the Portland Trailblazers, Janet made the excited comment: "Oh, on Tuesday they will be playing in Portland for the playoffs." She wasn't even concerned that she wouldn't be alive on Tuesday to watch it. Afterward, they headed back to the motel having enjoyed a full day, the last full day of Janet's life.

On their drive back, Janet asked Ron to make a stop. "Pull over at the supermarket," she stated. "I want to get some almonds and a banana for my breakfast tomorrow." It seemed like an ordinary day in the life of Janet. She gave no indication that she was fearful about what tomorrow would bring, only that she wanted to be sure to get her nourishment right up until the end.

When they arrived back at the motel they dressed for dinner and Janet picked out Ron's tie, as she had done for so many years. Carroll joined them for a wonderful French meal, which consisted of escargot, a hearty steak, and a bottle of wine that Janet selected. The waitress was a Vietnamese girl, and Janet lost no time in engaging the young woman in a conversation. Before long, the girl was pouring out the story of her escape from Vietnam. Janet had been teaching English as a second language, and she had taught many Vietnamese students over the course of her lessons. She was taking a sincere interest in the girl, which was characteristic of Janet, as she loved engaging with people and learning about their lives.

After dinner, they retired to their hotel to prepare for a good night's sleep, as they were all exhausted by the events of the last several days. Janet put on her nightgown, got directly into bed, and was fast asleep in no time, just like a newborn baby. On the contrary, Ron was awake the entire night watching his beloved wife taking her last breaths. Ron had a habit of running his foot down Janet's leg when he got into bed. He panicked when he realized he would never share that experience with her again. That precious leg of his beautiful wife would be gone tomorrow.

Arising at 5:45 a.m., they spent time in each other's arms hugging and cuddling before Janet's departure. Janet was insistent that Ron turn on the television set at 6:00 a.m. to watch the French Open tennis match being played in Paris. However, to her disappointment, she had forgotten about the time difference between Portland and Detroit, so it wasn't scheduled to come on until 9:00 a.m., and by that time she would have left to meet with Dr. Kevorkian. Janet became quite upset because it had been their tradition to watch the French Open every year.

She showered and dressed in a black skirt and a white silk blouse while the tears continued flowing between them. Janet wrote out a letter to take with her, which stated she was of sound mind, had Alzheimer's, and did not want it to take her down.

∞

Final letter written by Janet E. Adkins

I have decided for the following reasons to take my own life. This is a decision taken in a normal state of mind and is fully considered.

I have Alzheimer's disease and do not wish to let it progress any further. I don't choose to put my family or myself through the agony of this terrible disease.

Janet signed the letter and handed it to Ron to take to the front desk to get several copies made. To his dismay, the copy machine was not accessible to guests. He reluctantly handed the letter to the clerk, realizing that time was of the essence. His heart pounded in his chest while his mind ran wild with thoughts of a thwarted plan. He feared that if the clerk were to read Janet's letter, he would surely notify the authorities, which would have aborted the scheduled event. His anxiety was put to rest when the contents of the letter went unnoticed and the copies were handed back to him. When Ron returned to the room, Carroll had arrived with a personal note for Janet to be read by one of Dr. Kevorkian's sisters once she boarded the van.

At nine o'clock sharp, Margo and Flora arrived at the motel to escort Janet to her final destination. As Carroll and Ron walked Janet outside to the car, the event played out like a heartbreaking scene from *The Love Story*. However, the tape from this scene could not be rewound. If there was any turning back, now was the time, but Janet didn't hesitate for a moment. She was prepared to follow through with her plan. After she and Ron kissed goodbye and expressed their endless love for one another, Janet climbed into the front seat of the car. She waved goodbye and blew kisses to Ron as the car drove out of sight.

"Goodbye, my love," Ron whispered softly as tears flooded his eyes. That was the last he ever saw of his brave and courageous wife.

∞

Janet's Journal—*The Mists of Avalon,* by Marion Zimmer Bradley

The old man said when they departed,
"Remember that history is all around you both
behind and before you and no one can be sure
he won't go stumbling onto yesterday around
some corner of today. And you Niniane,
my dear, I shall see you again if not here then
somewhere else, perhaps in Avalon.
For whether we go backwards or forwards
it is all one because it has happened.
Whatever has been is, and always will be ...
Go with love, and with God
or Allah, it is all one"

7

A Date with Death

From the moment Janet left the motel, the exhausting and torturous waiting game began for Carroll and Ron. Much like the anxious parents awaiting the birth of their first child, Carroll and Ron sat next to the phone waiting to be notified of Janet's exit. The hours on the clock went around and around and still no call. When the phone finally rang, it was one of Dr. Kevorkian's sisters calling from Dr. Kevorkian's apartment. She advised that a problem had occurred. When Margo, Flora, and Janet had arrived at Groveland Oaks Park at 9:30 a.m., they found a distressed Dr. Kevorkian. While he was setting up the suicide machine, the bottle of thiopental, the vital ingredient that was necessary to end Janet's life, had fallen off the device, causing half of the solution to leak out. Dr. Kevorkian was faced with the dilemma that there might not be enough of the drug to cause Janet's death. Because of the mishap, and the inevitable delay in the schedule, the unlikely foursome got back in the car and made the ninety-mile round trip to Dr. Kevorkian's apartment. Ron could hear Janet in the background saying, "I love you, Ron."

The interruption in the schedule allowed Janet every opportunity to change her mind, but even with the setback, she remained steadfast in her quest to end her life. With the imminent delay, Carroll and Ron checked out of their rooms and waited in the hotel lobby for the final call, which would confirm Janet's death. At noon, Dr. Kevorkian and the clandestine group arrived back at their original destination and began preparing for Janet's departure. For the next two hours, Janet waited in the car with Margo while Dr. Kevorkian and Flora attended to the final details. Like an impatient traveler whose flight has been delayed, Janet waited anxiously for permission to board the vehicle that would launch her into the next dimension. According to Janet's belief in the afterlife, she would be propelled into the spirit realm, followed by the opportunity to reincarnate back to earth if she chose.

Janet's situation was reminiscent of the story of *Alice in Wonderland,* where the White Rabbit pulled his watch out of his pocket and kept repeating, "I'm late, I'm late, for a very important date," suggesting that Janet had a date with death and that time was of the essence. Both Alice's and Janet's adventures took place under strange and twisted circumstances that projected them into another reality.

The twenty-two-year-old van was rusty and worn, but Dr. Kevorkian had gone to considerable effort to make the inside comfortable. He placed clean sheets and a pillow on the bed and hung curtains for privacy. When the invitation came for Janet to enter the van, she climbed aboard and was directed to the quarters prepared for her. She stretched out on the bed, leaving on the clothes in which she had arrived, and relaxed her body as if she were planning on taking a peaceful afternoon nap. Dr. Kevorkian cut small holes in her nylon stockings at the ankles, attached electrocardiogram (EKG) electrodes to her ankles and wrists, and covered her with a light blanket.

When it came time to insert the needle that would deliver the deadly solution into her veins, Dr. Kevorkian made several frustrating attempts before he was successful at finding a vein that would accept the needle. Janet had frail and delicate veins, and Dr. Kevorkian was not the first to experience the difficulty in locating one that would cooperate.

Once the preparations were complete, Margo read Janet the following letter from Carroll:

∞

Letter from Carroll

My Dear Friend,
My heart weeps for you and for all of us. Keeping this vigil, watching you say goodbye over and

over to those you love will change my life forever. My knees shake, my being feels broken and I don't know how to say goodbye. . . except to just say, goodbye my friend.

Shalom, Janet. You leave us with love. Peace to you. I will miss you and there are no words to tell you how very much. You have helped make my life richer. You are leaving us with courage. I am in awe, in pain. I love you.

Margo then read the Lord's Prayer and Psalm 23, which had been selected by Heidi, Neil's wife:

Psalm 23

Yea, though I walk through the valley of the shadow of death, I will fear no evil for thou art with me.

After the readings were complete, Janet had no hesitation in pushing the button. Her final words to Kevorkian, as she drifted off to sleep, were "Thank you, thank you, thank you."

Dr. Kevorkian replied, "Have a good trip."

Six minutes after activating the suicide machine, Janet was confirmed dead by the EKG. She had died peacefully and painlessly and was on her way to the next realm.

Back at the hotel, with nerves on edge, Ron feeling as though he was near exploding, thought he might have a heart attack. Then, as if by magic, a warm, wonderful happy feeling came over him. He looked at his watch, and it was 2:30 p.m. He turned to Carroll and stated, "She's gone now." It was an overcast day, and at that moment, the clouds parted and the sun came out. Normally, Ron was a disbeliever of accounts such as this, but this experience made him a true believer of something far greater than what he believed. A few minutes later, the long-awaited call came from Dr. Kevorkian confirming that Janet had died at 2:30 p.m. and that everything had gone as expected.

Meanwhile, back in Detroit, Carroll and Ron were in a time bind to make their flight to Portland. They still had some unfinished business to attend to at the funeral home. They had to return their rental car and check in at the airport. With adrenaline running high, Ron darted in and out of traffic, making the hour's drive back to Detroit a frightful experience for Carroll.

Their first stop was the funeral home to arrange Janet's cremation. Prior to their trip to Detroit, Ron had purchased cremations plans, sight unseen, for Janet and himself. The plans allowed cremation services at a variety of locations, which included Detroit. The shabby cremation facility was a mirror image of the rusty old van: located in a run-down part of town where the buildings were dressed with iron bars to keep out uninvited guests. They were greeted at the door and ushered into a very small, unorganized office by a man who seemed unconcerned with their flight schedule. Ron became irritable and frustrated as the man moved sluggishly about his business. Lacking any sense of urgency, he instructed Ron to complete forms and pay a fee for the service. Ron listed the cause of death as "she died in a van" and informed the man that he could find Janet's body at the county morgue. With business complete, Ron and Carroll continued their frantic drive to the rental car agency, returned the vehicle, and made a mad dash to catch their flight.

Adrenaline flowing and breathless from running, they arrived at the Detroit Metropolitan Airport. Fighting their way through the crowds of travelers, they were startled to hear their names being paged over the airport loudspeaker. Ignoring the page and the inevitable outcome, they were stopped at the gate by a plain-clothed Michigan State police officer and escorted to one side. The officer began interrogating them inquiring about Janet's death.

"Did you know that your wife committed suicide?" the officer questioned in a puzzled tone.

"Yes," Ron replied.

"How long have you known about your wife's intentions?" the officer asked.

"I've known for the past year," Ron confessed.

Because he wasn't expecting a confession of that magnitude, the officer was confused by Ron's honesty, leaving him baffled and unable to resolve the situation. Ron was insistent that they had a plane to catch and convinced the officer to let them board.

Shortly after taking their seats, they were approached by a stewardess who asked them to identify themselves. Insisting that they get their carry-on luggage, they were escorted off the plane. Upon exiting, they were again confronted by the same officer, who picked up where he had left off, asking more questions. Frustrated with the situation, the officer told Ron that he was going to call his boss. Because the officer didn't have anything on which to legally hold them, Ron forced the issue. He advised the officer that they needed to get back on the plane and get home to their waiting families. Ron assured the officer that he would call him from Minneapolis between their flight to Portland and answer any more questions he might have.

Emotions twisting with fear, like two flies caught in a web, they again boarded the plane with a temporary sigh of relief. Carroll was an extremely attractive woman, and to any stranger who may have overheard the conversation or observed their frantic behavior, they might have conjured in their minds a scenario of a murder mystery involving the original trio. Janet, who had been present just days ago on the flight to Michigan, was now dead under mysterious circumstances. Now, both Ron and Carroll were traveling companions who appeared as fugitives on the run.

As soon as their plane touched down in Minneapolis, Ron called the police department as promised. The officer started his interrogation once again with the same line of questioning. Avoiding the questions, Ron informed the officer that they had another plane to catch. He promised they would talk again after they reached their destination. Once he was securely strapped into his seat with the plane heading for Portland, Ron knew that his life as he had known it would never be the same. His keen sense of awareness told him that trouble lay ahead as a result of Janet's date with death.

8

Media Circus

Stepping off the plane, Carroll and Ron were greeted by his three sons; relatives from British Columbia; Carroll's husband, Dick; and the media. They were invaded by the flashing of cameras and bombarded with questions by the local television networks. The press finally let up once the family's distress became obvious. After arriving back at his apartment, from that moment on, the phone rang off the hook. Janet's cousin, Lou, answered most of the calls and took messages. For Ron, the intrusion from the news media was unbearable.

The following day, it was decided to have a press conference due to the volume of calls and the family's inability to deal with the invasion of their privacy. The press conference was held in the cabana of the apartment complex and was attended by a group of reporters who asked numerous questions. The most shocking question that was directed to Ron by a reporter was, "How do you feel about you and your sons being charged with conspiracy to murder your wife?" Although Carroll, Ron, and his three sons were considered suspects in Janet's death, charges were never formally brought against them.

Prior to Janet's death, Janet, Dr. Kevorkian, and Ron had agreed that they wanted to keep a low profile. After Dr. Kevorkian had put a call into the police to report Janet's death, the police had detained him and spent several hours questioning him about his involvement. They also impounded his van along with 'The Mercitron' and eventually seized the videotape for evidence of Janet's interview with Dr. Kevorkian. The authorities didn't know what to do about the situation because it was the first of its kind. Once they felt they had collected enough evidence, they let Dr. Kevorkian go home. As he was leaving, he was informed to keep the incident confidential. However, by the time he got home his phone was ringing nonstop. Someone connected with the police department appeared to have leaked the story to the press. Ron was certain that Dr. Kevorkian hadn't released the sensitive information. Ron hadn't told anyone either, so it was concluded to have come from the police department. Both Carroll and Ron were shocked that it had gotten out before they arrived home in Portland. Carroll also experienced the disrespectful invasion from the media. She found the entire process obscene. While she was at Ron's apartment, the news stations paid a fee to interrupt his private telephone calls while cameramen and reporters showed up at the door unannounced.

Once the autopsy report was complete and it was confirmed that Janet's brain was riddled with an advanced case of Alzheimer's disease, the authorities concluded their investigation. Satisfied with the cause of death, Janet's body was released for cremation. Her ashes were eventually sent to Oregon, where they were scattered over the Pacific Ocean at Cannon Beach.

The memorial service was held the following week, on Sunday, June 10, 1990, at the First Unitarian Church in Portland, Oregon. The press filled the balcony, and the church overflowed with friends and relatives who had come to pay their last respects. The string quartet Janet had personally selected played to the audience as family and friends wept openly at the loss of their beloved Janet. The service was led by Janet's pastor, who had been her personal advisor for many years. He addressed the audience with passion, and he made it known that he had respected and supported Janet's decision to end her life.

Excerpt from Janet's Memorial Service

How do we assess the life of Janet? Vital in life, Janet has become famous in death. When I met with Janet, I was always impressed by her essential composure. The peacefulness with which she told me about her plan to end her life is an abiding memory. I do not think that Janet

intended to become a pioneer or crusader for death with dignity. In effect, that is what has happened. The public attention that her death has received, is an indication of the level of interest in this phenomenon. I supported Janet's right to decide when she planned to end her life. She was very concerned about the grim prospects of her continuing loss of memory to Alzheimer's. Her decision not to undergo pain and suffering is one that I can support wholeheartedly. I know she died because she did not want to reach the point where she could no longer make that decision. She desired control over her own decision in these matters. All of this has reminded me of a letter that Virginia Wolf, the most distinguished female novelist of the twentieth century, wrote to her husband Leonard before she walked into the ocean and took her own life.

$$\infty$$

A Letter from Virginia Woolf

Dearest,

I feel certain that I am going mad again. I feel that we can't go through another of those terrible times. I shan't recover this time. I begin to hear voices and I can't concentrate, so I am doing what seems the best thing to do. You have given me the greatest possible happiness. You have been in every way all that anyone could be. I don't think that two people could have been happier until this terrible disease came. I can't fight it any longer. I know that I am spoiling your life, and without me you could work. And you will I know. You see I can't even write this properly. I can't read. What I want to say is that

I owe all the happiness of my life to you. You have been entirely patient with me and incredibly good. I want to say that everybody knows that. If anybody could have saved me it would have been you.[1]

Just six days after Carroll played out the final scene in her best friend's life, she stood before the crowd and spoke to them in a soft and steady voice with composure and a loving smile. Addressing Janet's friends and loved ones, she spoke of the grieving that had been present in their lives with Janet over the past year. "Today we come together to celebrate Janet's life and to remember her as she had once been, a cherished friend, a beloved wife and mother. Janet no longer belongs to only us. Now she belongs to the world." Carroll spoke of the family Janet left behind:

Janet loved her family so much. She loved and adored Ron, her life's companion. And when I say life's companion, I say that with emphasis. All of you know that meant a constant and continuously growing relationship. For Janet, if there was no growth, there was no life. Didn't she always challenge us to think beyond our old and established positions about everything? Didn't she just hate it when she saw any of us thinking that we were finished and had all the right answers? Janet loved to be involved in everything, and she did love to win. Janet taught me to play chess, and we played by mail. She won the first game, I won the second game, and we never played the third game. Janet believed that there was no sling or arrow; that there was no affliction or set back that one could not

---

[1] Virginia Woolf, letter to Leonard Woolf, March 28, 1941, accessed July 29, 2019, https://www.smith.edu/woolf/suicidewithtranscript.php.

overcome. She saw more than one of us through bad situations with encouragement, and helped us to become determined to learn, and to fight, and to prevail.

When she was told that she had this terrible disease, Alzheimer's, and that there was no way for her to win, she won anyway. In doing so, to paraphrase a famous poet, *'she fired a shot heard all over the world.'* She didn't mean to do that, she even wanted us to try and find a way to keep others from knowing that she had Alzheimer's. She kept herself from the jaws of depression, and I don't know how she did that. Even to the very end, she had an abiding faith in the comfort and spirit of God, and in the power of love. She lived her life as a pioneer, and that is exactly how she chose to leave this life.

Carroll read a poem that Janet had sent her years ago. Yellowed with time, it was covered with pinholes from being attached to the various walls during her life. This poem says a lot about Janet and how she felt about the adventures in life.

∞

Janet's Journal—*The Waking,* by Theodore Roethke

I wake to sleep and take my waking slow,
I feel my fate, in what I cannot fear,
I learn by going where I have to go.
We think by feeling, what is there to know?
I hear my being dance from ear to ear,
I wake to sleep and take my waking slow.
Of those so close beside me, which are you,
God bless the ground,

I shall walk softly there and learn,
By going where I have to go.[2]

After returning to Seattle, Carroll was also sought out by the press. She was quoted in *People Magazine* and appeared on several television talk shows. "I don't think Janet ever thought her death would be an issue," she stated. "I think Janet thought she would go quietly to Michigan and that would be the end of it. I guess we all did. How naïve we were. I think that Dr. Kevorkian must have known it would create some havoc in the world because he made a videotape of himself interviewing Janet and Ron in the motel room. I can remember watching Janet look to Ron to finish her sentences. She was having trouble expressing herself in a way that she had been used to. For a person who had been used to being extremely bright and articulate, it was very difficult for her to no longer be able to do the things we take for granted."

Without personal time to grieve, the family was thrown into the spotlight both nationally and internationally. The shocking and amazing story of Janet Adkins made front-page headlines all over the world. *Newsweek, Time, People, Vanity Fair, Mirabella, Ladies Home Journal, The Economist,* and other foreign magazines, along with national and international television. Ron and his sons were invited as guests on numerous talk shows, including *Sally Jesse Raphael, Larry King Live, Sixty Minutes* of Australia, and *Ted Koppel's Nightline.* Dr. Kevorkian, Janet, and the family that she had left behind became famous overnight. They were caught in the middle of a heated controversial debate over doctor-assisted dying. Dr. Kevorkian took center stage on *Geraldo Rivera, Good Morning America, Nightline,* and *Crossfire.*

Always dressed professionally, Ron sported a black suit with a bow tie. His gray hair was neatly cut above his ears and his mustache and goatee were neatly trimmed for his television appearances. For someone who had just lost his companion of thirty-four years, he presented a tremendous amount of composure. He was amazingly

---

[2] Theodore Roethke, "The Waking," accessed July 29, 2019, https://www.poetryfoundation.org/poems/43333/the-waking-56d2220f25315, originally published in Collected Poems of Theodore Roethke (New York: Doubleday, 1961).

articulate and well-spoken as he detailed a synopsis of the events leading up to Janet's decision to end her life. As if Janet herself had prepared him to address the world, he became an excellent spokesman for Janet's cause. He fought valiantly, defending his position and a patient's right to die with dignity.

"Janet was a most unusual woman," Ron always told the audiences. "She was very intelligent and exciting. She was always on the forefront of thinking and always brought new ideas to the conversation. When the bomb was dropped on the twelfth of June last year, it meant that her mind was going to be taken away. She was fully aware of what Alzheimer's meant and that she would be losing the things she loved to do. She told the boys that she planned to deliver herself. They, of course, were upset because Janet had taught them that there wasn't anything in life that they couldn't overcome if they just worked hard enough at it. They felt disappointed that she was giving up."

Sometimes Norman and Ronald accompanied their father on television appearances. Neil declined to be interviewed.

Norman was twenty-nine at the time of Janet's death. He was a handsome young man, always dressed in a dark suit and tie for talk show appearances. His brown hair was cut fashionably, extending just above his shoulders, and like his father, he, too, sported a mustache and neatly trimmed beard.

He told the audience that the family had discussed Janet's situation and urged her to join a study group before giving up. He pointed out that the statistics were discouraging at that time with only a two in ten chance of positive results. The only result one could hope for was that the test drug would slow the disease.

Their third son, Ronald, was twenty-six at the time of Janet's death. He displayed a small frame with a slim and well-proportioned build. He was handsome like his brothers but stood out among them, as he was the only blond in the family.

Like his brother Norman, his fashionable hair hung just above his shoulders, and his beard and mustache had been neatly trimmed for his appearance. Looking at the three men side by side, there was no doubt they were cut from the same cloth.

However, his brothers and dad displayed outspoken personalities, whereas Ronald had always been a quiet observer. He spoke softly as he told the audience when he first learned of his mother's disease he was in denial, not wanting to accept that it was true. Janet had always taught them that they could overcome anything with their mind, and he didn't understand her reluctance to fight the disease.

Ron told the audiences, "My wife was the most up person you would ever want to meet. I wish all of you could have met her. She would spark your life. She was always optimistic. She was up during the whole last year. I was the one who couldn't sleep at night. I was the one who lost weight. I would be crying, and she would be holding me. Even up to the last day in Detroit she was propping me up. She was so happy that Dr. Kevorkian would accept her. I want to point out that she was not depressed in the least and she was very cognizant and rational. That is a point that must be brought out."

Then Norman shared a piece of the puzzle that put everything in perspective. "Mom's philosophy for as long as I can remember, was that if something like this were to happen this is what she would do. I remember hearing that early in my life, not understanding what it meant."

Ron informed the audience: "We were members of the Hemlock Society, which believes that people should be able to exit with dignity in a humane peaceful way. We are a society that is more humane to animals and relieving them of their suffering than we are to human beings. We need a humane society for humans."

PART II

Janet and Ron's Life Together

9

Eyes Wide Open

Janet's Childhood

Janet's grandparents, Adolph and Magdelena, were of German descent. It has been said that Janet resembled her grandmother Magdelena, who was a beautiful and loving woman. Her grandparents began their married life together in North Dakota, making their living as farmers and eventually moving north to Canada. Adolph was a strict father and a hardworking man who had the responsibility of supporting a wife and eleven children.

Janet's mother, Vi, was the oldest of the eleven children—six boys and five girls, with twenty-nine years between the first and the last born: Vi, Vernon, Vera, Adeline, Lorraine, Bill, Bert, Kenneth, Raymond, Eunice, and Bruce. A talented family of musicians, they often gathered together to sing and dance while different members of the family played tunes on the piano, accordion, violin, and guitar.

Janet's Journal—Author Unknown

***This day begins a new life
with twice as much music.***

Janet's ancestors were raised as strict Baptists. Adolph and his sons helped to build the Baptist church in the prairie town where emotional revival meetings were held in oversized tents out in the fields. A generation that was ruled by a fearful God rather than a loving God, the majority of the family went their own way, taking up different religious beliefs. As can be expected, Janet's grandfather was very upset by his children's defiance because he believed once a Baptist, always a Baptist. Some of the children found themselves rebelling against their parents' strict religious ways.

∞

Janet's Journal—Author Unknown

There is the old saying that God and your folks
give you the face you're born with.
But you earn the one you die with.

Vi, being the eldest in the family, was sent out to work in the fields with the adult men when she was just nine years old. Vern, who was a year younger than Vi, was sent along to work with her. The two children harnessed a team of horses, plowed, planted, and harvested the fields while the younger sisters stayed back at the house and prepared the meals.

Working in an all-male environment, Vi became pregnant at the age of fifteen. She was barely sixteen when she gave birth to a son she named Ralph. The child's birth father and his wife, who already had seven children of their own, raised the child with his half brothers and sisters.

∞

Janet's Journal—*Evergreen,*
by Belva Plain

We are driven by random winds,
blown and crushed under passing wheels,

or lifted to a garden in the sun.
And for no reason at all, that anyone can see.[1]

In 1934, Vi married Janet's father, Einar, and they made their home in Longview, Washington. Because it was during the Depression, they had a quiet ceremony. The following year, Vi gave birth to Janet on September 10, 1935, at Longview Memorial Hospital.

Vi was a generous hostess and excellent cook who frequently opened her home for gatherings when her family came to visit from Canada. She adored Janet and took pride in sewing dresses for her darling daughter and showing her off to visitors.

When Janet was two years old, Vi's sister, Lorraine, who was then twenty years old, moved from Canada to live with Janet and her parents in Longview, Washington. Janet's life was greatly influenced by her aunt Lorraine, who took to Janet as a mother would to a child. They developed a strong bond that would sustain their relationship throughout their lives.

Janet was an intelligent child with a keen curiosity about everything with which she came in contact. She marveled at the sound of music and learned to sing along while Lorraine played the piano. Over the next four years, Aunt Lorraine grew attached to Janet, taking responsibility for Janet's early development. When Aunt Lorraine left for her night shift at the Weyerhaeuser Mill, Janet was left to the care of her parents, who were showing early signs of alcoholism.

In 1943, Janet's parents moved to Portland, purchased a house, and took positions working in the shipyards. Janet went to live with her father's parents in Longview, Washington, for the next year while Vi and Einar got settled in their new home and their jobs. The following year, Janet was reunited with her parents in Portland. When Christmas arrived, Vi's parents, along with their two youngest children, Bruce and Eunice, moved in with Janet and her parents for several months.

During that time, Janet and Eunice bonded. Although Eunice was Janet's aunt, she considered Janet a sister as the two girls were

---

[1] Belva Plain, *Evergreen*, reissue ed. (New York: Dell Publishing, 1987), 341.

just nine months apart in age. Janet nicknamed Eunice "Zany," which was descriptive of her playful sense of humor and wild abandon. As a young child, Janet displayed a strong personality that convinced Eunice that she had best go along with whatever Janet wanted. Her father often delighted in buying dresses and shoes for both his daughter and granddaughter. When he returned with his treasures, inevitably Janet would have a dress that fit with matching shoes while Eunice would be left with a misfit dress and unmatched shoes. Although it seems humorous now, as a child Eunice felt that it was very unfair that Janet always got the better deal.

By the time Janet was eight years old, it was obvious that her musical talent was progressing. Aunt Lorraine encouraged Vi to buy Janet a piano and offered to give Janet lessons. She did not consider herself a professional by any means, so a classical teacher was located for Janet. Vi used to tell Janet, "It isn't good for you to wash dishes if you want to play the piano." So instead of washing dishes after meals, Janet practiced her piano, leaving the undesirable chore to someone else. Life began to change dramatically for Janet as Vi and Einar increased their use of alcohol.

∞

Janet's Journal—Author Unknown

We must all look at ourselves and the ill
that we have done, and if we are to survive,
we must have great compassion on ourselves.

When Janet entered her teenage years, her parents' drinking advanced to an intolerable state. Eunice can remember a time when she stayed with Janet and her parents for the summer. She recalled wonderful memories of sleeping under the stars and rolling cigarettes to smoke, but her memories were always overshadowed by the drinking and fighting that went on between Vi and Einar.

Vi had always told Janet that men would take advantage of her. Vi, it appeared, had developed a distorted view of men and her own sexuality as a result of having had Ralph out of wedlock and the rough life she had lived around men. Janet tried to teach her mother to forget the past and not dwell on it so much, but Vi was never able to release herself from the guilt that was attached to it.

Janet confided in Eunice that she had blocked out her teenage years and never wanted to talk about them. Because of her upbringing, she believed that sex was an awful thing. She told Eunice that it wasn't until her late twenties that she realized how good sex could be.

Janet's family members were the keeper of secrets. If they didn't want her to know something there was no possibility of changing their minds. They considered unfortunate life experiences to be "bad things," and "bad things" were not to be spoken about. Janet thought that, perhaps, if they could have looked at things differently, they might have understood that "bad things" were just a part of life and were a way of teaching life's lessons. Maybe then, they could have let go of some of their fears that held them back in life. But try as she might, Janet could not convince them to reveal anything about their past. They had a mind-set, and it was not about to be changed, at least in her generation.

∞

Janet's Journal— *The Forest Calls Back,*
by Jack Mendelsohn

Not until the last moment of life
should the longing and growing end.
One should die with his eyes wide open
searching to see the open horizon,
even while dying.
Living life as deeply, and in as fulfilled
a manner as possible is the
best preparation for what may come next.[2]

During her freshman year in high school, Janet developed a strong friendship with a girl named Helen. They both had a personal love for music and met through their involvement in the school band.

---

[2] Jack Mendelsohn, *The Forest Calls Back* (New York: Little, Brown, 1965).

Helen played the oboe, sax, and piano. Janet played the flute, French horn, string bass, and piano.

Janet possessed the innate ability to draw out Helen's strengths, and she recognized that quality in Janet as one of her greatest gifts. Self-conscious and shy, Helen had a hard time excelling at the piano, yet Janet constantly encouraged her to continue to practice. Helen was grateful to Janet for the personal attention, which ultimately resulted in a noticeable improvement in her skills.

As their friendship grew, Janet began to confide in Helen about the terrible conditions in which she was living. With the overbearing presence of alcohol, Janet's home life had become intolerable with her parents' constant fighting. Her house went from a state of intense madness to a state of extreme loneliness when her father, Einar, was gone for weeks at a time. His job as a government lumber inspector required his constant travel. While Einar was away from home, Janet's mother, Vi, took the opportunity to take to the bottle and disappear for days, leaving Janet to fend for herself. More than once, Janet found that she was locked out of the house and forced to sleep on the porch.

∞

Janet's Journal—*Out on a Limb,* by Shirley MacLaine

*If you are trying to fall asleep and your mind is
bouncing around with all kinds of social
problems that won't quit, here's what I do.
I think of what would make me,
at that moment,
the happiest person in the world.*[3]

Discussing Janet's situation with her parents, Bill and Betty, Helen received permission for Janet to stay with her family whenever she liked. She admired Janet's capacity to make new friends and to easily adapt to new situations. Janet's curiosity and her willingness to explore and challenge new ideas were intriguing to Helen. She saw

---

[3] Shirley MacLaine, *Out on a Limb* (New York: Bantam Books, 1983), 282.

Janet's self-confidence not as arrogance but, rather, as a statement that she could overcome any obstacle despite her family environment.

Helen had no doubt that Janet's mother, Vi, loved Janet and tried to be a good parent when she was sober, but the disease of alcoholism clouded her vision more often than not. Vi didn't have any specialized skills and had spent her years working as a fry cook, waitress, housekeeper, and a welder at the shipyards during World War II, making little more than enough money to buy her liquor. Helen tolerated Vi and actually liked her when she wasn't drinking. She thought that Vi might have settled for a marriage that was not good for her as a result of having had a baby out of wedlock. Helen had a dislike for Janet's father, Einar, finding him to be a difficult person to be around.

One evening, Helen was visiting at Janet's house because Janet didn't want to be alone. Vi had gone out for the evening, and Einer was working out of town. Vi came home intoxicated with a strange man tagging along in a similar condition. She looked at both Janet and Helen and said, "I want you to meet this old friend of mine." Then she looked at the man and said, "What's your name again?" Janet was upset and embarrassed by her mother's behavior, and she painfully kept her facade that everything was normal at home.

∞

Janet's Journal—*A Deadly Shade of Gold*, by John MacDonald

The physical act, when undertaken for any
motive other than love and need,
is a fragmenting experience.
The spirit wanders, there is a mild feeling
of distaste for one's self.
She was certainly sufficiently attractive,
mature, totally eager,
but we were still strangers.
She wanted to use me as a weapon against
her own lonely demons.

I wanted information from her.
We were more adversaries than lovers.[4]

Janet began to spend more and more time at Helen's house and became very close with her parents. As self-confident as Janet appeared, Helen found it humorous that Janet was usually nervous when having dinner at her mother's, Betty's, table. One evening, Janet was attempting to cut a piece of meat that was covered with catsup when it flipped off her plate flying across the table. Janet was mortified by her own clumsiness. A blush of pink coursed through her cheeks as she repeatedly apologized for her awkward behavior.

The two girls soon came to understand that they were drawn together due to similarities that they had in common. Helen's mother was a strict schoolteacher who provided a stable disciplined environment, whereas Helen's father was an alcoholic who caused upset quite frequently in his relationship with her mother. Although he was not as bad off as Einar, there was still that element of alcoholism that Janet could not escape. At least they had each other, and Janet was never completely alone after they became friends. Aside from their interest in music, they loved to play games and go to movies. They joined a high school sorority club called the Cosmo Ki and became involved in extracurricular activities.

∞

What Janet wrote in Helen's Roosevelt Ranger Yearbook

Helen,
You are a wonderful friend and I feel lucky that I have your friendship. I hope that you have lots of fun going to college and take your music seriously. You're so friendly to everyone. I know you'll make just as many and more friends at college as you have at Roosevelt. I'll always remember all the fun and good times we've had

---

[4] John MacDonald, *A Deadly Shade of Gold* (Philadelphia: Lippincott, 1974).

together. I hope we have lots more. Lots of good luck to you, Helen.

Love, Janet.

Janet's family life deteriorated completely when Einar drew out his government retirement money and purchased a tavern on the northwest side of Portland. He and Vi became their own best customers, and eventually, the business went downhill until they lost everything. Einar took to living on the streets and panhandling in downtown Portland. Sometime later, after Janet and Ron were married and had children, she ran into her father on the street while shopping with her boys. As she handed a dollar to the poor beggar, she was mortified when she recognized the man as her father. Living a rough life, Einar died as a result of being kicked in the head while he was passed out on the street.

∞

Janet's Journal—*A Deadly Shade of Gold,*
by John MacDonald

It is so strange about the dead. Life is like a
big ship, all lights, action and turmoil,
chugging across a dark sea.
You have to drop the dead ones over the side.
An insignificant little splash
and the ship goes on.[5]

---

[5] MacDonald, *A Deadly Shade of Gold.*

10

Early Imprints

Ron's Childhood

Ron was born in 1932 to Dell and Emily Adkins at Albany General Hospital in Albany, Oregon. Albany is located in the heart of the Willamette Valley just sixty-nine miles south of Portland, Oregon. It is known as a quaint little town where turn-of-the-century houses line the streets. Albany was the original home of the Calopooia Indians before being settled in 1848 by the early pioneers. Ron's ancestors were part of the early pioneers who had arrived by covered wagon and settled northeast of the town of Albany on Knox's Butte. They farmed the fertile land, and to this day, the Willamette Valley is prolific in raising crops of wheat, grain, and hops used by brewers.

Dell Adkins, Ron's father, was one of five children with three brothers, Wayne, Alfred and Larry and a sister named Alice. All the children were born and raised on the farm and eventually moved into the city of Albany. Unlike his roughneck brothers who often resorted to fighting to get their way, Ron's father was a quiet sensitive boy with a gentle disposition. He carried a sense of class about him and used his intelligence and wit to find his way in life.

In his early adult years, Ron's father developed a heart condition, which limited his ability to work and confined him to the house for a year. He filled his time with reading and enrolled in an electronics course, which at that time was a new industry. Of the four boys, he was the most mechanically inclined, which served him well throughout his life.

Ron's father and his two brothers, Larry and Al, started a firewood business while Wayne went to work for the railroad. As a young child, Ron was mesmerized by the humming sound of saws and the crackle of axes slicing wood. He often stood in awe, watching the belted saw devour enormous slabs of wood. For the family, the distinctive smell of wood chips permeating the humid summer air was a promise that money would soon be earned to put food on the table. Once the wood was cut and stacked, it was sold and delivered to the town's people to provide them with their basic source of heat.

Ron's father became the talk of the town when he successfully converted the wood stove to one that was heated by oil. The wood business continued to do well until a conflict arose between two of the wives over who was going to answer the phone and take the orders for the wood. The disharmony resulted in the business splitting apart, with each brother and his wife going their separate ways.

Alfred, Ron's favorite uncle, took his wife, Alice, and left town. Because of the Depression, their only means of survival was to live like their pioneer ancestors, camping out and hunting for food in the wilderness. They did some gold mining with Ron's great-uncle in southern Oregon and later moved on to cattle and potato farming in Northern California.

Ron's father branched out and started a gravel business partnering with logging companies in building logging roads. He had a good mind for business and successfully converted his wood hauling truck into a gravel truck. From that one truck, he built a business that ran four trucks at the peak of his gravel business. Like most boys, Ron was excited to accompany his father on the truck. Their drives would take them up dusty twisted roads where the eagles soared high and the deer ran free. The husky men, with sweat dripping from their bodies under the blistering sun, always had a kind word for Ron and seemed genuinely glad to see him. They could be heard hollering from the road, "Hey, little feller. We could sure use your help in building a road today." The business continued to do well, providing enough income for Ron's father to move them to a new home.

This was one of the happiest memories of Ron's childhood as the relationship grew deeper between him and his father. As a surprise, his parents presented him with a streamlined tricycle with fenders, which was the hottest thing in town. To Ron's delight, he became the envy of every child on the block, and the tricycle became the showpiece of the neighborhood.

Ron was a skinny child with a slight build, blue eyes, brown hair, and oversized ears. He was well liked by his peers, and by the time he entered the first grade at Central School, he was a self-confident and well-balanced child. His mother, Emily, enrolled him in xylophone lessons and he began to develop his love of music. The evening breeze often carried the tunes from his xylophone while his dad played along with his harmonica, violin, or banjo. Ron was blessed with musical talent from both sides of his family, but primarily it came from the Oxley side. Grandfather Oxley, Uncle Joe, Ron's mother, and her sisters were gifted vocalists who sang solos at church. Two of the sisters eventually made recordings and sang on the radio. Music was truly the lifeblood of this family.

∞

Janet's Journal—Author Unknown

Those who wish to sing always find a song.

Once again, Ron's father moved the family so he could take a job working on different logging roads. This move took them to Powers, Oregon. His father located a whimsical summer cottage on the Coquille River for his mother and son. The breathtaking beauty of the river and the solitude of the forest were the perfect setting for Ron's healthy development as a young boy. When his father was home, he loved spending quality time with him fishing on the river and the special times when his mother joined them with a picnic lunch. They were a family, and that was the most important thing in the world to Ron.

He was an energetic child with a mischievous disposition, and he took delight in playing practical jokes on both his mother and his friends. When he was six years old, he deliberately locked his mother in the bathroom by turning the key and removing it from the keyhole. He took great delight in this prank until his mother threatened him with severe punishment if he didn't let her out. However, that incident didn't put an end to his pranks with his mother. He was willing to risk punishment by continuing with his bad behavior. The pranks and jokes continued with his friends and became a permanent part of his personality that followed him into adulthood. His life was filled with the love and security, of what appeared to be a strong family unit, but that image would soon be shattered.

∞

Janet's Journal—Author Unknown

We all fail each other, especially those
we love most dearly. And is it so strange?
Wasn't Jesus singularly unsuccessful with
a great many people?
But love is what it's about, isn't it?
Not success.

Ron's mother was the daughter of Fred Oxley, who was a telegraph operator and a stationmaster for the railroad. Fred worked in a number of different towns throughout Oregon, and he worked as a minister for the Apostolic Faith Church in Albany. The family consisted of three girls and one boy: Emily, Mildred, Alpha, and Joe.

Grandfather Oxley was a talented singer and a well-respected minister. Ron often attended church camp meetings where he was proudly introduced as the grandson of the former Fred Oxley. The people of the church raved about Fred Oxley's wonderful voice and his gift as a minister. They were careful to keep the secret that haunted the family. Several years before Ron was born, Fred Oxley came down with a thyroid condition when he was in his early forty's. A goiter, caused by a lack of iodine, developed, with the hideous growth protruding from the side of his neck. The pain was grossly unbearable, and Grandfather Oxley became despondent. In an act of despair, he left home in the late hours of the evening with nothing more than a bedsheet. In the dark of the night, he found his way to the railroad tracks, where he laid himself down and was ripped to shreds by the next train traveling through his area. Yet, another suicide in this family dynamic, which would carry down to Ron's future sons having suicide on both sides of their family trees.

As a child, an attempt was made to shelter Ron from this disgraceful family incident. But, as children often do, Ron listened to the whispers of the relatives and the townspeople. The horror of that night had a way of leaking out, even to the ears of a child. Ron still remembered the piercing pain in the pit of his stomach when he overheard people telling the story of having to pick up his grandfather's remains, which had been scattered over the railroad track. What was left of Grandfather Oxley was placed on a rubber sheet and hauled away to the morgue. This was Ron's earliest recollection of a family illness that had been followed by a tragic suicide. His journey of questioning the meaning of life and death was beginning to take hold.

∞

Janet's Journal—Author Unknown

After Jean-Marr died very young of cancer
I looked at his still face.
Death isn't at all what you imagine
I told myself, a rendering, a tearing.
It's more like a logical conclusion,
a door you go through
which opens into something else.
Which is why country people who see things
more simply, say "pass on" instead of die.

Ron started the fifth grade in Powers, Oregon, surrounded by families who were considered mountain people. They were very poor and it was not unusual to see kids with bare feet at school. It was during this time that his mother took ill and had her appendix removed. She never fully recovered after that operation, and she began showing signs of a greater illness to come.

Within months, Ron's father moved them again, this time to Tillamook, Oregon. Ron was faced with adapting to yet another school. To cope with all these changes, and the continuous role of being the new kid on the block, Ron developed a coping method: by becoming the class clown. It was compounded by the fact that he was dyslexic, a condition that was not recognized at that time. Looking back, Ron remembers the humiliation of consistently reversing numbers and concepts. He had great difficulty spelling, and he was overtaken by the severity of punishment for not being able to spell. It particularly affected his writing ability when he had a good story to tell. Fortunately, by the time he reached college he had found a teacher who recognized his problem and identified a method to assist him with his spelling. Ron's humiliation over this affliction was eased when he discovered that George Washington also had trouble with spelling.

He finished up the school year in a one-room schoolhouse with only one teacher for twenty-five students ranging from first to the eighth grade. The room was heated by a potbelly stove, and each student had his or her own desk with an inkwell and a seat that flipped up with a storage unit underneath. Ron's experience was enhanced by the fact that he was the only boy in the entire school. The twenty-four girls with their hair bound in braids and their flirtatious grins were a memorable educational experience for Ron. By the time he entered the sixth grade, his mother's health was failing, and he was taking care of his mother every day. His father was gone for weeks at a time, and he was forced to take on the role of the man of the house. When his father was home, he spent his after-hours hanging out with his employees at the local tavern. When he finally returned home smelling of beer, cigars, and cheap perfume, Ron's mother would be furious. Ron would be witness to their constant fighting and bickering.

∞

Janet's Journal—Letter 1869, by George Sand

I would like the little ones to be shown only the sweet and the good of life.

94

Until the time when reason can help them to accept or to fight the bad.[1]

On one occasion, Ron's father took him and his mother on a temporary job he had in Newport, Oregon. After putting them up at the Newport Hotel and joining them for dinner, his father disappeared for the rest of the evening, which added to Ron's suspicion that he was up to no good. His withdrawal from the family and his inconsiderate behavior only added to his mother's stress and accelerated her deteriorating health condition.

Ron was saddened to see his mother in such agony, both physically and emotionally. Her hands shook all the time and she had equilibrium problems, which affected her walking. She had a hard time getting around, with one foot always dragging behind her. Her mind was still in excellent form, but her body was deteriorating. This was an ironic twist, which was just the opposite of Janet's illness to come. How could Ron have known that his mother's illness would be preparation for his role with Janet's disease?

∞

Janet's Journal—Gloria Steinem, about her mother

Perhaps the worst thing about suffering is that it finally hardens the hearts of those around it.[2]

Ron's mother's condition continued to decline. When she was finally admitted for medical testing, she was eventually diagnosed with multiple sclerosis. Mildred, his mother's sister, had already taken in Grandmother Oxley after Grandfather Oxley's suicide. She graciously opened her home to Ron's mother, but ironically there was *'no room at the inn'* for Ron. Just eleven years old, he was taken from

---

[1] George Sand, letter to Gustave Flaubert, at Croisset Nohant, February 24, 1869, accessed July 29, 2019, https://ebooks.adelaide .edu.au/f/flaubert/gustave/f58g/letter106.html.

[2] Gloria Steinem, "Perhaps the Worst Thing," AZ Quotes, accessed July 29, 2019, https://www.azquotes.com/quote/947188.

his mother and sent to live with his dad's sister, Betty, in Portland, Oregon. As any child would be, Ron was stricken with intense sadness and grief with the separation from his parents.

$$\infty$$

By Ron Adkins

When you are out at sea all you can think about is keeping your sail set and holding onto the tiller. You don't have much time to think about where you are going or why you are there.

Aunt Betty had been married five times. She spent her evenings sitting around the house with her mother drinking coffee and smoking cigarettes. The conversation was always centered on gossip where they spent the majority of their time talking badly about men. Ron started smoking in the seventh grade and spent many nights drinking coffee, smoking cigarettes, and listening to the gossip of the '*hens in the hen house.*' His favorite uncle, Al, was more of a father to him than his dad ever could be at that time in his life. He convinced Ron that he should ignore the hens, as their cruel gossip and constant complaining were sure to catch up with them one day.

Ron's father's visits to see his mother began to decline, throwing suspicion on his intentions and his whereabouts. Eventually, he let it be known that he had a girlfriend named Opal. She began to show up during the holidays, including Christmas, when all the family was together. As a result of his involvement with Opal, he started divorce proceedings. The Oxleys were furious when he filed for divorce, listing Ron's mother as an '*unfit mother.*' A divorce was granted, and his father ran off with Opal, leaving Ron to fend for himself.

Ron carried a tremendous amount of resentment toward his father and Opal. His anger was exemplified by the fact that his father had run off with another woman when his mother was sick. His father was keenly aware of the fact that Ron was greatly affected by his lifestyle, but he did nothing to rectify the situation. In later years he recognized that his choices had affected Ron's life, and he attempted to make it up to him.

Ron stayed with his Aunt Betty for a year, and then his grandmother Adkins took him into her home. Even in 1948, grandparents were raising grandchildren, much as they are today. He lived with his grandmother on her acreage and took care of the farm while she worked as the head chef for the Riverside Golf and Country Club. With an extra teenage mouth to feed, money was tight as was to be expected. Ron was required to help in any way that would bring additional income to the household. When all the neighborhood kids were out playing, his time was spent with his grandmother, emptying the drop pans for a thousand chickens and tending to the vegetable garden. He loved his grandmother and was grateful to her for taking him in, but he longed for a normal home life with his parents.

It was a very depressing and difficult time for Ron to be without his parents during his seventh and eighth grade years. One day the principal called him into the office and inquired about his obvious behavioral change. He had always been the class clown, and now his personality was reflecting one of darkness. He told the principal that he had been shuffled around like an old dog since his mother had been taken away from him and his father had run off with Opal. Unfortunately, the schools did not have therapists in those days, and Ron was left to fend for himself to sort out his feelings of abandonment and despair.

∞

Janet's Journal—Ralph Waldo Emerson

On the debris of our despair
we build our character.

Opal was a woman whose face was masked with deceit and lies. She fussed over Ron and tried to take his mother's place. Ron's mother was a proper woman with high morals and ideals. On the contrast, he considered Opal to be a low-class individual. For Ron, watching his father slipping away from them was very upsetting.

Opal's announcement that she was pregnant with his father's child shocked the whole family. He informed Ron's grandmother that he and Opal would be moving into the farmhouse. Grandmother

Adkins was absolutely furious about the situation, and Ron's resentment continued to grow. His father lost his gravel trucks, went bankrupt, and took a job as a mechanic. Within a short time, he was back on his feet and had earned enough money to buy a house. About the same time, Grandmother Adkins sold her acreage and moved to Long Beach, California. Ron was left with no choice but to move in with his father and Opal since he had nowhere else to go.

Five children were born to his father and Opal. The children were raised in a tiny cottage with cramped living quarters. As the family grew in size, his father built bunk beds for the children that projected off the walls in the closet. Ron was left to sleep on the couch in the overcrowded front room of the house.

Life to Ron was like living in no-man's land. Opal had no concept of cleanliness or motherhood, for that matter. She slept all day and did nothing to add to the well-being of the family. The rancid smell of soiled diapers permeated the air and was quick to send an empty stomach into rapid convulsions. She hated cooking, and dishes were left to pile up on the counters until maggots found the last morsel of food. The house was filthy and had become an open invitation to rodents seeking out their next meal and a warm place to nest.

∞

Janet's Journal—*Out on a Limb*, by Shirley MacLaine

*Work hard, don't lie,
and try not to hurt anyone.*[3]

Opal and Ron's father were alcoholics. Their constant fighting created an intolerable atmosphere in which to raise their family. When Opal was in a drunken stupor, she went after Ron's father with a butcher knife, with the deliberate intention of doing him bodily harm. As a child, Ron held the belief that he was unique and that he

---

[3] Shirley MacLaine, *Out on a Limb* (New York: Bantam, 1983), 295.

was the only child who had to live in these horrid conditions. These were very depressing times in his life.

∞

**Janet's Journal—*Baltimore 1692*,
by Anon**

*Speak your truth quietly and clearly and
listen to others even the dull and ignorant.
They too have their story.*

That Ron's mother was not going to recover became evident, so her family sent her to live with members of the Apostolic Church. Ron tried his best to maintain a relationship with his mother, traveling by bus to visit her on Sundays when she lived in Portland. She was eventually moved to Grants Pass, which made the long twelve-hour round trip more difficult. Their visits were spent in small talk that carried little to no importance. She commented on the fact that she was proud of Ron for attending high school, as she herself had received an education and graduated from high school. His father, on the other hand, had dropped out of grade school and had never gone on to high school, which was fairly common in a rural community.

Watching his mother lose her husband, her family, and her dignity was extremely difficult for Ron. In her eyes, she had been diminished to nothing. All the belongings of her entire life were placed in a small cedar chest at the end of her bed. The fact that she could not be a mother to Ron only intensified her sorrow. When he visited his mother, her tears flowed like an untamed river as she apologized for her illness and expressed her undying love for him, her only child. Watching her lying there, unable to move, trapped in her small, useless body was a humbling experience for Ron. Her mind was intact, but her body was only a shell of the woman who had once been a refined and elegant human being. His mother dying at the young age of forty-five was bittersweet. He was glad that she was relieved of her suffering, but he knew there would always be an emptiness and void in his heart.

∞

Janet's Journal—*One Fearful Yellow Eye,* by John MacDonald

Every day, no matter how you fight it,
you learn a little more about yourself
and all most of it does is teach humility.[4]

Ron established a family connection with his uncle Al and aunt Alice, who were openly accepting of other people's lifestyles. He was amused by their love of pulp-fiction western magazines and the fact that the other relatives labeled them as lazy because they always had their nose in a magazine while everyone else was out working the fields.

During his freshman year of high school, he took an interest in electrical engineering. He enrolled at Benson Polytechnic public high school, which was the most unique technical boys' school west of the Mississippi. The school offered technical courses in preparation for college engineering. He was in his element as he studied electric theory and engineering courses, which was something that really caught his interest.

Ron worked during the summer months for his uncle Al on his sixty-acre farm in Oregon City, plowing and hoeing. One summer he made seventy-five dollars and was able to purchase his first trumpet from the band director at the school. Thus began his musical career. He started out playing the trumpet in the freshman band. By his senior year he was playing the French horn and string bass. He was recognized for his talent and ability and received invitations to join the All City Band, All City Orchestra, and Junior Symphony.

This new interest made his life complete in a way he had never known. For the first time in his life he was someone to be admired. People looked up to him and wanted to share in his glory. This carried over to his education and he maintained excellent grades and achieved honor roll status.

---

[4] John MacDonald, One Fearful Yellow Eye, trade paperback ed. (New York: Random House, 2013), 222.

The band director, Norman, became Ron's mentor. He instilled in his students the notion that they had the capability to accomplish anything they set their minds to. As a result of that affirmation, the band took first place three years in a row for the Rose Festival Parade in Portland, Oregon. The students beamed with pride over these accomplishments, which propelled them in their abilities and self-confidence. Ron became the president of the band and joined the union playing professionally in a jazz band his senior year.

Norman made a tremendous impact on Ron's life, so much so that he named his second son after the band director. Many of the band members went on to play with big bands and symphony orchestras all over the world. Even to this day, whenever Ron attends a class reunion, his classmates still attribute their success in life to Norman and to his belief that they could accomplish whatever they set their minds to. This motto eventually became the foremost theme among his three sons.

His self-confidence and interest in life had finally taken a turn for the better. However, up until his junior year in high school, the conditions that he continued to live in were mortifying. He was without a bedroom, sleeping on the couch night after night. In the cramped quarters, and without a corner to call his own, the only privacy that could be found was to lock himself in the bathroom to practice his music. With the notes bellowing from the French horn and bouncing off four walls, he was successful in drowning out the sounds of the screaming children and the vulgar language coming from Opal.

On one particular day, in the cold of winter, he was invited over to a friend's house after school. Billy's warm, cozy house smelled of freshly baked cookies and hot cocoa that his mother had set out on the table for them. Billy proudly showed Ron his private bedroom and the model airplanes he had built. He had all the things Ron wanted as a boy but could never have. Ron left Billy's house with a heavy heart. He carried a chip on his shoulder with an attitude that life was not fair. He had been born into a bad situation, and it didn't seem right that his friends could have what he couldn't have. It hurt him deeply, and he wallowed in his feelings of despair. On the way home he made a Christmas wish for a loving family who would provide him the love that he desperately needed, along with a nice warm house with a bedroom all to his own. As if by magic, his wish was granted when Grandmother Adkins moved back to town and graciously opened her home to him once again.

∞

Janet's Journal—Author Unknown

I've discovered that to be happy
we must have someone to love,
something to do and something to hope for.

Ron continued to excel in high school. His entrepreneurial spirit was enhanced on joining Junior Achievement and studying the art of business. Very soon he was elected president of JAC Wood Products Company. His company created a board of directors, sold shares of stock, and designed and manufactured a footstool that won national honors in the wood products division. Junior Achievement became the foundation for his success in business.

He graduated from Benson High School in 1951 with a technical background and started college that same year. He was the first person on the Adkins' side to graduate from high school and the only one to graduate from college. Sadly enough, the only family members who attended his graduation were his grandmother Adkins and his aunt Betty.

∞

Janet's Journal—Elizabeth Kübler Ross

There is no grief more deeply felt
than the loss of a childhood.

His father stayed married to Opal until their children finished high school. After twenty years of marriage, he divorced Opal and went to live with his sister Betty. She introduced him to her friend, an absolutely charming woman in her fifties who was a beautiful and lovely individual. They eventually married and spent several happy years together traveling in their recreational vehicle while spending their winters in Arizona and their summers in Portland.

One summer day, his father and his wife went fishing on the Columbia River. While returning to Portland, they were involved in a fatal automobile accident. Although they had both been wearing seatbelts, his father was killed in the accident, and his wife sustained severe injuries. Ron was filled with grief over the incident, but he was grateful that his father had spent several good years of his life with a wonderful woman. Once again, he was left to deal with the loss of a parent and his issues of abandonment that he had felt as a child.

He enrolled at Vanport College, later named Portland State University. He took a job at a music store in Portland during the day and worked dance jobs by night. He had planned to attend Oregon State in Corvallis to get his engineering degree, but because the location was not feasible in terms of making a living, he resigned himself to staying in Portland and attending Vanport College during his freshman and sophomore year.

He worked at the music store during the day, and in the evenings, he played in nightclubs. As his popularity increased, so did the demand on his time. He was now playing the string bass as many as six nights per week. It soon became evident that his focus had changed from engineering to music, business, literature, and the arts. He was a gifted musician and found that he received an intense emotional release through his music, particularly when he was playing jazz. When he allowed himself to ad lib his chorus and melt into the creativity flowing through him, the result was a climactic release of all the pent-up emotions of his existence.

The band director, Norman, continued to have a great influence in his life. He had a summer reading band and offered open invitations to all the young musicians around the city. It was a great way for Ron to get acquainted with other musicians and meet students of the opposite gender. That was the first glimpse of his future with Janet.

11

To Love and Be Loved

Janet and Ron met while playing in the Summer Reading Band. One evening Ron joined the group with his friend Floyd who played the trumpet. Floyd's girlfriend, Marlice, was a flute player who had brought along her friend, Janet. Ron and Janet were invited to double date with Floyd and Marlice, and that was the start of their three-year steady relationship.

Janet was young at the time, just sixteen, and Ron was nineteen. To Ron, Janet was beautiful, intellectually stimulating, and striving to be the best she could be. She was a good musician who had a talent for playing multiple instruments. She played the French horn, string bass, flute, and piano, which were a very unique and complementary combination. They bonded quickly after discovering that they had both come from similar backgrounds of neglect and abandonment. For Ron, it was love at first sight, but not so for Janet. She had a crush on another boy at the time. She eventually decided to take her friend Helen's advice that Ron was a much better catch and that she had better snag him while she still had the chance.

Janet's Journal—Author Unknown

*"Damn," said Niniane when she realized
she was in love with Robert Irwin.
He asked her why she said "damn"
and she answered,*

*I suppose because it's bound to
interfere with my freedom.*

They married on August 5, 1955, at the White Temple Baptist
Church in Portland, Oregon. When they exchanged their vows Janet
was nineteen, and Ron was twenty-one. Janet's parents were drinking
heavily at the time. Janet had invited them to the marriage ceremony
but had no idea if they would come. Janet's aunts wanted to get
involved in planning the reception and insisted on using good china.
Material things and appearances were never important to Janet, and
she was content to keep things as simple as possible by using paper
plates.

Helen was honored when Janet asked her to be the maid of
honor at their wedding. Ron asked his friend Calvin to be his best
man as he had been his best friend through grade school and high
school. There was no way that any of this group could have known
that Janet, Calvin, and Helen's youngest son, Johnny, would all die
by suicide. In later years, Calvin broke a hip that would not heal.
Under the influence of a mind-altering pain medication, Calvin
jumped to his death off a bridge in Newport Beach, California. In
later years, Helen's son, Johnny, died a similar death. Was this just a
coincidence, or was this group of souls destined to come together?
Ron's relationship with Janet and this new experience of love brought
a passionate element into his life, which was to love and be loved. He
hadn't known love since being separated from his mother at an early
age. He never felt accepted by his father, and he believed that his
father would never have deserted his wife and son if he had truly
loved them.

∞

**Janet's Journal—*A Severed Wasp*,
by Madeline L'Engle**

*Part of life is getting used to living
with the things that will always hurt you.
Once love has been awakened,
the flame never entirely dies.*

She knew and accepted that it
is quite possible to love more than one person
simultaneously, ultimately, adding to
rather than taking away from the other.[1]

In the beginning of their relationship both Janet and Ron were very insecure because of their lost childhoods and the terrible conditions they had endured. They fought continually about insignificant things, each trying to gain a sense of control over the other. Ron was tremendously jealous of Janet, even more so after they married. He loved her dearly and feared losing her because he had lost everything else in his life.

He used to tease Janet, even up until the last days of her life in Detroit. He told her that she had fallen in love with his horn playing, and then she had fallen in love with him. She always denied it, but he believed it to be true, and he still believes it to this day. He has always believed that when a man and a woman are in a love relationship, one loves more than the other, and the one who loves the least controls the relationship. This was certainly true with them throughout their thirty-four years of marriage. Ron put Janet on a pedestal, and he allowed her to pull his heartstrings.

∞

Janet's Journal—*Madame Bovary*,
by Gustave Flaubert

At the bottom of her heart, however, she was
waiting for something to happen.
Like shipwrecked sailors, she turned
despairing eyes upon the solitude
of her life, seeking afar off some white sail
in the mists of the horizon.
She did not know what this change would be,
what wind would bring it to her,
towards what shore it would drive her,

---

[1] Madeline L'Engle, *A Severed Wasp* (New York: Open Road Integrated Media, 2017), 306.

if it would be a shallop or a three-decker,
laden with anguish or full of bliss
to the portholes.
But, each morning as she awoke, she hoped
it would come that day; she listened
to every sound, sprang up with a start,
wondered that it did not come; then at sunset,
always more saddened,
she longed for the morrow.[2]

Their honeymoon was spent on the Oregon coast. Ironically, the only hotel that had a room for the night just happened to be the same hotel where Ron's father had put his mother and him up for the night while he was having his affair with Opal.

Upon returning from their honeymoon, a letter was waiting for Ron from the draft board. He was stunned to find out that he had been drafted and that the draft board had no record that he was a full-time student. To his dismay, it was too late to reverse the order. It was a traumatic time for the newlyweds. They had just rented an apartment and set up housekeeping. Now Ron was expected to report for duty in December.

He was assigned to basic training at Fort Ord, California, for three months, leaving Janet behind in Portland. One day he was called out of the ranks and given an audition for the army band. By a strange coincidence, the member who auditioned him on the French horn had taken lessons from the same horn teacher that Ron had in Portland. He played exceptionally well and passed the audition with flying colors. He was immediately sent to Fort Dix, New Jersey, for training in the army band school. Upon graduating, he was eligible for assignment to any army band in the world.

His first assignment was to play in a band in France. It was a fantastic opportunity, but he was unable to appreciate it at the time because he was experiencing intense grief and depression with the separation from his new bride. The emotional pain that he felt as a young man, growing up without parents, had diminished to a tolerable state when he met Janet. But now, that familiar gnawing

---

[2] Gustave Flaubert, *Madame Bovary* (New York: Shine Classics, 2014), 35.

feeling had returned with the fury of an enemy that intended to rip his heart from his very soul. But, as fate would have it, he was offered an outstanding assignment in Orleans, France, to play in the Seventy-Sixth Army Band. Because the master sergeant of the band training school had grown concerned with Ron's circumstances, he went out of his way to make certain that Ron's new assignment would include his bride.

Ron arrived in France in the spring of 1956, and Janet joined him four months later. By the time Janet arrived, he had located a quaint chateau that had been built in 1640. The accommodations included a private bedroom with the sharing of the common spaces. They lived at the chateau for four months until an apartment became available from a trombone player who played in the band. When he moved out, the apartment was offered to Janet and Ron. Their new home was located directly across the street from the French Caserne, a French military complex that had been taken over by the US army. It was the headquarters for the Com-Z, which provided ammunition and supplies to American soldiers in Germany in case of a Russian breakthrough. The new location allowed Ron a painless commute to work. He began his day with a short walk across the street to join the army band for their 7:00 a.m. concert of marches. The music was a welcome greeting to the soldiers and generals as they arrived for duty. Their new home was a marvelous set up for Janet, as she would have frequent visits by the band wives when they came to shop at the Caserne.

They were living a unique experience that most people would never know. They were on the other side of the world in a glamorous, beautiful country filled with history and romance. Opportunity had come knocking on their door. Ron's assignment took him all over Europe and introduced him to the culture of the European world while the band played tribute to the souls who had been buried in the World War II cemeteries.

One of the more memorable occasions in their lives was the opportunity to sing in the chapel choir retreat with vocalists from all over Europe. On February 21, 1957, Janet and Ron were personally invited to attend a retreat at the Usareur Religious Retreat House Alpine Inn, in Berchtesgaden, Germany. The clinic director, Edwin Wilson, was a student of orchestral conducting at the Bavarian

Staatliche Hochschule fur Musik, Munich, and he was responsible for founding the Protestant Choir Clinic as a means of promoting music in the military chapel program.

The backdrop for the scene was one out of a fairy tale. The immense jagged mountains towered over the tiny village on that bitter-cold day in February. The brilliant rays of sunlight reflected rainbows that danced and spun across the icy snow with each chord sung, from the songs that they were singing, such as "Come, Let Us All This Day" by Bach, "Let All the Nations Praise the Lord" by Leisrin, "In Death's Strong Grasp the Savior Lay" by Bach, "I Will Lift Up Mine Eyes" by Sowerby, and "Let Down the Bars, O Death" by Barber.

How their lives had turned around in such a short time was amazing. They were truly blessed with a life of abundance that was full of unique experiences that were a rarity to most people of the world. They were free to spread their wings like birds released from a cage. But most of all, they felt extremely fortunate to be living oceans apart from their alcoholic families who had been a negative influence on their lives.

They found they were one and the same with this new country and soon settled into the life of a French married couple. They learned the ways of the French people and discovered that they had a craving for new and unusual foods. They frequented quaint French restaurants and dined on delicacies that were rarities in the Western world. Upon the completion of one of their favorite meals, the only remnants that remained on the plate were a pile of tiny fragile bones that looked similar to toothpicks. As their romantic evening came to a close, the sounds of Janet's giggles could be heard as Ron ribbitted sweet-nothings in his bride's ear.

That Ron would be stationed in France for some time became evident. He arranged for a woman to come into their home and teach Janet French. Because Ron was traveling all over Europe, he was not allotted the time to learn the French language. However, he continually teased Janet by insisting she allow him to take a young French girl who could teach him the ways of the French.

∞

Janet's Journal—*Languages of the World,*
by Charles Berlitz

It has been said that living in the world and
speaking only one language is somewhat
equivalent to living in an enormous mansion
and staying in only one room.
Those who acquire more than one language
find fascinating new and different vistas
opening before them, not only of practical
opportunity but for the fulfillment of intellectual
curiosity and the fascination of looking at the
world from a background and viewpoint
of another culture.

As Ron matured, he became more serious about life. He had decided early on that he didn't want to have children, and he intended to place his focus on building a career in the business world when he got out of the army. He still carried resentments toward Opal for hooking his father with her pregnancy. He had been obsessively cautious during his courting years, and he had no intention of ever getting a girl pregnant. He was certain in his own mind that this was not a path he wanted to take. He didn't want to be forced into a situation that would control his destiny like his father's entrapment with Opal. He had determined long before meeting Janet that the only reason he wanted a woman or a wife was to have a companion at parties or business functions.

Ron underwent a metamorphosis while in France. The magic of the beautiful country drew him into the love mode. A delightful child, Marcia, whom Janet took care of while her parents were traveling in the band, was responsible for changing their lives. Children became the main topic of discussion. That Janet wanted six children and Ron didn't want any was clear, so they compromised on three.

Janet became pregnant with their first child while in France. She stopped smoking only to find that she had zero tolerance for others' smoke. The slightest hint of smoke on Ron's uniform would send her reeling to the bathroom. He would have to change into fresh clothes before he would be allowed into the house. As Janet's belly grew, so did his anticipation of a new member to their family. When her time came to give birth, Janet was taken to a French retirement home that had been converted into an army hospital in a little village outside Orleans. It was a beehive of activity filled with the moaning, groaning, and terrifying screams from the army wives who felt isolated and alone giving birth in this foreign land. The head pediatrician examined Janet once. Then he went off duty for the next three days, leaving an inexperienced staff to cope with Janet's labor.

To keep his mind occupied during those three days, and to act as a deterrent to witnessing the excessive pain his wife was experiencing, Ron turned his attention to the music playing inside his head. By counting the contractions and using the rhythm of those contractions, he formed the tempo for the music of a ballet. He chose sections of the hospital for the setting and visualized the nurses spinning round and round to the tempo of each contraction. Faster and faster they spun until they reached the exciting culmination, which would result in the birth of their child.

When the doctor finally returned from his leave, Janet was exhausted and nearly hysterical from experiencing three days of intense labor with a baby that was now in fetal distress. The doctor immediately stimulated her uterus and pulled out their infant son with forceps. All too late in this case, it was discovered that Janet had a lazy uterus, which became vital information for future pregnancies.

Thousands of miles from his parents' homeland, Neil was the product of their romantic bliss. Born to young lovers in Orleans, France, on January 10, 1958, Neil was a gift from God in its purest form. Their dark-haired, blue-eyed baby was deeply loved and wanted from the moment of his conception.

∞

Little Man—Written for Neil, by Janet Adkins

He's just a little man, our son,
Soft, tiny, pink and leaning

Sprung from this amalgamation of love
For life and meaning.
He's just a little man, our son,
He coos and smiles and romps and plays,
Our hearts turn over and are won,
By his each endearing, charming way.
School begins, the years do speed,
And he all too quickly grows up tall.
He's borrowed we are told, take heed,
Enjoy and love him, time will call.
He's just a little man, our son,
And with God's hand to guide,
He'll wax and grow
Till he'll become, a man, of strength and pride.
He's now a bigger man, our son,
Ours once and now adult and grown,
He's our bequest as we pass on, the answer
To our "why" is known.

Nothing could have prepared Ron for the surge of emotion that pierced his very soul when he laid eyes on his newborn son. As tears of joy welled up in his eyes, he took the precious baby into his arms and vowed that his son would never experience the home life to which he and Janet had been exposed. Filled with gratitude and love for his wife and son, Ron gave thanks for the gift of life and for this new responsibility entrusted to his care.

∞

<u>Janet's Journal—Levin at the birth of his child,</u>
<u>*Anna Karenina*, by Leo Tolstoy</u>

All he knew and felt was that what was
happening was what had happened nearly a
year before in the hotel of the country town at
the deathbed of his brother Nicholas. Only that
was grief and this was joy. But that grief and
this joy were equally beyond the usual

113

conditions of life. They were loopholes as it were, in that ordinary life through which there came glimpses of something sublime. And, in the contemplation of this sublime, the soul was exalted to inconceivable heights, of which it had before had no conception, while reason lagged behind unable to keep up with it.

While in France, Janet met Carroll, who would become her lifelong friend and the woman who would later accompany Janet to her death. When the young women met, Carroll was nineteen and Janet was twenty. Carroll considered herself narrow-minded in her views about life due to her upbringing in the Lutheran Church. On the contrary, she viewed Janet as open to everything and willing to challenge every new idea that came along. Janet asked personal questions that Carroll would never have thought to ask because, in Carroll's opinion, they were much too private. Once exposed to Janet's way of thinking, she began to view things from a completely different perspective.

Janet and Carroll found themselves alone in a strange country, oceans apart from their family and friends. While Carroll's husband and Ron were traveling in the army band, the women bonded through their pregnancies both giving birth to healthy boys. In addition to motherhood, they passed their time playing silly card games and teaching Bible school.

∞

Janet's Letter to Betty and Bill (Helen's parents), January 13, 1958

Just finished nursing the baby and have an hour till lunch so thought I'd scribble a few lines. Wednesday we get to go home from the hospital and from then on we'll be on our own with the baby. I don't feel too nervous or worried because Neil is so big, and he seems to be taking to the breast quite well. He's actually fat, just like you

114

said your Gracie was. I guess he ought to be, being 22 days late. I was beginning to think he didn't ever want to come out. I was in labor for 3-1/2 days. Poor Ron must have made 50 million trips out to the hospital and each time I was still in the labor room. But we're so happy with our boy. We're ready to have 3 or 4 more.

Today little Betsy is one year old. We sure enjoyed getting the picture from Helen and I can't wait to see her in person. Well, from now on, the time should go fast. Only four months left for us over here.

Oh, Betty, would you mind too much if I sent some of our things to your place? We want to start packing and sending as many things home as possible. Would you have room to set them upstairs until we get home? Be honest, now.

Gosh, I feel so good I almost wish I were going home today. Two of the mothers are leaving today and that leaves just three of us here. But, with all the pregnant ladies here there should be more coming in soon.

I told Gracie I'd send all my maternity clothes (Helen's too) home, and she's welcome to use any of them she wants. (Personally, I can't wait to get home to try on my red jumper). Gracie should be about in maternity clothes now. I bet she looks cute. Tall, slim people look so much better in them than short people. But, I sort of enjoyed wearing them.

Tell Gracie that there's absolutely nothing as wonderful as having a baby. You know what I did? The doctor showed me the baby as soon as it was born, and it was crying, and all I could do was cry, too. I was so happy and so relieved that he was alright after being pushed around in labor so long—and so happy, too, that he was a boy because that's what Ron had his heart set on.

I didn't tell you what he looks like. He's not at all like we had him pictured. He's just his own self. He has long, straight black hair, big fat cheeks, round face, dimpled chin, maybe he has my eyes, and I don't know whose nose. His feet are so long, and right now he's peeling all over. Quite a little rascal. We'll take pictures and send them as soon as we get home.

Well Betty, this is all for now and hope you'll write us a long letter soon.

Love from Janet, Ron and little Neil.

P.S. Incidentally you're a good baby predictor.

Six months after the birth of their son, Ron was granted a discharge from the army after completion of a three-year term. The time had finally arrived to return to the States.

12

Mental Illness Is a Killer

With his beautiful wife and child, they boarded a plane to Portland, Oregon, having arranged to stay with Bill and Betty until they found a suitable place to live.

When Janet reconnected with Helen's parents, she learned that Helen, her childhood friend and bridesmaid, had given birth to a son while Janet was in France. In later years, Helen's son, Johnny, was diagnosed with a bipolar mental condition. With his first psychotic break, he was hospitalized at Fairfax in-patient facility for adolescents. After that, it became a frequent event.

A highly gifted child, Johnny had many talents. One time while hospitalized, he received a letter stating that he had won $200 in a writing contest. He played the piano and the horn, he sang in the choir, and he was a musician in the Seattle All City Junior Symphony. Unable to sleep at night, Johnny would wake up everyone in the house by playing the piano at 2:00 a.m. One evening Johnny boarded an empty Metro bus. Tired of waiting for the bus driver to finish his break, he drove off with the bus and was stopped by the Seattle Police. The personal disruptions were now starting to venture outside the privacy of their home. Yet another incident occurred at Helen's place of employment. Called to the front counter at work, she was greeted by a police officer who had come to take her statement concerning a threat she had received. Apparently, Johnny had called the police department, imitated her voice, and requested assistance, indicating that she was being threatened on the job. It was a time in her life when she was hoping that they would reserve a bed for her at the hospital so she could get some rest and keep her sanity. All her time and energy were focused on Johnny.

As Johnny's condition worsened, Helen became concerned not only for her sanity but her safety as well. Arriving home from work, she found that Johnny had turned on every faucet, every burner, and every appliance in the house. The paint had begun to blister on the walls, and that the house was still standing was a miracle. When the police arrived, they were met with the unpleasant challenge of subduing Johnny, who was kicking and screaming as medical staff strapped him into the ambulance. After that episode, Helen disconnected herself from Johnny for her own safety. Like a battered wife trying to escape an abusive husband, she moved out without notifying Johnny. If Johnny needed her, she could be notified through her other two children. Shortly after moving, she received the tragic notification that her disturbed son had jumped to his death off the Seattle Aurora Bridge. Just eighteen years old, Johnny had taken his young life in a fit of desperation to end his emotional anguish.

Was it just a coincidence that Johnny and Janet had been stricken with terrible diseases that stole their minds? Or could it be that the mysterious power of attraction is much stronger than anyone realizes? Could it be that people attract other people or situations that carry common threads of life experiences, even though it may not be evident at the time? Could anyone have prevented these deaths? If Johnny and Janet had been locked away for their own safety, their deaths might have been prevented, but would the suffering and anguish have been prevented? Probably not, unless they were so medicated that they didn't know the difference. Then what kind of life would that have been? Helen helped Janet escape from a terrible childhood environment, but ultimately, she could not save Janet or her own son from taking their lives. Both Janet and Johnny had become someone different than the people she had known. Both had mind-altering diseases.

13

The Music Man

After hearing about student housing for low-income families, Ron applied for an apartment so he could attend college to complete his senior year. It was an affordable way to live and attend school at the same time with rent being twenty-eight dollars per month. The apartment unit housed a variety of interesting people ranging from welfare to medical students. These students provided them with an intellectual stimulus that added intense color to their lives.

While living there, Janet gave birth to their second son, Norman. Born on October 20, 1960, Norman entered this world as a high-spirited child. Staring into the eyes of her newborn son, Janet recognized something deep and profound. If the eyes are truly the windows of the soul, Norman's reflected the ancient wisdom of an old, wise being who had been carried over for many lifetimes. Janet always told Ron, when she looked into Norman's eyes, that he knew far more than she did. She also perceived an independent spirit in him, one that she knew would challenge her in this lifetime.

Janet's Journal

My God how I'd like some uninterrupted time; to think, to read, and to write. Two little boys take my constant care. One just now said, "I yuv you mommy." Two little sons, busy and eager, crying and pleading to be channeled along a worthwhile path of existence. Tis a great job at

hand for me and I am proud. What will they be
when they are grown? No thoughts of this sort
enter their minds now.

Upon completion of his senior year, Ron applied to several stock brokerage firms in Portland. He was invited to join a firm, but since the position was not immediately available, he accepted a job at a grade school in Forest Grove teaching music for kindergarten through sixth grade. He entered the position with apprehension, as he had no previous experience teaching vocal music. His misgivings were soon put to rest when the students nicknamed him the *'Music Man.'* Folk musicians, including Peter, Paul, and Mary, were popular at the time, so Ron learned to vocalize and play the guitar. These were good times for Janet and Ron. Janet taught piano, developed a base of students who she worked with on a regular basis, and sought to improve her own skills.

∞

Janet's Journal

I've been studying piano this year. I worked on Debussy's Ballade, Chopin Etudes, and Waltzes. Lots of Bach and some Bartók and Scriabin. My thinking is that I'd better get lessons in before the boys begin and we can't afford it. I manage to get in a good hour of practice a day. About three weeks ago I accompanied two of my flute playing friends in a Telemann Trio Sonata at Pacific University in Forest Grove. The piano was a brand-new Baldwin Grand and very stiff, but the concert went well, and the experience was good for all three of us because we hadn't played in public since college days.

They made friends with couples who had children the same age as their two sons and formed a musical group with other musicians in Forest Grove. It seemed like the perfect place to raise a family as

Janet gave birth to their third son, Ronald, a blond, green-eyed baby who entered this world on February 23, 1964. If anyone had inherited the philosophical side of Janet, it was Ronald.

∞

Janet's Journal—Ronald

Ronald William is fifteen months old now and Mr. Sweetness himself.

∞

Janet's Journal—Norman

Norman was just wheeled into surgery for a hernia operation. It's routine and simple, but it's still an anxious experience for a parent. We have a private room so that I can stay at night, which is a comfort to both Norman and me. Seeing sick children here on the pediatric ward is a bit much. I could never be a pediatric nurse.

∞

Janet's Journal—Neil

Neil finished first grade this year and seemed to like school fairly well.

He has lately been asking why he's the smallest boy in his class. He frequently steps on the bathroom scale to see if he's growing but we tell him it doesn't matter what size he is; it matters how he acts and feels inside. And he says, 'Like a walnut'. The shell isn't the important part the inside is. He speaks in metaphors and thinks and acts just like Ron.

While working as a music teacher for the school district in Forest Grove, Ron received a new desk. He surprised Neil with a huge cardboard box that had contained the desk. Like young boys will do, Neil immediately went to work making a play fort out of the box. His creativity and playful nature inspired his mother in her writing.

∞

Janet Adkins—To Neil—*Cardboard Boxes*

In my basement I do play,
At fun pretend games all day.
Cardboard boxes are down there,
I build huge buildings everywhere.
A trailer house I build sometimes,
And live in it, it's hard to climb.
And sometimes I'm the driver man,
Of a huge long train or moving van.

They associated with teachers who were interested in music and sang in the Congregational Church choir. They formed a group that sang Madrigals, the songs of fair maidens that were sung to royalty in England after supper. The group consisted of eight vocalists: two basses, two tenors, two altos, and two sopranos. They met once a week and occasionally performed publicly.

∞

Janet's Journal

I love to sing my favorite Madrigals. "The Silver Swan," "Hark All Ye Saints," "Weep Thee No More Sad Fountains," and "Sweet Day." I'm a real Madrigal nut.

It was a small-town atmosphere, and nearly everyone in town sent their children to Marty Warner's Castle Nursery School. The school was situated in a classic, old four-story house. The school provided a child's dream atmosphere, which had a slide that ran between floors. The gleeful screams of the children could be heard as they went up and down the slide. Some of the creative activities involved sculpturing clay and baking bread. Marty providing transportation in her Volkswagen bus was a good thing because the parents would have had a difficult time convincing their toddlers that it was time to go home. The children bonded, as did the parents, which created a desirable environment for raising a family.

Janet's Journal—Norman

Norman is going to nursery school and is a character. He loves people, chewing gum, trains; peanut butter sandwiches exclusively, teddy bears, kittens, swimming pools and little girls. He says, Daddy, why do little girls have such soft skin?

Janet loved reading and philosophy. Her life was greatly enhanced when Brooke came onto the scene. Brooke was a classy elderly woman in her eighties. She had moved to Forest Grove after the death of her husband and settled in this small university town. People were usually fascinated with her, but some were a little put off. Janet found her to be a most unusual woman who offered an exciting expansion into the world of intellectual thinking.

Janet's Journal

Ron and I attended several great book discussion sessions and read Plato, Aristotle, Thoreau and a book of the Bible. The discussion shed new light on them because the group was made up of ordinary people, not authorities with inflexible opinions.

After two years of teaching music, Ron took a position as a stockbroker with a brokerage firm in Portland. A young firm, it eventually grew from five brokers to two hundred with offices up and down the coast. It was the time of the bull market and Ron believed that he could walk on water. Everything he touched turned to gold. He became a principal in the firm and was extremely successful. He was a natural, and by his second month, he had earned more in one month than he had earned his entire year in teaching. He was doing so well financially that he was able to take his family on vacation every time he had a good month.

Janet's Journal

Ron continues to love his job as a Stockbroker but he goes up and down emotionally when the market does. I admit he works longer hours than teaching, but we're breathing better financially. The important thing is he's found his niche. We are currently investing all our money.

Although Ron was doing well by his standards, his peers did not look on his profession with respect. Many were unfamiliar with stocks and bonds and misunderstood the brokerage business. Some of those who knew him were convinced that their beloved *'Music Man'* had fallen into a deep pit with the sharks and snakes and that he would soon be devoured. As he continued to earn more money and their lifestyle began to change, the resentment and distrust continued to increase among some of his peers. What was viewed as *'Ron's secretive business dealings'* became the topic of conversation at many group gatherings. To some, he was dealing with the dark side, and to others, he had become a more interesting and colorful individual. But no one could understand how he could work less and sustain their cost of living. It just didn't make any sense, and suspicions ran rampant that he might be into something illegal. Some of his music friends made the frequent comment, "What in the hell do you do for a living?"

∞

Janet's Journal—*The Forest Calls Back,* by Jack Mendelsohn

He was a man of integrity, complete integrity,
And a highly intelligent philosophical person.[1]

Ron continued to stay active in the army reserve band as he had a three-year commitment upon discharge. He served as the director and chief warrant officer of a forty-five-piece marching band, a sixteen-piece big band, a combo, and a choir. The position carried all the duties and responsibilities of a company commander in terms of weapons and equipment. He attended band training school where he was drilled in the intricate movements that went along with performances for special ceremonies. His band played magnificently in parades and concerts for three fulfilling years.

Music was his passion, and he continued to play dance jobs by night. He became a well-respected jazz musician and played with The Mills Brothers, The Platters, Doc Severinsen, and Jimmy Rogers. He was driven by his desire to achieve success. His musical talent was the one thing he owned and something that no one could ever take away from him.

Ron's self-confidence was running high when he purchased their first home in 1963 for a costly $16,000. It was a small home on Westwood Drive with a partial view in the West Hills area of Portland. When they were young, the three boys loved spending quality time together as a family in the comfort of their family home. The home was unique and inviting in many ways. The family gathered most often in the main room, where the floor was heated by pipes under the floorboards. On cold, snowy nights, they loved curling up on the warm floor with a blanket. Janet sat nearby reading books the children had selected from the local library. Other nights, they spent time as a family playing musical instruments.

---

[1] Jack Mendelsohn, *The Forest Calls Back* (New York: Little, Brown, 1965).

Their next move was a step up. They purchased a lot with a breathtaking view of Mount St. Helen's and Mount Hood and built a home overlooking the city of Portland.

At an early age, Neil and Norman, like their parents, possessed a talent for music and were encouraged to play the piano. Their custom-built home was spacious and provided more than enough room for two pianos. Upstairs was a spectacular loft, which presented the perfect setting for a Steinway grand piano. The Spinet piano was downstairs in the family room, and Neil and Norman continuously argued over who would play which piano. Disciplined to rise each morning at 6:00 a.m. to practice before school, one of them would play upstairs on the grand piano, and the other would play downstairs on the Spinet. The early-morning hours were filled with the clamoring tunes of two young boys, who would rather be sleeping than following their mother's orders. Janet's bedroom was just down the hall from the grand piano, and she could be heard hollering over the music, "No, that's wrong; you need to do it again." Neil chose to practice on the downstairs piano, which allowed Norman to get away with playing the blues and not worry about having to learn something he wasn't interested in playing. That was always comical because the two boys would see who could race to the downstairs piano the fastest, so they could avoid the scrutiny of their mother's critical surveillance.

Janet and Ron believed in instilling positive mental attitudes in their children. Their boys were disciplined to do positive affirmations and visualizations every night. "I love myself unconditionally" they would write out five times and then repeat it aloud five times. Every three to four weeks they would be given a new affirmation to recite.

As Ron's success grew, so did the jealousy among some of his peers. They had become the envy of their friends as the *'Music Man'* moved up in stature.

14

The Perfect Child

Neil's Childhood

As the firstborn, Neil was a responsible and obedient child who seldom rocked the boat. It's Neil's belief that Janet did the best she could to provide him with the type of home that she never had, but intuitively, he felt in his heart of hearts that something in the relationship was missing. He was aware of his mother having been neglected as a child, and it became more and more evident to him by the lack of physical and emotional connection between them.

Early on, it was his observation that his mother was a controlling and dominating individual. To him, that she controlled people by asking them questions was obvious. Whenever he asked her a question, it was always returned with another question rather than an answer. He grew to resent what he believed to be a manipulative tactic, and he saw it as a shield that guarded and protected her emotions, feelings, and darkest secrets. He had no idea who this mother of his really was. Try as he might to win her love, there was usually a condition attached. It seemed as though he always came up short, feeling as though nothing he did was ever good enough. For him, being a perfect child, who in his mind could never gain the acceptance of his mother, was frustrating and stressful. He became driven to gain his mother's approval.

Janet was a magnet who drew in people of all statures in life, including the wealthy and philosophers. She had something about her that was very unique, and she was a master at the game. With her extraordinary technique of subtle questioning, the unsuspecting persons were soon spilling their hidden thoughts. People would leave baffled and unburdened, with a sense of relief similar to an experience in a confessional. The oddity of the entire experience is that the individual knew little to nothing about Janet. Neil thought she was as unattached to strangers as she was to him.

Janet could be likened to the Pied Piper who mesmerized the town's people with her magical spell. She had the ability to draw out information and to offer her unique expression of wisdom for which people hungered. But the irony of the situation was evident in Neil's heart. Although she was a good mother and provided for his physical needs, he felt that she was blind to his emotional needs. Neil was lacking a deep emotional connection with his mother that became apparent to him long before he ever left home.

Janet was a very unpretentious person who had little or no interest in material things, while Neil was very materialistic and had dreams of becoming rich. When he was thirteen, Janet encouraged him to mow lawns to learn what it would be like to work with his hands. Showing signs of an early entrepreneur, Neil lined up all the yard jobs then hired his friends to mow the lawns while he did other things. According to Neil, he did this in defiance of his mother's wishes. His rebellion was upsetting to Janet because he wasn't working with *'his own hands,'* which was the way she thought it should be done.

As a young adult, Neil was extremely ambitious and quickly learned that he could make money in business. When he was ready to expand his career from yard work to something more artistic, he put his creative talents to work designing hippie earrings. He sold them to the buyer of Meier & Frank, the largest department store in Portland. At age seventeen, he struck up a friendship with a Prince from Saudi Arabia who was a student at Lewis and Clark College. With his dad's encouragement, he took an interest in the import–export market and flew to Saudi Arabia to do a business deal with the prince.

An independent young man, Neil was known to make impulsive decisions. On his return flight, he made a side trip to France to visit some friends. He decided to stay on and attend a French school for half of his senior year in high school. This, of course, caused a problem when he returned to the States because he did not have clearance from his previous school. It took some doing, but he finally convinced the school to accept the credits he had earned in France.

With his new language skills that he acquired in France, a common bond was created between Neil and his mother. Because they were the only two people in the house who could converse in French, the other family members felt excluded because no one had any idea what they were talking about.

Socially, Neil was very involved in school. In grade school he was elected student body president. In high school, he was captain of the track team and junior assistant scoutmaster in Boy Scouts. With his mother coaching him to improve his times in running, he excelled in track and cross-country. He won the mile event at the city track meet his senior year in high school.

15

Genes are Everything

Norman's Childhood

A high-spirited child full of energy and seldom tired, Norman, the middle child, required constant attention. When he was four years old, he fell into a fishpond and nearly drowned. On another occasion, while learning to ride his older brother Neil's bike, he wiped out at the bottom of a big hill. To Neil, that someone other than him was watching out for Norman was clear, as he had calls with death on more than one occasion.

Frequently disrupting the neighborhood, Norman would be brought home by an angry parent. They had their side of the story, and Norman had his. He found great satisfaction in convincing his mother to accept his side of the truth over the neighbor's. But then again, there were always two sides to every story, and the truth depended on who was telling the story.

Norman was a fun-loving child but one who insisted on pushing the envelope. He had a thirst for life and was an intense spark in the family. Like his grandfather, he was mechanically inclined and business-minded. Excited by change, he was always open to participating in something new, but many of his choices were upsetting to his parents, including his choice of friends. Norman became adamant that he was not going to follow the family rules and do what was expected of him. He became defiant, particularly with his mother, as she had strict rules about times to eat and the way she expected her children to participate as a family member. Like most parents, Janet had reasonable expectations about his performance in school, as a member of the track club, and in practicing the piano.

Much like his dad, Norman was a jokester and loved to make people laugh. During his younger years, many incidents took place that could be construed as pranks. As parents, Janet and Ron had made a concerted effort to ensure that their children were given every opportunity for a successful life. But as fate would have it, their life was thrown into an upheaval when Norman entered puberty.

His fun-loving nature changed and his unruly behavior put him at odds with his mother, as they each fought for control over the other and he became defiant and challenging at every turn. Many times, Ron was called home from work because Norman was out of control. All of Ron's and Janet's attention was focused on Norman, as the effort was made to help him fit into the family.

This was a difficult time as a family, but particularly for Janet as she was burdened with all the detrimental feelings of guilt that are typically associated with a mother whose son has gone astray. This was not what she wanted for Norman or her family. Janet was a controller, and she could not handle the fact that Norman would not play by her rules.

Norman's recollection of his relationship with his mother was one of acceptance. He was able to use cuss words and speak his mind in the way he wanted to, and there was never any offense taken by her. She always seemed interested in whatever was going on in his world, and she was curious as to what was *'hip'* in his generation. She wanted to know what was *'cool'* and what wasn't. However, Mother Superior saw things much differently. She described Norman as an unrefined young man with a lot of rough edges. His grades continued to decline, and he was determined to break the rules and challenge authority at every turn. At fourteen, he was still under the house rules and was expected to play by those rules, which had been set by his mother. If the rules were not kept to Janet's liking, a price would have to paid. Of course, Norman seldom had intentions of keeping the rules.

∞

Janet's Journal

Had hassle with Norm after three-hour Saturday night talk about good intentions. Didn't start the dishwasher, didn't leave notes, and was thirty-five minutes late for dinner. Didn't even feel any of this was wrong.

As Norman became more involved with his friends at the Catholic school, he started experimenting with taboo substances. In addition to alcohol, he was experimenting with marijuana and other drugs. His behavior became intolerable, which fed a continual battle between Janet and Ron. Norman was taken to numerous counselors, but he was clever; before long, he had the counselors buying into his story. He told them what they wanted to hear, and he played them like a piano. Nothing Janet and Ron tried made any difference in his behavior.

Unable to deal with Norman's continual disruption to the family unit, he was eventually legally emancipated. Arrangements were made for Norman to live with a Catholic family who lived up the street. Being nearby, Norman kept frequent contact with his biological family.

∞

Letter to Norman—from Mom, Dad, and Ronald

How is it for you? We think about you all the time in so many ways. I'd love to hear about your classes, Norm, your teachers and new people you're meeting. I know new situations are hard sometimes, but I also know that it's easy for you to make friends. Remember that you're our son and we love you. That may mean more to us than it does to you right now but keep it tucked away

133

in the back of your mind so that you will always
know it.
Love, Mom, Dad & Ronald.

As parents, Janet and Ron had always had very high hopes for
their children. Their dream was to start a new generation, and they
were determined not to follow in their parents' footsteps. This was
the family they always wanted and never had growing up.

Ironically, life didn't work out the way they expected. They had
both believed that the environment was the main factor in raising a
family. They soon came to believe that genes were the dominant
factor playing a much larger part in the family dynamics than the
environment. Norman was proof of that theory. He had taken on the
traits of the alcoholic grandparents and many personality traits of
their ancestors. He had a wild streak that was not apparent in his
brothers, Neil and Ronald. Oddly enough, Janet thought that, as a
young boy, Norman was her most exciting child, and she considered
him to be her prize.

∞

Janet's Journal

*I'm a strong believer in genes for explaining the
unusual range and assortment of personalities we
have living under one roof together. I also feel
that the longer I live the less I understand.*

16

The Philosopher

Ronald's Childhood

As the youngest son, unlike his two older brothers, who were extremely vocal and dominating, Ronald was a quiet, sensitive child who was invisible most of the time. He often went unnoticed taking in more of his surroundings than anyone ever realized. Janet respected his strength in silence and undoubtedly recognized the philosopher carefully hidden within. To Ronald no one else in the family except for his mother seemed to be the least bit interested in hearing what he had to say. Curious as to what he was thinking, Janet always made it a point to silence the family so he could have his chance at the podium. "What do you think, Ronald?" she would say. In a sense, she became his facilitator, which made him feel that his opinion mattered.

Janet instilled in him the belief that there was more than one way to do things and there was more than one way to believe. She encouraged his individualism and self-discovery. Although he had been raised Unitarian, there was a time when he wanted to be an altar boy for the Catholic Church. He talked with the priest, attended a summer program, and was permitted to serve at church, even though he wasn't Catholic. On another occasion when he expressed his interest in the Muslim faith, Janet purchased him a Koran so he could study the Abrahamic religion.

Ronald's experience of his mother was one of deep love and affection. During his early years, Janet was a nurturing stay-at-home mom while his dad was working. Arriving home from school, Ronald would be greeted with a warm hug followed by a tall glass of ice-cold milk and a plate of snickerdoodle cookies. He vividly recalls the days when he and his brothers were in track and cross-country. Every Saturday, Janet would come into their rooms and wake them up by writing a numeral one on their chest with her finger. This was a reminder for them to do their best and envision themselves running the race. She always told the boys that they were number one and that there wasn't anything they couldn't do.

∞

Janet's Journal

Ronald is completely absorbed in jazz piano. He plays in a group and has two part-time jobs and banks every check.

Ronald was grateful to be able to travel abroad with his family during his teenage years. He respected his parents for providing him with the opportunity to experience other cultures. He was well aware of the financial sacrifices they made for those family trips. Rather than saving for retirement, they chose to enjoy life in the now. One particular flight on Piedmont Airlines turned out to be a frightful event. Traveling through turbulent air, Ronald will never forget the look on his mother's face as she looked over at him and his brothers and mouthed the words "I love you." Even though she may have been terrified herself, her face showed no signs of distress. That was his mother, always in control of the situation.

17

Liberation

During their child-raising years, the demands became greater and greater on Janet. The men in her life required more and more attention. Their teenagers needed constant taxi service to music lessons, sports, Boy Scouts, school activities, and so on. The boys were not known for their neatness, so someone always needed to clean up after them. The pets needed to be fed and bathed, and the three young men always needed to be reminded of their chores. The job of being first sergeant fell on Janet's shoulders.

Angry with her family of four men, Janet wrote the following letter:

Janet's Journal

The solution seems to be that I get a job in order to remove myself somewhat from your lives. This will mean that more responsibility will have to be taken by the four of you. I'm sick of trying to teach responsibility and then being chewed out by you, Ron, for trying to teach it. I simply cannot live with rude irresponsible people. I think I serve you all and show interest in your problems and your studies. I listen to you and offer understanding when the market is good or bad. I offer organizational help when things are stressful for each of you, and also any other kind of help from finishing up a clean-up contract so you can go to Malibu . . . to picking you up at 1:30 a.m. or 2:00 a.m. because you've drank too much.

You all take for granted and expect the meals to be ready and the laundry and cleaning to be done. You expect me to be available to all your needs, whether to taxi you somewhere, budget the salary or hold your hand. I also expect to be treated decently with respect for my person with help when it's needed and with a growing responsibility to do willingly and with a happy heart the things that are yours to do. This is not asking too much. When things are out of harmony let's all try to bring them back into harmony. Going off in a corner and thinking 'poor me' doesn't bring back harmony. The more we all try to do this the easier it will be. We all have needs. What are your needs right now Ron?

During a time when Janet and Ron were involved in a political campaign for a Libertarian presidential candidate, they opened their home for a fund-raiser. With the presidential candidate as their expected guest, everything needed to be in proper order. Looking over the deck at the picturesque view of Portland, it was a grand view not only of the city but also of several marijuana plants growing on the hillside below their home. Norman had been responsible for the plants, and they had gone unnoticed by his parents until a guest pointed it out. Janet just laughed and said they would handle the situation. Without proper time to dispose of the plants, Ron instructed Norman to place black plastic garbage bags over the top of the plants.

∞

Janet's Journal

It depressed the hell out of me last night to watch Town Hall and see how many young people are habitual users of marijuana. Whatever happened to natural highs? Then again, the adult friends we have, all use too much alcohol, ourselves included.

For their twenty-fifth wedding anniversary, Janet's relatives came down from Canada to celebrate. At the time, Janet couldn't have cared less if anyone came or not. She was having problems with Norman, so much so that she later went and stayed in a motel and didn't tell anybody where she was. She just needed to have a couple of days for herself, and she wanted to get away from the crazy making.

During these difficult years, Janet took time for herself, spending occasional weekends at the beach in an attempt to find her solitude.

She took a job working for the Schick Center in Portland. The center was developed for controlling smoking and weight loss. Janet's friend Carroll was managing the organization at that time and was instrumental in getting the job for Janet. Previously, when they had been living in Forest Grove, both Janet and Ron had taken up still-life painting. Now that Janet was working for the Schick Center, Ron was amused when he thought of a still-life painting that he had painted some years earlier. The picture depicted an ashtray on a table with a cigarette that had smoke drifting up into the sky. He thought it ironic that the smoke was not still, but the cigarette did *'still-life.'* Now, Janet was working with smokers to stop their smoking before they stilled their lives.

For the first time in their marriage, Janet was working full-time. She began to take an interest in the women's liberation movement and the emancipation of women's rights. As she rapidly expanded her world, Ron's security became threatened as Janet made comments that were outside the boundaries of their marital relationship. When Janet began discussing new concepts and ideas, which included thoughts about an open marriage and the fact that she would like to have three husbands, Ron was shattered. His belief had always been that when he married Janet, he would be married for life. In his naive world, the concepts of having three husbands and an open marriage never crossed his mind.

Once the seeds were planted, his jealousy and fear of losing Janet grew to such proportions that distrust erupted in their relationship. Like a rumble of distant thunder, that change was coming was evident. Change was threatening because it fueled Ron's uncertainties about their future together. Although Janet made it appear that she was just playing with the philosophical viewpoint of an open marriage, he was always on guard as a result of her comments. Because of his jealous nature and his suspicious mind, the only way he could find peace in their relationship was to put on blinders. In other words, he preferred not knowing. So, the subject was never brought up again, and he never asked. However, his anger and resentments festered and showed up in other areas of his life, such as exploding with rage when it was least expected.

As a young child, Ron vented his anger by crying and throwing tantrums. But now as an adult, the hidden dragon within was beginning to show itself in another form. Although he never laid a hand on Janet, his fiery dragon was unleashed in the form of road rage. If someone cut him off the road, his rage would surface like an animal's survival response in the jungle. In one instance, he became so enraged with a driver who had cut him off that he actually jumped out of his car and went up to the driver's window. If the driver had had a gun, he might likely have used it to defend himself against the onslaught of anger that was being spewed at him.

∞

Janet's Journal—*A Credo—*
For My Relationships with Others,
by Thomas Gordon

You and I are in a relationship, which I
value and want to keep. Yet each of us is
a separate person with his own unique

needs and the right to meet those needs.
When you are having problems meeting
your needs, I will try to listen with
genuine acceptance in order to facilitate
your finding your own solutions instead
of depending on mine. I also will try to
respect your right to choose your own
beliefs and develop your own values,
different though they may be from
mine.[1]

During those years, they enrolled in personal growth classes and were able to work through many of their personal conflicts. One thing they learned was to take accountability for their own feelings and their own perceptions of how they viewed each other and how they interacted in their relationship. But for Janet, she had taken a stand to liberate herself from the controls put on her by the members of her family and later by society.

---

[1] Thomas Gordon, A Credo—For My Relationships with Others, Journal of Humanistic Psychology 12, no. 2 (1972): 77–78.

18

Marlow and Beyond

In 1977, Ron became involved with a company that offered him an opportunity to represent their financial products in Europe and the Middle East providing tax shelters to American ex-patriots. A very exciting proposition for both Janet and Ron, they were elated with the possibility of living in Europe. Ron accepted the position, sold his book of brokerage clients, and left for England. Janet stayed behind to rent out their house in Portland.

Ron set up an office in London and found a place for the family to live in the quaint village of Marlow on the Thames River. He later discovered that his favorite poet, T. S. Elliot, just happened to have lived in the same town while he was writing CATS.

<hr/>

Janet's Journal—September 3, 1977

Ron left today at 4:15 p.m. for London. Neil, Ronald, Dominique, Carroll, Nick, Tom, Kati, Janie and I saw him off. A happy departure filled with expectancy. Last night's dinner together at L'escargot was beautiful. Talking, sharing, and expressing love and appreciation, saying it all. Hearing that Ron is not afraid to die, that if he were God he would not do it differently. Ron is a different person now. He has changed and I like the changes. I feel excited about new beginnings. I hope he likes my pocket agate and note.

Prior to this time, Ron had carried a chip on his shoulder about life. He believed that if he were God, he would have laid out the program of life with more direction. He would have left specific information as to what life was all about. As he grew in his life experiences, he shifted his context to one of more openness and acceptance of the other person. He began to see life from a different perspective. He decided that the way God had laid life out *for people to find out what it was all about'* was through their own learning and self-discovery. Much like a poem, as the reader, he could discover the many meanings in life from his own perspective and experience.

For many years, Ron had been a bit of a hypochondriac. He had lived with the fear that he would get sick and die before he had raised his family. Now, with his new personal growth and his new understanding of life, he felt that they were all part of the universe. He believed that nothing is lost it just changes form. Energy continues, perhaps reincarnates, in another form in a different galaxy. His new attitude of being *'okay with death'* gave Janet comfort.

∞

Janet's Journal—September 8, 1977

The house has been filled with people these last days. Not much time to reflect. I got up at 7:00 a.m. and went for a walk this beautiful fresh morning. Stopped at the top of Westwood and 14th and looked out far upon the river and pockets of gentle fog. I awakened thinking about Norman. Ronald started eighth grade yesterday. And so much more. . . .

Ironically, Neil had been accepted to the American College of Paris right at the same time the family was moving abroad. When Ron arrived in Europe, he checked into a hotel in London and then went to Scotland for several days. When he returned to his room, he found Neil sleeping in his bed. Neil, having a knack for getting around red tape, had successfully talked his way into Ron's room. Ron's anger was still festering over Janet's comment on wanting to have three husbands. He took a long walk with Neil through Hyde Park and told Neil that he would never give one-hundred percent of himself to any one person again. He had found from his own personal experience that he had made a mistake. From that day forward, Ron guarded his heart and vowed that he would never be vulnerable again. Neil stayed with him for a couple of days then left for Paris.

Janet arrived in England with Ronald and Norman in October. Ronald enrolled in the eighth grade at Great Marlow School. Norman was seventeen at the time, and in England, at that age, he would have already completed primary school and gone on to college. Because Norman hadn't completed high school, he found that he didn't fit into the system. He passed his time playing jazz on the piano and hanging out in the local pubs where he was of legal age to be served.

Janet's Journal—Marlow, England
November 18, 1977

I sit in our upstairs bedroom. It is 4:45 p.m. Friday and the moon is up as I look out over Marlow. Lights are on now at 5 p.m. and the moon is bright (half-moon). I think of friends on the western coast of the United States where it is 9:00 a.m. for them. Norm and Ronald are watching BBC on the telly downstairs. The house is clean, the laundry done. Tonight Ray and Sue are coming here for a drink before we take them out to LaChandelle for dinner. Marlow is a beautiful old quiet small English village thirty miles west of London with 15th and 16th century buildings. I love to market there every day. Without a car, it takes a daily trip to keep the home supplied with food. I bought a little cart with wheels. People are friendly and helpful. We're just four blocks from town and I walk the public footpath to town that is lined with trees and birds, an old wooden fence, which ivy clings to.

It's a very different time for our family. We are not surrounded by a wall of friends here as at home, though letters filter through to give us the love and support we need. It is a time to be resourceful to find new ways for each of us. Ron is in the financial world in the big city of London

Norman is looking at his life wondering whether to stay at Great Marlow School or go to college at High Wycombe. Norm managed to get a light load of classes. Beginning to know more and more that music is important to him. Mentioning an interest in becoming a stock-broker. Spending his evenings skate boarding and visiting the neighborhood pubs where the men play darts and billiards.

Ronald is feeling homesick and lonesome for his friends, but hanging in there making a good adjustment to his many classes and new people at Great Marlow. Ronald is taking history, drama, math, woodworking, English, American literature, art, games, technical drawing, biology, PE, physics, geography, humanities, and chemistry. WOW! But some of those classes meet just once a week. It's a big adjustment and the boys must wear black or gray slacks, dress shirts and ties, v-necked sweaters and oxfords (positively no jeans). Ronald is enjoying his family, Norman especially. I think he counts the days till we go home, hoping it is right after Christmas. I hope he and Norm receive a letter or two soon. I know how important it was for me to get the letter from Mama and from Peggy and Bob.

We rent a car on weekends and go around to see as much as we can see. Neil came from Paris last weekend (some French holiday) and we had the neatest family weekend together that I can remember in a long time. Norm is even being a delight some of the time. Last weekend we went to Oxford, which was absolutely overrun with people (Christmas shoppers) and cars. We split in a hurry and went to a quiet little restaurant that Ron knew in Henley—on Thames and had a three-hour dinner with good conversation and Beaujolais. I'm going to sample the Dry Sock Sherry I bought and then take a leisurely bath before Ron comes home.

∞

Janet's Journal—December 6, 1977

Ron's business venture is not happening, at least right now. He was unable to get his visa and leave with Ray to Saudi Arabia November 26th. Ray went and will come home sometime this week. Time is very different over here. Everything takes much longer. Ray said it would take three or four weeks to accomplish their mission in Saudi Arabia. Ron is frustrated, I think, and anxious. Norm seems restless and edgy. Probably I am too. Ronald is sort of quietly homesick, but hanging in there. I wrote about ten Christmas cards today but it wasn't easy. I've been pouring out so much in letters. I think it's a time for filling up. I may spend the rest of the day reading. Neil called from Paris last night to thank us for the money we sent him. I think he was a little homesick. What does life bring next?

Ron's position was short-lived when the tax laws changed, affecting the sale of the product. He had an office in London on Curzon Street in the Mayfair District, which he shared with Ray, his English partner. They attempted to get a business going that involved an investment fund that purchased and sold famous English paintings. However, when they were unsuccessful in raising funds to make the business profitable, it was decided to close the office. After less than a year in England, Ron made the decision to move his family back to the States.

Before they returned home, he took his family to Paris to spend Christmas with Neil. Norman insisted on traveling to Paris by himself and was nearly thrown off the train. When he arrived in Paris, he joined a group of college kids who were drinking wine. They came across an unattended moped, and Norman didn't waste any time in taking it for a ride. A Gendarme stopped him, and fortunately for Norman, he escaped the punishment of a cold night in jail. Norman finally met up with the rest of the family and joined them for a road trip to southern France.

After returning home from Europe in 1978, the family moved back into their home in Portland and picked up their lives where they had left off with their friends. Ron went back to the stock brokerage business but unfortunately, he had to start his business from scratch, as he had sold his entire book of clients when he left for London.

Janet went back to work at the Schick Center and attended night school to get her teaching certificate to teach English as a second language (ESL). She accepted an exciting position at Portland Community College teaching ESL to students from Vietnam, Russia, Iran, Iraq, Brazil, and Eastern Europe. She loved helping people and received great satisfaction by working with students who were willing and eager to learn.

∞

Janet's Journal

I love teaching English as a second language. The students are so eager to learn and so grateful. Some of their cards to me say, "For my Best Janet Adkins. And thank you very much for your help, and I just want to say thank you again and again. The past two months was the best chance and more help for me, because I was in your classes. I never forget. Goodbye forever and my name is Yang Thao." Yang has four children and no husband. He was killed in Laos. Just being with these students is so important to me. Seeing all the adjustments they're making, enjoying their smiling faces and sense of humor. Laughing together over English mistakes. We have been learning Christmas songs. Last Thursday we sang "Silent Night" in English, Vietnamese and Spanish simultaneously.

Janet's life was full. She loved teaching and she filled her extra time with literature, playing the piano, traveling and tennis. Both Janet and Ron loved to play tennis and joined a tennis club which provided the venue for Janet to play in tournaments around the city.

∞

Janet's Journal

Ron and I both enjoy playing tennis three or four times per week. He hates it when I beat him.

Ron took an interest in the oil business and was offered a position as vice president of finance for an oil company in Victoria, Texas. The position was exciting because he worked with investors in limited partnerships. He raised money privately for the company and took the prospective investors on tours of the site. He was successful beyond his wildest dreams when he made $350,000 that year. Not bad for a year's work. He put two-thirds of the income back into the drilling of gas wells. The following year was another success.

∞

Janet's Journal—February 5, 1978

Sunday morning. Ron is in Texas, Norm working, Ronald at Mt. Hood at a snow scout overnight. Delicious being in the house alone.

The business had its ups and downs. Although it made a lot of money, it lost a lot of money as well. One particular project resulted in developing a natural gas field in Victoria, Texas, where a number of wells were drilled that tested positively. The figures they had worked up from geologists indicated a fantastic potential for success. As a matter of fact, if they were as fantastic as indicated, Ron would never have to work a day in his life again. He dreamed of living on the French Rivera without a worry in the world. But, unfortunately, although the wells did very good at first, they eventually watered up and declined in value.

∞

Janet's Journal

An ice storm this week with school closures, no heat, no lights, and inch or two of ice on the trees. Two huge limbs fell from the oak tree. The roof, bird feeders, deck railing are all draped with icicles. The birds came sliding into the deck like ice skaters. We managed to get the car out of the garage to go to L'Auberge for Neil's 21st birthday. Pioneering does become weary after a few days spending all one's time cooking, heating water, cleaning up, confined to one room for warmth. Ronald says he likes to sit; it brings everyone closer. The thaw begins and the electricity came on yesterday afternoon and went off at 5 a.m. We each took a shower, got a load of clothes washed, armed the house before it went off again! Night sounds of an avalanche of ice roaring off the roof, crystals escaping from the trees, a branch cracking off; the day sounds of chain saws, cars spinning their wheels. The thermometer reads 33 degrees outside the kitchen window. Jack, one of Ron's business associates, didn't make it in this morning from his house on Hewett Blvd., a wooded area. He said his area looked like a battlefield.

When finances were good, the Adkins family took trips to exotic places enjoying the warm, sunny climates of Tahiti or Hawaii. Janet drove a silver Mercedes, and Ron, a red Porsche. Now that they were living in the fast lane, Ron's jealousy and fears began to surface again. Entering the *'swinging era,'* they lived the life that one reads about in books or magazines. This was a new experience and one that carried a bitter-sweetness for Ron. They attended frequent parties that involved potlucks, dancing, and soaking in hot tubs into the wee hours of the morning. This new experience was exciting but also dangerous because it set the tone for infidelity, which meant that their marriage might not last. Playing with fire, the possibility was that someone would get burned. Ron never knew of any infidelity, nor did he care to know. He was content to wear his blinders and avoid unnecessary pain.

THE ADKINS
FAMILY'S PHOTOS

Emily and Dell - Ron's Parents

Einar and Vi - Janet's Parents

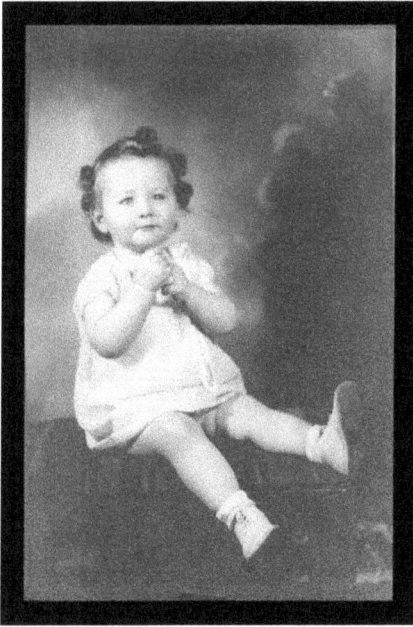

Janet's Baby Picture

Janet's Childhood Photo

**Janet's
High School
Graduation**

Janet Playing the French Horn

Ron, Age 17
High School Band

Ron, Age 21
Playing the
String Bass

Janet and Ron's
Wedding

Helen (Bridesmaid),
Janet, Ron,
Calvin (Best Man)

Einer, Janet, Ron, Grandma Middleton, and Vi

76th Army Band Coligny Caserne Orleans, France

Ron's Dance Band Concert - France 1951

Ron, Janet
and Carroll
in France

Janet and Baby
Neil in France

Janet and Baby Ronald in Forest Grove

Janet and the Boys in Forest Grove

Janet, Ron, and Boys
Music Night

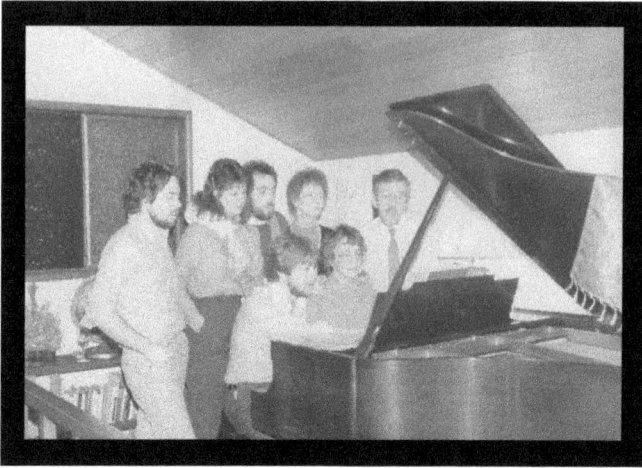

Family Night at the Piano

Ron and Janet Playing Music at a Campground

Janet and Ron Hiking

Janet Hiking at a Glacier

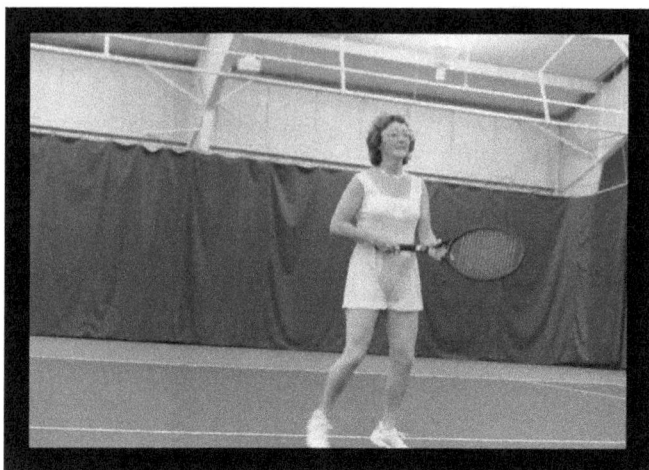

Janet Playing Tennis

Carroll and Janet

Ron and Janet in the Tree of Life

Janet and her Vietnamese Students

Janet and her Grandsons

Neil, Ron, Ronald,
and Norman

The Adkins Family –
Norman, Ron, Janet, Neil, Ronald

Ron and Janet Adkins

PART III

Janet's Dynamics of Family and Friends Learning about Janet's Illness and Choice to Die

19

Freedom from Control

Graduating from high school and selecting a college, were important steps in Neil's life. Although he viewed his mother as a caring individual, he resented her attempts to control his future. With Janet's insistence that he attend Oregon State, he deliberately chose a college in Paris, France, to gain his freedom and distance himself from his mother's control.

Janet's Journal

I like it when Neil comes home from work at 11:30 p.m. He comes into my room to sit and talk, our only time to see each other. Next Thursday he leaves for Paris.

Arriving in Paris, Neil was elated to finally experience his freedom, He was able to relax and allow his new identity to emerge. He smiled more readily and started to enjoy life. However, even though he was on the other side of the world, that Janet was still trying to maintain control over him was evident. The frequent letters he sent home were constantly scrutinized by his mother, an English major, and sent back to him with corrections, which only added to the resentment he already felt, and he stopped writing altogether.

He took an apartment on the seventh floor of a large building in the Latin Quarter of Paris, a one-room maid's quarters, small and expensive, with noisy pigeons squawking and scratching outside his window. The apartment, which had an adjacent view of the Eiffel Tower, was located just a couple of blocks from the college on a parkway overrun with vendors.

Neil's daily routine started with a morning jog around the Eiffel Tower, passing through a bustling market where the town folk handpicked their fresh produce, meat, and fish for the day while the delicious aromas of fresh baked goods permeated the crisp morning air. There would be days when he'd sit for hours reviewing his studies and watching people go by. He was especially amused by the neighborhood school-children parading by in their school uniforms. Laughing and giggling, they playfully chased each other up and down the streets of the Latin Quarter. Returning home from his daily adventures, he was faced with the arduous task of climbing seven flights of stairs, as the elevator to the apartment was always broken.

Life in Paris was like waking up on vacation every day. He soon discovered that there was an overabundance of English-speaking girls and very few English-speaking boys, which made it a paradise for a young man his age. He was naturally drawn to beautiful women. He loved to charm the girls, and his heart skipped a beat when they exchanged glances. Much like Janet, he had the ability to engage in intimate conversations with complete strangers.

For the first several months, he enjoyed dating many girls. His evenings were taken up with clubs where he danced his way through the night. Mornings were spent eye gazing with beautiful French girls over tea and croissants; afternoons, hanging out at French cafes with his best friend, Greg, watching girls and discussing life. His school studies were most definitely overshadowed by the excitement of Paris.

In November, he fell in love with a girl named Valerie, and time stood still. Valerie was a gentle and soft-spoken girl, the opposite of his mother, Janet. Being his first love, his feelings were intensified by the incredible beauty and romance of Paris. They spent their mornings in cafes discovering one another and their afternoons visiting museums and studying the culture of France. On the weekends, they took trains into the country and spent their nights at village inns. They attended classes together and hung out with friends at quaint little bistros tucked away in some small corner of the city. The food that they sampled was '*to die for*' and included some of the finest delicacies in all of France. For Neil, the intense experience was electrifying, one that will be embedded in his mind forever.

The following year, he made plans to attend college in Hawaii. Valerie's parents insisted she attend Bethany Nazarene College in Oklahoma, so he changed his plans and followed her there. He had not been raised as a Christian, although he had always been drawn to the Christian faith. He recalled a time in Boy Scouts when he had attended a vesper service and felt a strong spiritual connection. Sharing that experience with his mother, she downplayed the event and told him that Jesus was just a man. When he became an Eagle Scout, it was a requirement that all scouts believe in God. At the time, he wasn't sure of his beliefs, and Janet threatened to go to the Supreme Court to state his case if that would have kept him from becoming an Eagle Scout. He finally advised the Eagle Review Board that he believed in a Supreme Being, and that was acceptable to them.

∞

Janet's Journal—*The Forest Calls Back*, by Jack Mendelsohn

Jesus told me that all men have to be good to one another, and not hate one another. It is not enough for one Shipibo to love another. There must be goodness among all men. Later Binder told me that he sees this as confirmation of his own view that a sense of humanity depends on no single race or religion. He advocated that they must broaden and universalize the ethics, which prevail among themselves, but which are normally denied to all outsiders.[1]

Neil and Valerie started back to school for their first semester at Bethany Nazarene College. Two weeks later, Neil realized he had made a huge mistake after receiving discipline from an elder. On a

---

[1] Jack Mendelsohn, The Forest Calls Back (New York: Little, Brown, 1965).

100-degree day, he had been playing tennis in a pair of shorts. Out of uniform with his legs exposed, he had broken the rules. That was all it took for him to be on the next plane to Hawaii. A short time later, Valerie joined him in Hawaii, and their relationship intensified.

His junior year of college, Neil followed Valerie to the University of Houston after her parents insisted she attend a college in their state of residency. Once again, having acted on impulse, he was faced with the realization that he had succumbed to his weakness with women. He was beginning to see that his hormones, rather that his heart and his intellect, were leading him. After meeting Valerie's mother, he was hit with the realization that if this relationship was to lead to marriage, he would be marrying Valerie's mother, and that was not going to work. Although he was only one term short, he went back to Portland and never completed his degree. Janet had always told him that he would never amount to anything without a college education. He intended to prove her wrong and show her that he could be successful without a college degree.

Janet's Journal

Neil comes home Monday from the University of Houston. A three-day Trailway bus ride. This is his senior year.

After arriving home, back in Portland, Neil took a job and got seriously involved with a woman named Laura. That he attracted a strong woman, much like Janet, wasn't surprising, and the relationship was doomed before it ever began. While involved with Laura, he was introduced to a woman named Heidi, who lived in the same apartment complex. An instantaneous attraction, they found themselves talking for hours and sharing life experiences. When it became evident that their attraction to each other was evolving, he made the decision to break it off with Laura because he wasn't in love with her. As fate would have it, Laura announced that she was pregnant.

Janet loved Laura like a daughter and informed Neil that, in no uncertain terms, he was going to do the right thing and marry Laura. He purchased a ring and went through all the motions of accepting his fate. But he soon realized that if he married Laura, he would be marrying a woman who had the same controlling characteristics as his mother and that it would never work.

Heidi was employed as a travel agent. At Neil's request, she arranged a trip for him to take Laura to the Caribbean Islands to see if they could reconcile their differences. When they returned, Neil was clear in his mind that he was in love with Heidi and that he was not willing to marry Laura out of duty. The relationship broke apart, and Laura delivered their son in August 1983. Janet immediately bonded with her first grandchild, Michael, and he became her new pride and joy.

In April 1984, Heidi and Neil married, igniting a fire between her and Janet. The relationship between the two women was a constant struggle right from the start, with both women vying for Neil's attention. Because Heidi was the first woman to join the Adkins family, she suspected that it was difficult for Janet to accept her. She knew that she had not been Janet's choice for Neil. Heidi, also a Nazarene Christian, carried a different spiritual belief system than Janet.

Heidi viewed Janet as a controlling woman who often imposed her views on the other family members. When getting together for family gatherings, conflict often arose between the two women because they both had their own way of doing things. Heidi enjoyed preparing an elaborate meal with a creative flair, whereas Janet preferred a simple meal without a lot of fuss. These seemingly insignificant conflicts fueled the fire between Janet and Heidi.

Two years prior to Janet's death, in the summer of 1988, what started as a trivial family incident was just the beginning of turmoil. From that point forward, a series of incidents were triggered that caused resentment and dissension among some of the Adkins family members for years to come.

The week prior to Labor Day, the family chartered a sailboat out of Anacortes, Washington, for a weeklong trip in the picturesque San Juan Islands of Puget Sound, as they had done in years past. When it came time to board the boat, Neil informed Janet and Ron that he and Heidi would be sleeping in the master's quarters. Janet thought that she and Ron, being the parents and the seniors, were entitled to the master cabin. Because Neil had paid for the boat, he thought that he and Heidi were entitled to the cabin of their choice. Disagreement over the sleeping quarters caused such dissension among the group that when the boat pulled into the dock in Roche Harbor, both Heidi and Janet refused to stay on the boat. Heidi told Neil that she intended to take a ferry home, while Janet insisted Ron pay for a room at the hotel. Being a holiday weekend, the hotel had been booked ahead for six months. Fortunately for Janet, a cancellation occurred just as they approached the desk.

When Ron and Janet returned to the boat the following day, they conceded to sleeping in the smaller quarters. Heidi had returned to the boat the night before, and she and Neil had taken the master quarters. With unresolved tension among the group and limited space aboard the sailboat, the next week was awkward as they sailed the seas. Attempting to avoid confrontation, Neil was caught in a compromising position trying to please both his mother and his wife.

Ron tried to explain to Neil and Heidi that he suspected something wasn't right with Janet, but Neil and Heidi rationalized Janet's behavior as a sure sign of menopause. The following year, Ron talked with the family again about his concerns with Janet's memory loss. Janet's diagnosis of Alzheimer's shocked everyone. Because the family didn't live with Janet day in and day out, for them to notice any significant changes in her behavior had been impossible.

When Janet announced the decision to end her life, both Neil and Heidi were shaken to their core because their faith in God had taught them that only God has the right to decide when it is time for a person to leave this earth. "God never promised us a life free of suffering," Heidi told Janet. "If I were in your position, I would place it in God's hands that he would put people in my life to care for me. God never fails to meet our needs if we trust in him."

Janet was talking about all sorts of ways to end her life: walking into the ocean or jumping off a building. In the hope of influencing her to give her illness over to God, Heidi invited Janet to an Easter pageant portraying the life of Jesus. Heidi hoped and prayed that Janet would have a change of heart. But over the following weeks, she witnessed Janet pulling the heartstrings of her sons. Toward the end, Neil told Heidi that Janet was placing threatening calls to him, stating, "I'm going to do it this weekend." Several times Neil told Heidi that he would need to make a last-minute trip from Seattle to Portland to try to talk his mother out of killing herself. It got to the point where Heidi couldn't cope with it any longer. Nothing in their lives mattered except Janet's decision to end her life.

Neil implored his mother to reconsider and asked her to participate in a program for Alzheimer's patients at the University of Washington that involved an exploratory drug treatment plan. He was both grateful and relieved when she agreed to attend the program.

Heidi thought that Janet's impending death was responsible for Neil's withdrawal in their marriage and had caused him to turn to the bottle. With chronic fatigue syndrome and a two-year-old child, Heidi was financially dependent on Neil. According to Heidi, Neil had become oblivious to the financial and the emotional needs of his family, leaving her to deal with the full responsibility for everything it took to run their lives. When he didn't come home at night, she believed that he was working long hours to support the family. She had no idea that he was spending his evenings in the taverns and many hours sobering up before he came home. When he told her that he was an alcoholic and had been drowning his feelings in alcohol, she was shocked. She had seen the alcoholic behavior in other members of the family but had refused to see it in her own husband.

Neil stopped drinking March 20, 1990, ten weeks before Janet died. He wanted to be sober to say his last goodbyes. Although Neil admits that Janet was not responsible for his drinking, he does believe that her impending death accelerated his drinking. He actually thought that he might have gone on drinking indefinitely had it not been for Janet's death. In a strange sort of way, he has Janet to thank for accelerating his drinking to the point of hitting bottom.

Sensing his unrest with Janet's decision, Ron placed a call to their family therapist to see about scheduling a time for the family to discuss their differences.

Notes from Myriam Coppens, Family Therapist

May 23, 1990—Some unfinished business exists between her oldest son, Neil and Mrs. Adkins. I suggest Mr. Adkins ask if Janet and Neil would both want to come in for some family counseling the following weekend.

May 26, 1990—Office visit with Neil first. Then jointly with Mrs. and Mr. Adkins. The session is mostly between mom and son. Janet is very appropriate and clearly competent.

During the session, Neil shared his thoughts with his mother: "You've controlled everything in your life. The very thing that you value most is being taken away from you, and you are still trying to control the exit."

Attempting to bring closure, he asked his mother to accept Jesus Christ as her savior. She informed him, "No," that her belief was that which encompassed a universal God. Neil responded, "What do you have to lose, Mom?"

Janet wrote Neil the following letter before she ended her life:

∞

Janet's Letter to Neil

I'm so glad that you have two wonderful sons. And maybe you will have even more. You have been a wonderful son who is growing and learning always. Enjoy everything with a passion for it all. The little things and not so little things. It's the best world I know! Neil, you are always so generous and caring. Heidi is very lucky. When I go for a walk in Washington Park I look at the buttercups and feel happy to be alive. Remember to get out in the wilderness it's so renewing. Take your children to see the flowers that grow in the high areas. Did I tell you all that I meant to tell you? All that I felt was important? You can never love too much. Love with a quiet peace within your heart. Make other people laugh. Did I tell you what a joy it is being a mother to you?

20

Flirtation with Death

Norman, the middle son, continued living on the edge, flirting with death at every turn. He took a career in the insurance business where his charm and wit were an excellent combination for successful sales but fed his self-destruction. As soon as he'd receive a large commission check, he'd purchase his drugs, along with a ticket to a foreign country.

On one occasion he woke up in Jamaica, and he had no idea how he had arrived at his destination. He found himself without his wallet and credit cards. On another occasion, he was involved in a crazy incident where he was free-basing cocaine and blew through $12,000 before hitting bottom. There was yet another life-threatening episode in which he went on a four-day bender without eating. This time, he had the sense to call his parents for help. Ron went to get him while Janet went directly to the store. She returned with some chicken soup and nursed him back to life. She knew that her son would die if he didn't do something about his habit.

Ron gave Norman phone numbers to several treatment facilities in Portland. He was accepted into Saint Vincent's Treatment Center and checked himself into the program only to relapse ten days later. He had always been determined to get whatever he wanted out of life. His determination finally worked to his favor when he was admitted into an outpatient program that allowed him to stay employed in the insurance business while going through treatment. He was able to stay in the mainstream of life, feel the pain, deal with his issues, and maintain his ability to function. For him, this was a far better choice than checking into a facility in a sheltered environment for forty-five days. He needed to deal with the stress of everyday life

183

while going through the program. The fee for the program was $5,000. He was a proud man when he paid it off himself eighteen months later.

Living sober was a frightening experience for Norman because he had to learn to live in the real world. He spent his days at Alcoholics Anonymous (AA) meetings and went to Cocaine Anonymous (CA). He soon discovered that Cocaine Anonymous didn't suit him because cocaine had never been his drug of choice. Alcohol had always been his first choice and one he always went back to. He'd drink anything, and he craved any type of alcohol available. He attended meetings on a regular basis in the basement of a one-hundred-year-old house in Portland. Coincidentally, his grandmother, Vi, had gotten sober in the same building twenty years earlier.

About four months into his sobriety, he latched onto a woman dealing with her own recovery issues. Two individuals, both struggling to find some sanity in their lives, it seemed as though they were matched right from the start. Instinctively, Norman knew that the relationship was destructive, but try as he might, he wasn't able to pull away from the intense sexual activity that bonded them.

Janet, sensing that the relationship was a detriment to his sobriety, wrote a note and taped it to the windshield of his car while he was attending an AA meeting. "Norm, you need to find somebody who cares for you and for who you are," indicating that he should leave the woman he was involved with. He was shocked because he had always had his mother's blessing for whomever he chose to include in his life. He told his dad that if his mother was that concerned over the relationship, then he must be a more codependently sick individual than he thought. That realization forced him into codependent treatment, which gave him the strength to end the eighteen-month relationship.

His girlfriend, however, saw things much differently. She believed the problems in their relationship were due to the controls and guilt trips that Janet forced on them. Six months before Janet's death, Norman's girlfriend sent the following letter to Janet:

∞

Letter to Janet from Norman's Girlfriend
November 27, 1989

Mrs. Adkins, I pray daily for your family. I have grown very fond of them. I haven't written this letter before because I didn't want the situation between us to get worse. I always hoped we could reconcile whatever was between us. I'm really not sure what it was. I think part of it was you didn't like the way I treated Norm, and I didn't like the way you treated him. I felt you always made him out to be the bad boy. Maybe part of our differences also was that we never got close. That was probably my fault, and I am sorry. I always wanted to be close to you and know you (you seemed so warm and caring). I just didn't know how, and I was afraid I would do it wrong if I tried. I think if you asked Norm, he would tell you I have a hard time letting most people get close to me. He is the only one that really knows all of me.

I'm sorry for any pain I have caused. I guess all of that really doesn't matter now though. I can not go on with the hiding, the control, and the snide remarks to Norm about our relationship. You won. I just hope that in the end you don't end up loosing. I believe your hanging your death over your family's heads will push them away. I don't believe that is what you want. I feel you just want a lot of love and joy from your family in your last days. They will get tired of the dangling and the guilt.

Remember the conversation at the beach, about your mother, that if she continued to make the family feel guilty they were going to quit calling. I don't believe the boys will do that with you, but there will be, and is, a lot of anger. It's really hard to enjoy someone when you're angry at them. I know all of your boys love you dearly, and I see why, when you let your inner light out. They all want to spend as much quality time with you as possible. Not because they have to though, but because they love you and want the memories of the specialness that is you. I think you would find that if you let go of dangling your death over their heads, and just enjoy, love and laugh with your family, everyone could find more joy in each other in this last stage of your journey together. Give them the gift that is you. I know this is not easy for you and your family, but God gave you time to enjoy your family, and them you. My grandfather didn't get that, and he wanted it, but was bed ridden.

It is a gift from God that you have the time to leave your family with happy memories. Please go live it up, and thrive on the individual ways that your sons love you. If you let them give of themselves in their own way, they won't leave you. They also want this time with you so they can have your smiles and warmth to hold, and warm their hearts when you are gone. Put the talk of death away. When the time is here you will know it, and you can more freely enjoy now. At least give that to your sons. Don't leave them with pain and anger in their hearts. The warmth, love and smiles are the grandest gift you can leave them with. I know if I was dying, I would want my children to see my specialness, and not the other sides of me that can be demanding, selfish and self-pitying. I would want to leave the good behind in their hearts and memories.

I don't know if this letter will do any good or not, but I see the pain and anger in Norm, and I would give or try anything that might erase that.

I'm not the one that is able to do that though, no matter how much I want to. I love him, and your family has become very special to me, even though I didn't know how to show it to you, and I was afraid to try. I have a lot of fears and insecurities, and those just make this whole thing harder for Norm, so I am choosing to get out of the way and let God do his handiwork. He can do things I can't. I love Norm and don't want to make things harder for him, but I also want love and attention. Be good to him, he tries so hard to please you and never feels that what he does is enough, and then he gets angry and pulls away. His intentions are good.

May God go with you and give you strength and courage through this final part of your journey. We have a saying in AA 'God will never give you more than you can handle,' although sometimes it doesn't feel that way. I will miss all of you and will be praying for you. I will also hold close to my heart that specialness that you have shown me, especially in the beginning.

P.S. I've told Norm if he wanted to stick up for the rights of our relationship I would stay around and love him through this. If he doesn't, I will not stand around and watch our relationship, which we have had to struggle with, destroyed by control and guilt games. I've done a lot of wrong in this relationship, but I am not the only one to blame. Most decisions made that had to do with my family, or your family, have been joint decisions based on circumstances. My family gatherings have suffered by my leaving early also.

I pray you can learn to accept your sons for who they are, and see that they have needs also. We are all God's children and wonderful just the way we are. When you criticize something or someone you are criticizing God's handiwork. I have also heard time and again what you don't like in someone else is really what you don't like about yourself, but are afraid to see it in yourself. I pray you don't throw away your last chance to find happiness and peace of mind with your family, your world and your life.

Janet gracefully responded:

∞

Janet's Letter to Norman's Girlfriend
November 30, 1989

Thank you so much for caring and wanting to write. You have to know that I'm the easiest person in the world to get to know. I'm really not complicated. I am what I am, and I say what I feel. You don't ever need to be afraid of me. Life isn't about winning or losing. Life is until it isn't. I want so much to continue to see my children and my grandchildren, don't you know. It seems strange that you don't understand how I would feel about having this dreadful disease. I would feel better if you could show me empathy instead of hurt. I'm not into guilt. I never have been into guilt.

When you have a loving family, it is going to be difficult, especially for Ron, but also for everybody. It seems harder to lose a mother. Fathers are usually the ones that go first. Mothers stay and help their families. I want each and all of us to be caring for each other. Be happy! Be as happy as you can be every hour and every day. Love life and smile with your wonderful smile.

Love, Janet

Janet had made her peace and expressed her feelings about guilt. As she stated, "I'm not into guilt." She was not into guilt, yet in the wake of her death, guilt was to be dealt with by everyone that was left behind.

After ending the unhealthy relationship, Norman met his present wife, Tami Jo, at their ten-year high school reunion. Like himself, Tami Jo had also had her go around with drugs. With her sobriety, they made a strong couple that supported each other through their changes. Janet was fond of Tami Jo and believed she was a good partner for Norman. She gave them her blessing before she died.

Once Norman sobered up and had his life on track, he was faced with the agonizing truth of his mother's decision to end her life. Believing that his mother really had Alzheimer's was hard for him because what signs she presented seemed insignificant at the time. He loved challenging her at a good game of Scrabble and had learned to memorize all the numbers on the letters so he could score the most points. Winning didn't seem like a victory once he became aware of her handicap. He had noticed little things. Janet would tell him, "I can't make the stereo work. There is something wrong with it." He would check it out, and it would be working just fine. Her long-term memory seemed intact, but the here and now was definitely a problem.

Norman was angry with his dad as he felt he was to blame for reaffirming Janet's illness. The situation was confusing to him because he had always been taught to speak positive affirmations. If he affirmed and reaffirmed something, it would come to pass. Ron had been trying to convince him of Janet's illness for some time, but he had refused to believe it as fact. Blaming his father was easier than to face the truth of the matter.

Discovering Janet's plans to meet with Dr. Kevorkian was even more terrifying for him. According to Norman, this was not the way it was supposed to go down. He knew what his mother's position was on death, as he had discovered a recipe for death by barbiturates in the kitchen recipe box many years earlier. However, knowing that fact didn't make it any easier. He supported his mother's decision because he knew that was what she wanted, so he didn't try to change her mind. Instead, he became angry with Neil for trying to force his

Christian beliefs on their mother. Janet was a Unitarian and had her own belief system. With her impending death, Norman didn't think that she needed to be confronted with her spiritual beliefs.

Like the other family members, Norman requested a private counseling session with his mother prior to her death to discuss any personal differences that may have been unresolved.

Note from Myriam Coppens, Family Therapist

May 26, 1990—Phone call from Mr. Adkins. Norman, another son, would like to come in with mom. Date set up for Monday, May 26, 1990. Two-hour office visit with Norman and Janet. Very moving. Very appropriate. This will be my last visit with Janet.

Janet and Norman discussed an incident of resentment that he had carried around for years. When he was a young child, he had gotten into trouble, and Janet had punished him by having him stand facing a corner of the wall. After a short time had passed, she told him that his time was up. Apparently, he didn't hear her, and he continued to stand there for what seemed like two hours until she came back from the neighbor's house. During the counseling session, he talked to his mother about his unresolved anger about that childhood incident. Hearing Janet's side of what happened helped him understand that her intent had not been to administer cruel and unjust punishment.

Then Janet revealed her anger toward Norman concerning the worry he had caused her over the years. When he used to drive his motorcycle through the neighborhood drunk at night, she worried all the time that she would get a call that he was dead. Sharing their frustrations, they completed with tears and hugs. Norman felt fortunate to have had this special time with his mother.

He wrote Janet the following letter the day before she left for Michigan:

∞

Letter from Norman to his Mother

I just wanted to write a few things to cheer you up. Did you know that when I was a young boy of about eight, I stole two of your wonderful freshly baked chocolate chip cookies and darted out the door? I was not to eat these cookies as it was very close to dinnertime. When I was running to a safe place to enjoy my cookies, a bee decided to fly under my tongue. Before I could remove him, he stung me. I was unable to enjoy your batch of cookies and I missed dinner that night. I love you, Norm.

On the day of Janet's departure, Norman walked with his mother and his brother, Ronald, through the concourse at the Portland airport. Neil hadn't joined them as he was against Janet's decision to end her life. They stopped at a coffee shop to say their final goodbyes, and they watched Ronald breakdown with uncontrollable sobs, knowing it would be the last time he would see his mother alive. With all that occurred for the past year, Norman was numb and unable to cry. As a family, they had gone through many false hopes with Janet's illness, and her date with Dr. Kevorkian had already changed once. Norman wasn't really sure she would go through with it, and he was more comfortable staying in denial.

21

Heartbreak and Fatherhood

Like his two brothers, Ronald struggled with alcohol and enjoyed the party scene. In 1984, while attending the University of Oregon, he met a young woman at a fraternity party. Distracted from his studies, school took a backseat to his new relationship. Finishing out the school year, it seemed like the perfect time to fulfill a childhood dream of living in Alaska. In 1985, he dropped out of school, purchased a car, and drove the picturesque highway to Anchorage, Alaska, with his girlfriend. Living with careless abandon, they found their lives changed when they discovered they were soon to be parents. Desiring to be near family, they moved back to Portland where his girlfriend gave birth to their son, Bryan, on August 11, 1986.

Their relationship was a stormy one that ebbed and flowed over a six-year period. Although Ronald deeply loved his son, it was clear that marriage to this woman was not in the best interest for either of them. Their son, Bryan, went to live with his mother, and Ronald moved back into the family home, sharing custody of Bryan. As time went on, that Bryan was living in a precarious situation became obvious to Ronald. When Ronald arrived at Bryan's house to pick him up for the weekend, he was most often met by shady characters hanging out at the house.

On one particular evening when Ronald had been drinking heavily, it became evident to him that life was becoming intolerable. Angry and frustrated with the direction that his life was taking, he got into an altercation with his mother. His dad was gone on a business trip, and Janet was in bed reading a book when Ronald stormed into her room. She was startled by the intense anger spewing from him as his nostrils flared with rage while he shouted at her. "I'm frustrated with my life!"

"You need to get a job! Just get out there and find one!" she screamed back.

"You're not in my shoes, and you shouldn't be telling me what to do with my life!" he retorted.

As Janet started to get out of bed, he grabbed her arm and pushed her back down on the bed. Raising his voice even louder, he pointed his finger at her and ranted, "You don't know what I am going through! I have a child to support!"

It was a bad time in Ronald's life, one that was never talked about again. Even after he got sober in 1988, it never came up. That incident still haunts him to this day, and he regrets that he never apologized to his mother prior to her death.

When he first learned about his mother's illness and her intent to end her life, he was grief-stricken. Janet had spoken openly about her philosophy on death for many years, but knowing that didn't make it any easier. Meeting at the apartment on her last day in Portland, Ronald was surprised to see how comfortable his mom was with her decision. She was packing her bags as if she were going on a vacation, while checking a list of items that needed to be addressed.

Pointing toward the kitchen, she said, "Ronald, you can eat the chicken breast that I've cooked, but be sure and make something for Dad when you come back. Promise me you will take care of Dad. He doesn't cook, and he doesn't do laundry. I've done everything for him over the years, and I want to be sure that he is taken care of after I'm gone."

Ronald handed Janet the following letter before her departure:

∞

Letter to Janet from Ronald

I'm writing this in the car, so I hope you can read this. I just want to say Thank you for being you. You have instilled in me that life is wonderful and to experience everything it has to offer. (You do this and always have.) Mom, I remember

when I was little when we were living on Westwood Drive that you told me some people are Giants and to me you will always be a Giant. Enjoy this wonderful journey and remember that I am always loving you. Ronald or as Norman puts it '*Buck Wheat.*'

22

Tragic Sorrow

Eunice, Janet's aunt from Canada, and her husband, John, looked forward to their visits with Janet and the family. Eunice admired their beautiful home with its view of Portland. Janet had no interest in keeping her home up to the standards of perfection, and that was one of the many things that Eunice loved about her. Whenever she came to visit, Eunice took over the cooking so Janet could visit with the guests. Janet would get the conversation going by asking questions, as she satisfied her curious nature by discovering what was going on in other people's heads.

Eunice believed that Janet had a magnetic power over Ron, influencing him to think the way she wanted him to think. To Eunice, Ron seemed willing to go along with whatever Janet wanted. If Janet wanted to take a trip to Europe and they didn't have the finances, they would go anyway. If Ron wanted to stay home and relax, and Janet wanted to go hiking, they'd go hiking. Janet had always wanted to take a ride in a glider. Ron had no interest, so she went by herself and was thrilled with the experience. Another time she took a hot-air balloon ride in Palm Springs. She did what she wanted to do, and Ron respected her for her choices. Ron admitted that Janet had a magnetic power over him, and it was fair to say that he was content to live with her terms.

When Janet wanted Ron to accompany her on a trip to Nepal, he declined because he was emotionally uncomfortable with the poverty in that country. He had some concerns about her taking the trip because he had noticed little incidents that were occurring on a frequent basis. Periodically Janet would become confused with her sense of direction. Eunice had noticed it too. More than once she had observed Janet go the wrong direction when she exited a door. Because Janet was traveling with a friend and neighbor to Nepal, Ron relaxed a bit and trusted that she would be in good hands. Janet had a fabulous time trekking in the Himalayas and sent Eunice a picture of herself riding an elephant.

∞

Janet's Journal—Dag Hammarskjöld, Secretary General of the United Nations

When the morning's freshness has been
replaced by the weariness of midday,
When the leg muscles quiver under the strain,
the climb seems endless, and suddenly
nothing will go quite as you wish,
it is then that you must not hesitate.

Every year, Eunice and John stayed at Janet and Ron's home in Portland while John played in golf tournaments. On one particular visit, Eunice noticed that Janet was having trouble with crossword puzzles. That wasn't at all like Janet because her expertise working with those types of puzzles had been very advanced. Eunice mentioned it to John, and he responded that he wasn't the least bit concerned.

The following year when they were visiting again, Eunice asked Janet, "Do you find that your mind isn't as good as it used to be?" Janet replied, "Ever since I was in Nepal I haven't been the same. I got sick and lost ten pounds. I thought I had a parasite, but I was checked for that and it was negative."

After that day, Eunice noticed a steady decline in Janet's memory.

Later in the year, on their way to San Diego, Eunice and John stopped in Portland for another visit. By that time, Janet had been diagnosed with Alzheimer's and was undergoing some tests.

"I have a potion in case my future isn't positive. I've marked a date on my calendar," Janet told them.

"Janet, you cannot do this!" John exclaimed, trying to dissuade her.

But by then Janet had already made up her mind. Nothing in the world could have changed her mind. Over dinner, Janet seemed to be her usual upbeat self. By looking at her, one would never know what she was facing. She acted as though nothing was wrong. Understanding Janet's way of thinking was hard for John and Eunice.

The following year, to Eunice that Janet was deteriorating was obvious. She could no longer play the piano, read, or keep score in tennis. Seeing Janet lose her abilities was extremely sad for Eunice because Janet had always had a brilliant mind and was so active. She supported Janet's decision once she was able to accept the fact that Janet indeed had Alzheimer's.

"I know how awful the disease is, and I don't want to see you end up in an incapacitated way, not having control of your person. I want to remember you as you are," Eunice told Janet.

"I want you and Aunt Lorraine to look after Mama while I go to heaven to be with Grandma," Janet replied.

∞

Janet's Letter to Her Aunt Lorraine

Dear Aunt Lorraine,
You have been such an important person in my life. It will be hard to leave you. I just want to tell you how much you have meant to all of us. Please take good care of mama and love each other ten times more than usual. I will always remember how much you helped us with tiny babies and medium sized babies and grown up babies. They have been a part of you and you have been such an integral part of them. You have loved them all so much. Keep loving them and keep loving all of your large and wonderful family. They are all exceptional, I think. I am so glad you were in my life.

I love you, Janet.

Aunt Lorraine is not sure what choice she would make if faced with a terminal illness. "Sometimes I think I would not want to live if I had an incurable disease," she stated. "If people have no more hope, it isn't fair that they should suffer. I never did believe in doctor-assisted dying, but as the years go by, I notice how much people are suffering."

She has dreams of buying a new home with all new furniture. Janet would have been excited about the possibility of a change in residence for her aunt Lorraine. She would have said, "Go for it, Aunt Lorraine. Go for it!"

John was adamantly against Janet's decision to end her life, and it caused many heated debates between Eunice and him.

"She's far too young to kill herself. She is not far enough gone," John exclaimed on more than one occasion.

"But, John, she can't wait too long," Eunice responded, knowing that Janet's time for making a rational decision was running out. "It is great that she is going to do something."

"You just can't take your own life," John stated. "It's just not right."

As a Canadian police officer, John's job was to save lives, not take them. When he first learned of Janet's plans, he didn't really believe that she intended to go through with it. In his line of work, he had heard a lot of people say they wanted to kill themselves, but it never amounted to much, so he didn't take it seriously. When he learned that Ron was a member of the Hemlock Society in Portland, he was shocked. For many years in Canada, committing suicide was a crime. If a person attempted and failed, he or she could be charged with a crime, so a person needed to make sure the first attempt was successful. Taking one's life was totally against John's way of thinking.

John had seen a lot of failed suicide attempts. He had also seen a lot of dead bodies. It was a bloody mess and never a pretty sight. He had seen people who'd survived slashed wrists and slashed throats. On one cold day in November, when the rain was falling and the temperature had dropped to 38 degrees, a young woman had attempted to take her life. After slashing her wrists and her throat, she had fallen off the fire escape into a ditch. A passing motorist found her four hours later. That she survived was no small miracle.

Always a heated argument between them, John and Eunice could not agree on Janet's decision to die.

∞

23

Be Bamboo

Judy met Janet in 1962 while living in Forest Grove. It didn't take long for the two women to discover that they had many things in common. Their husbands were music teachers in the Forest Grove schools, both Judy and Janet were accomplished musicians, and they both had children around the same age who attended school together. Family was important to them. Judy still remembers how excited Janet was when she shared the news that she was pregnant with her third son, Ronald.

Although they loved their families, their interests were more than just recipes and diapers. For Judy, Janet was a ray of sunshine, leading her out of the tunnel of housewife mentality into an open field of new discoveries. She was intrigued by Janet's interest in new ideas and philosophy. Janet presented a new way of thinking that went far beyond the norm. Judy looked forward to their times together where they would spend hours discussing the books that they had read. Judy was a music major, and prior to meeting Janet, she had not been exposed to literature. Janet brought a new level of interest in her life. Just the idea of reading a book, discussing it, and exploring the plot or the threads woven throughout the story was very exciting to Judy.

∞

Janet's Journel–Francis Bacon

Some book are to be tasted,
Others to be swallowed,
And some few to be chewed and digested.

Judy thought Janet would have made a good Barbara Walters because she had a special ability to connect with people. Her unique style of asking questions opened a person up, allowing them to tell her more and more about him or herself before they discovered what was happening. In an odd sort of way, Janet's tactic actually assisted the other person in developing a thought or an idea that he or she hadn't considered.

While Judy was recuperating from a back injury, Janet visited her. For Janet, it seemed like an appropriate time for her to share the diagnosis of her illness with Judy.

"I have Alzheimer's disease, and it's progressing," Janet whispered in a steady voice.

Refusing to believe what she had just heard, Judy responded patronizingly, "Janet, we all forget things."

"No, Janet replied. "I'm serious. I really do have Alzheimer's." When it finally struck Judy that Janet was, indeed, being truthful, she was totally dumbfounded and felt embarrassed that she had not reacted as a supportive friend. It was nearly impossible to grasp the fact that her dear friend who stood before her could possibly be losing her mind.

At that point, Janet made a startling statement that Judy was not prepared to hear. "I don't want to live to see the disease progress, and Doctor Kevorkian is going to deliver me."

Believing that she would eventually reincarnate, Janet blatantly stated to Judy, "Well, I guess I'm not going to come back very soon, am I?"

In Judy's mind, she had no doubt that Janet was absolutely determined to end her life. Janet didn't want her body walking around doing and saying ridiculous things when she wouldn't mentally be there anymore. To Janet, death wasn't when her physical body died; it was when the essence of who she was wasn't there anymore. She didn't want to experience the deterioration and the degradation of her person. Janet's composure in facing death was in knowing that she had a dignified way out.

∞

Janet's Journal—
Here Comes There Goes You Know Who,
by William Saroyan

*You betray honor, you betray yourself, and you
betray the human race when you believe the
way to truth is the way taken by the mob.
When you agree because it's convenient,
when you accept, when you conform,
when you don't go after the truth
as if it had never before been seized.*

After Janet left, Judy spent the afternoon playing back in her mind the events that had occurred with Janet earlier that day. Still stunned by the information, she placed a call to Janet.

"I want you to know that I'm with you all the way. I care for you and want you to know that I'm here for you if there is anything I can do."

Judy recalled a calligraphy sign that hung in Janet's kitchen: *'Be Bamboo.'* To Janet, that meant that one should be flexible and bend with the wind.

"Be Bamboo," she said to Janet.

Judy berated herself for not having recognized the early signs of Janet's illness because more than one red flag had gone unnoticed. Looking back, there had been a time, several months before, when a group of friends had met at Washington Park for a picnic. The entire afternoon, Judy had the feeling that something wasn't quite right with the group, but she couldn't put her finger on it. Usually the group jelled and carried on lively conversations. But on that day, the conversation kept falling dead with periods of silence, leading the group to break up earlier than normal. Later, she realized that the conversation had died because Janet hadn't kept it going, like she had always done before, with her relentless questioning of what was going on in everyone's lives.

Another red flag went unnoticed when she called Janet to give her directions to a restaurant. Janet handed the phone to Ron, stating,

"Ron, you are better than I am at understanding directions." Shortly after learning of Janet's condition, Judy received a call from a friend planning a group weekend at their beach home. Janet and Ron were among the group of invited guests. Sensing that Judy was keeping something from her, the friend began pressuring her. "What is with you? I know something is wrong."

Trying to hold back, Judy could not keep the dam from bursting, and the news of Janet's impending death came spilling out. Janet and Ron were obviously trying to cover things up as best they could because many of their close friends were unaware that anything was wrong.

After spending the weekend with Janet at the beach house, any doubts Judy may have had about Janet's condition were soon put to rest. In the morning while preparing breakfast, she asked Janet to make the coffee. Janet wasn't able to figure out how to put the percolator together. Where the coffee went and how to get the basket into the coffeepot were confusing to her. When it came time to eat, Judy took the quiche out of the oven and handed Janet a knife and spatula. Janet was able to cut up the quiche, but she had no idea what to do with the spatula.

On one particular evening, Judy met Janet and Ron for dinner. This was no ordinary dinner, as the conversation was centered on Janet's plans to end her life. During the evening, they informed Judy that they were busy making final arrangements. Janet started talking about Dr. Kevorkian in an upbeat tone of voice that expressed extreme relief. She advised Judy that she had looked at every option she could think of including jumping off the balcony of her building, taking pills, or getting a gun and shooting herself. But to Janet, none of those options seemed like a viable alternative, as none were guaranteed to do the job. She also feared that it might be traumatic for the family. Janet described Dr. Kevorkian as her salvation. She was so happy to have found him. She couldn't believe that she had seen him on television. Her only problem with the plan was her fear that Dr. Kevorkian might change his mind and back out on her.

Janet frantically exclaimed, "What if something happens to him?"

Ron assured her. "He'll be there when you are ready."

But Janet's greatest fear that he might not be there propelled her determination to meet with him sooner than later.

Over dinner, Janet divulged all the details of her planned exit. She described the three bottles that were suspended from the death machine, and she told Judy that Dr. Kevorkian would instruct her as to how to activate the machine. Strange as it seemed, Janet had accepted her destiny. She displayed no evidence of sadness or regrets.

Janet went on. "I want Ron to remarry. I know he will be remarried within a year. You know Ron. He'll probably get some woman with big boobs." They all laughed. Janet went on to say, "Judy, I never thought I would get to the other side and find out before you. We have talked about this so many times and I'm going to beat you. I'm going to know before you." Then Janet once again made the comment, "I won't be coming back anytime soon."

Judy never tried to talk Janet out of her decision. Knowing Janet like she did, it made perfect sense to her. Judy told Janet that she would feel the same way if she were in her position and would make exactly the same choice.

Leaving the restaurant, Janet turned to Judy and stated, with grateful acknowledgment, "I want you to know how much this means to me that we can talk about this. I can't talk about this to everyone. Just being able to talk freely and openly is a big relief. It has just helped me so much."

To Judy, Janet had obviously found the perfect solution to her dilemma. The last time Judy saw Janet was at a concert they attended together. She told Judy that she had set a date with Dr. Kevorkian and that Ron had purchased round-trip tickets for both of them in case she changed her mind.

"I'm not the least bit interested in a round-trip ticket," Janet proclaimed. "Ron just wants me to know that I have the option of changing my mind."

"Janet's exit has the possibility of causing a lot of publicity, even internationally," Ron pointed out.

Janet looked at Ron with disbelief. "Oh, Ron, don't be silly. Of course not!"

That thought hadn't occurred to Judy, but when Ron mentioned it, the scenario certainly sounded probable. They were soon to discover that no one was prepared for the magnitude of publicity that would be generated by Janet's death.

Their conversation ended with the discussion of Janet's memorial service and Ron asking Judy if she would like to speak at the memorial. Judy said she would be honored, and then they said their tearful goodbyes.

∞

24

Clueless in Portland

Shirley and Dell met Janet and Ron while living in Forest Grove, an artistic college town filled with intellectuals. They soon discovered that they had children and music in common, which fueled their friendship spanning more than thirty years. Shirley's husband, Dell, was an easygoing, laid-back man, who directed the band at Sunset High School for twenty-five years.

A feisty woman full of spirit and spunk, Shirley was blessed with high energy that was both a gift and a curse. There was a time in her life when she thought that she would go out of her mind because life to her was so boring. The mundane existence of a housewife was the worst possible situation that she could have created for herself. She despised her role as a homemaker and was unable to find a way to make her life fun. She constantly fantasized about running away from home and contemplated ways in which her husband would cope with raising their three children after she left.

∞

**Janet's Journal—*The Empty Copper Sea*,
by John MacDonald**

*Now listen to me. I really do love you.
And as much as I love you and want you,
I can't be somebody's remedy,
some kind of medicine for the soul.*

I have to be my own person.
I have to take complete charge of my life.[1]

Whereas Janet was interested in philosophy and deep conversation, Shirley and Janet's relationship was quite the opposite. Although Shirley and Dell were conservative, they found Janet and Ron interesting because they were always delving into something new. Janet was a constant searcher, and to Shirley, Ron seemed willing to go along with whatever Janet wanted. Dell often told Shirley that he thought Janet was doing outrageous things as a gimmick to get attention.

When the Bhagwan Rajneesh came to Oregon, Janet and Ron participated for a day in spiritual activities. Shirley was quick to voice her opinion. "You are nuts! Don't do this. This is stupid. They're crazy! They're awful!"

"Give them a chance," Janet retorted.

When Ron announced to the group that Janet and he were taking a class in wine tasting, Shirley and Dell were stunned because nobody did that sort of thing in their circle of friends in the early seventies. Janet and Ron were always on the cutting edge of something new and delved into everything that came along. They continued their quest for personal growth. When Janet and Ron were involved in the EST courses, Shirley's mind went crazy with thoughts of them sitting around naked in hot tubs contemplating their navels. She could not understand what the attraction was for them.

Whereas Janet was viewed as a searcher, Ron was viewed as the jokester. Seldom serious, Ron was known for his bad jokes. Sometimes his jokes were funny, but at other times, Shirley and Dell found them to be just plain irritating. Although there was an occasional annoyance between them, Shirley and Dell actually looked forward to their next escapade with Janet and Ron.

Janet loved influencing her friends into thinking the same way she did, and she wanted the whole world to have the same experience. One time she brought up the subject of birth control with

---

[1] John MacDonald, *The Empty Copper Sea*, trade paperback ed., introduction by Lee Child (New York: Random House, 2013), 267.

210

Dell. Full of enthusiasm she excitedly asked Dell, "Have you tried foam? It gives you freedom of expression."

"No," Dell replied with flushed cheeks and embarrassment in his voice.

Another time Janet asked them, "Have you ever made love the French way?"

"I don't even know what the French way is," Dell admitted.

"You should try it. It's really fun!" Janet responded.

"What! Are you out of your mind?" Shirley exclaimed.

Shirley could never understand Janet's way of thinking. She thought that for someone so open about her sex life, Janet didn't seem to fit the image. Janet was attractive in her own way, but she certainly was not a glamorous woman by any means. Janet didn't dress to be noticed, and she didn't seem to be the least bit concerned about the latest fashions. Her hairstyle and clothes were very conservative, and she wore little to no makeup. In Dell's opinion, Janet dressed like a dowdy housewife and Ron wanted to keep her looking that way. Shirley thought Janet should sharpen up and get something wild for her lifestyle. To Janet, those things were not important, and Ron was content with her just the way she was.

Shirley recalled a time when Janet had her heart set on going to France to teach English as a second language. She confided in Shirley that she didn't follow her dream because Ron told her if she made that choice, he would not be there when she got back.

As close as Janet and Ron were with Shirley and Dell, they did not share Janet's diagnosis which left Shirley wondering what was wrong with Janet.

Looking back, Shirley thought that if she had paid attention to her intuition, she might have realized that her brain was a constant receiver of information. But, unfortunately, most of it went straight to her subconscious, where it was stored only to be revealed long after the fact. That had been her experience when she shared with Janet the circumstances that had played out at a birthday party. The couple hosting the party had invited a friend of theirs whose husband had Alzheimer's. Of course, Janet's interest was piqued when Shirley described the scene to her. The Alzheimer's patient had been very pleasant and had been smiling through the entire dinner party. But it was like having a three-year-old child at the table. He burst out with inappropriate words and just sat there smiling. His wife was determined to take care of him to the end, and she refused to put him in a home. He didn't disrupt the dinner or bother anyone, and he got along just fine. But he couldn't be included because he wasn't able to comprehend the conversation. Janet's expression said nothing to Shirley that would indicate that she was facing the same prognosis.

Another time after seeing the movie On Golden Pond, Shirley had described a scene to Janet that involved Henry Fonda's character, who had wandered away from home in search of strawberries. She told Janet it was just too bad that he couldn't have been left there to die. It was the natural order of life and time for him to go.

Shirley had felt the distance growing between them, and she thought that Janet was trying to end their friendship. Several times Shirley had called Janet to get together. Janet had made, what Shirley considered to be, a lame excuse on every occasion. Shirley didn't buy Janet's excuses, and her anger toward Janet began to build as her friend began pulling away. Shirley just thought that Janet wasn't being "good old Janet" anymore. She hadn't the slightest inkling that anything was wrong with Janet's health. Looking back, the clues were all over the place. But, because Shirley wasn't privy to Janet's secret, she was left to form her own judgments.

One time, Shirley called Janet to ask her opinion on a letter that she was writing to the editor of the Oregonian newspaper. She knew that Janet would be able to verify the facts that she was referring to in her letter.

"I don't know. I can't remember," Janet replied. Shirley just thought that Janet was being uncooperative and didn't want to talk to her.

Another incident stood out in her mind. Janet and Ron had invited Shirley and Dell to see the movie The Gods Must Be Crazy II. Shirley was dumbfounded by the movie, as it was not at all consistent with the Janet that she knew. Janet loved classy art and always selected movies that were beyond Shirley's comprehension. To Shirley, this movie, with its theme centering on a woman's skirt flying up every time she got in an airplane, was just plain stupid.

Shirley and Dell looked forward to the elaborate dinner parties that Janet created. Janet would host a party for any unusual reason, and everyone who was anyone hoped to receive an invitation. Janet would delight in seating large groups of people in crazy chairs around odd tables that didn't match. One particular party was in celebration of the straightening of her teeth. Janet introduced the dentist as her guest of honor. During the evening, she proudly showed off her newly straightened teeth to all the guests asking for their opinions of orthodontists.

One particular evening stood out in Shirley's mind as being quite unusual. The meal served that night was far too simple. She overheard what she thought was a strange conversation between Janet and Ron.

"Is the gravy done?" Ron asked Janet.

"I can't remember how to make the gravy," Janet replied. "Oh well, never mind," Ron stated.

The guests were served soup and bread that night. "They must be getting into a strange way of eating," Shirley told Dell. From Shirley's perspective, neither Janet nor Ron seemed the least bit concerned over the meal. But Shirley was concerned, as everything was always done properly with Janet. She viewed Janet and Ron as people of the world who did everything right. This most certainly was not the Janet she knew. That evening had seemed strange to her at the time, but she didn't know what to make of it. Janet and Ron just went along and pretended that everything was normal.

Shirley berated herself for missing so many clues—the same perception shared by many of their friends as well. If Janet didn't want them to know, they were left to form their own opinions about what was going on in their lives.

Ron once told Shirley that he and Janet were taking Vitamin E. "Do you know that Vitamin E is good for your memory? You should take it. Janet and I take it." Here, again, was another clue that Shirley had missed.

A friend of theirs, the principal at a middle school, had played tennis with Janet just days before she died. When someone had mentioned to her that Janet could not keep track of scores, she had replied, "Well, who can? That's not so unusual." Janet's illness had gone unnoticed by a good tennis player as well.

The last time they saw Janet, Dell was directing a symphonic band of eighty musicians. Shirley and Dell had invited Janet and Ron to attend the concert in downtown Portland at the concert hall. After the concert, they visited friends of theirs who had invited them to their home to view their antiques. Janet was very quiet that night and barely spoke a word. That was not at all like the Janet that Shirley knew. Later that night when they departed from their friends' home, Janet and Ron walked up the hill toward their apartment. As they walked hand in hand, Dell asked if they would like a ride up the hill. "Oh, no. We're going to be fine," Ron replied.

For Shirley, many strange signs that evening indicated that something might be wrong, but she didn't know what to make of it. She wonders how many other people missed the clues.

25

The FART Club

Peggy and Bob were family friends of Janet and Ron for over thirty years. They raised their four children in the same neighborhood in Forest Grove, Oregon.

Janet influenced Peggy in her way of thinking. Janet was the type of person with whom Peggy could be herself. There was never any pretentiousness. If Janet stopped by unannounced and Peggy was having a bad hair day, her house in shambles, and the beds not made, Janet didn't care. Peggy always felt comfortable in any situation that was presented where Janet was concerned. It probably had something to do with Janet not being a perfect housekeeper by any stretch of the imagination.

Peggy viewed Janet as a woman who was not the least bit materialistic and someone who needed very little to make her happy. Janet wore large, round glasses and most likely never considered contact lenses. Makeup, hairstyles, and the latest fads didn't concern her in the least. She was only concerned about what went on inside people's heads. For Peggy, Janet was one of the most interesting people that she could ever hope to meet. She liked the fact that Janet was inquisitive. "How do you feel about this or that?" Her questions allowed Peggy to stop and think, and her curiosity presented the impression that she was truly interested in knowing the real person. However, Janet didn't particularly like it if anyone questioned her. She wanted to be the one to start the conversation and get things rolling.

Discovering that they had much in common with their young families, they developed a deep, lasting friendship that included not only raising their children but also participating in adult activities.

Every Friday they played tennis. They named their group the FART club—Friday Afternoon Recreational Tennis.

They often took trips together. On one particular trip, they found themselves hiking in the remote foothills of the Canadian Rockies. Janet and Bob were always the brave and daring ones. While they hiked along steep ridges and narrow precipices, Peggy and Ron lagged behind. As the hike progressed, Peggy and Ron became frightened of the narrow trail. Knowing that with one slip they would fall hundreds of feet to their death, they decided to return to the safety of the lodge. Bob and Janet continued the hike, returning later that day. They spent the evening telling frightening tales of their climb while expressing their ultimate exhilaration with the challenges they faced.

∞

<u>Janet's Journal—July 1980</u>

Ron and I went for a ten-day trip with good friends to a place called Lake O'Hara in the Canadian Rockies. We hiked to the tops of prospects enjoying the wildflowers, mountains, lakes and beautiful sunshine.

Peggy and Bob viewed Janet as a gutsy woman. When she made up her mind to do something, there was no stopping her. She always took charge of her life and did what she wanted. On one occasion, Janet took a thrilling, but scary, ride in a glider. It was just another example of her daring sense of adventure that made her who she was. Having that kind of temperament might have had something to do with her decision to end her life. She wasn't going to live her life as an invalid and put her family through any hardships.

Janet and Bob were similar in their temperaments. They often bickered about who was going to be in charge because both liked to be boss. Peggy and Ron kept themselves amused by watching the two of them go at it. On a trip to France in 1982, Bob and Janet continually clashed over the itinerary, with both having an obvious difference of opinion. Bob finally gave in to Janet and told her she could be in charge the following day. He promised her that he would keep his mouth shut. They got a late-morning start with Janet being unorganized, as was her usual style. She knew exactly where she wanted to go, but didn't have a plan on how to get there. The day ended short of their intended destination with Bob chuckling to himself. That Bob and Janet had no intention of giving up their control was evident.

∞

Janet's Journal

We arrived in London on September 23, 1982. We shared a room with Bob and Peggy, took a nap, showered and then went out for a simple dinner in Covent Garden before attending the musical CATS, all the rave in London this past year. But frankly Ron and I were disappointed. Last night we discussed what might have made it better, in our opinion. First of all, there was very little story line, the dancing was very good, and some of the musical numbers were quite good. But it seemed long and repetitious. With a little more expertise, care, attention or creativity, it could have really happened. It felt like a near hit to me.

Every night the couples were given the choice of two rooms when they arrived at their hotel. Invariably, one room was always much better than the other. They made a pact that every other night one of the couples would have the first choice of rooms. On one particular evening, they arrived at a little medieval village perched on top of a steep hill surrounded by a wall. It just so happened that it was Bob and Peggy's night to sleep in the room of their choice. The suite they chose was charming. It had a four-poster canopy bed, and the windows were draped with luxurious maroon velvet drapes. Looking out the window there was a magnificent view of the countryside. Janet and Ron slept in a smaller room with a partial view of the countryside and a plain bed. Ron later informed Peggy that when Janet learned that the famous French writer Camas had done some of his writing in their room, she broke into sobs of disappointment. She would have liked the experience of sleeping in the same room that had been used by a famous writer. Settling for the luck of the draw, they made the best of the situation.

∞

Janet's Journal

Ron and I woke up at 3:15 a.m. and could not go back to sleep. We looked out our window at the moon at 5:00 a.m. Appreciated the valley below, then went back to bed and made love.

Their days were filled with sightseeing and new experiences that were much different from their life in the States. They respected the Europeans' freedom of expression, their openness, and their acceptance of their bodies.

∞

Janet's Journal

We had lunch and enjoyed the beach, especially Bob and Ron. They ogled more breasts than they believed could be possible. It was unbelievably warm there and the bare boobs were beautiful and natural. Ron and I walked to the end of the beach and saw a young topless mother whose 7-year-old daughter was sort of making imaginary designs with her hands on her mother's tummy.

Being in this strange and wonderful land could be likened to a dream. But all dreams eventually come to an end.

218

∞

Janet's Journal

Now we are on the plane headed for Seattle, then Portland by car. I feel a little anxious to go back to Portland. It was a wonderful trip. And now back to reality.

One evening in 1989, while the couples were sitting around the table, Ron opened the conversation by stating, "We have something we want to tell you."

"Oh? What's that?" Peggy asked with a keen sense of curiosity.

"Janet has Alzheimer's," Ron stated in a sympathetic tone of voice.

"Oh, that's nice, and what else do you have?" Bob replied with sarcasm.

When they realized that Ron was telling the truth, they were stunned. Janet informed them that her illness was in the early stages and that she had enrolled in a treatment study in hope that it might slow down the disease. Neither Bob nor Peggy had any idea how serious the situation was. Looking back, Peggy was certain that Janet had enrolled in the program for the boys, but her heart was never in it. As determined as Janet was, she had already made up her mind what she intended to do.

Peggy began to take notice of Janet's situation. She could no longer read music, and she couldn't do a crossword puzzle as well as she used to. One evening she had trouble making a layered salad for the FART club. Janet was never an organized person, but once she made up her mind to exit, she got her life in order. She made videotapes for all her grandchildren, she put movie slides together and set up family counseling, and she wrote personal letters to each of the boys, her mother, and Ron. She was not leaving without preparing her family.

Janet and Ron had numerous conversations with Bob and Peggy about Janet's intentions. They talked two or three times a week. Janet talked about jumping off her ten-story apartment building, renting a motel at the beach, and walking out into the ocean, taking her life with carbon monoxide poisoning in a garage, and all kinds of other alternatives. When she heard about Dr. Kevorkian and he agreed to do it, she was very excited, happy, and relaxed that she had finally found a solution.

"Once she made up her mind, she was determined to follow through, stated Peggy. I don't mean this in an unkind way at all, but I think Janet was a dramatist. She loved something different like the Bhagwan Rajneesh. She was very enthusiastic about him because he represented something different. This was just an important part of her personality. I think that was one of the reasons it appealed to her to seek out Dr. Kevorkian."

Many times, Peggy asked Janet, "Are you sure you want to do this? Can't you think of some other solution? Can't you wait?"

Janet adamantly replied, "No, I'm going to do it! I'm going to do it!"

Peggy often visited Janet's mother to take some of the pressure off Janet. Now an invalid, Vi lived in low-income housing. She put a lot of demands on her only daughter, and Janet felt guilty if she wasn't available at her mother's every call. Peggy frequently brought Janet's mother goodies and pictures of the family and took her to doctor appointments. Janet did just about anything her mother asked her to do. Tending to her mother after she was diagnosed with Alzheimer's became more and more difficult. Peggy thinks it may have been a part of Janet's decision to exit because she eliminated the stress associated with her mother. For Vi, losing her only daughter was very hard because she depended on her. After Janet's death, Vi frequently told Peggy, "It just can't be. It is so sad."

∞

Janet's Journal

Today seems filled with heavies. Mama fell six weeks ago and broke her hip and wrist. Recovery is real slow. That is where all my time goes. Her voice is weak and there is much pain as she tries to put weight on it in therapy.

Mama wonders if she can hire someone to take care of her in her apartment, when good Sam

(Good Samaritan Hospital) releases her, so that she won't have to go into a nursing home. I wonder if I can find someone. I stopped by Mama's apartment and saw all the old people trying to be cheerful. One old man on the elevator tells me that he will be 72 on Sunday and that his wife is in a nursing home. He says he's having a devil of a time getting along without her. Sitting at the dining room table, I look out, and the sky is very blue. The leaves on the tall poplar tree are shimmering in the gentle wind.

In her last few months, Janet put on extra weight due to frequent dining out. Bob loved teasing Janet about her weight, which only intensified the long-standing bickering between the two. "You're getting chunky, Janet," Bob teased. Janet really got mad at Bob, and Peggy didn't blame her. Bob was always in trouble with Janet.

The couples got together again for the last time the night before Janet left to meet with Dr. Kevorkian. After dining at a Greek restaurant, they went back to Bob and Peggy's house for an after-dinner drink. When it came time to leave, they stood in the driveway saying their last goodbyes. Peggy put her arms around Janet, hugged her for the last time, and stated, "Janet are you sure this is what you want to do?" Janet never cried or showed any emotion of being scared or upset about her decision. Peggy handed her a poem that she had written and waved goodbye as they drove off. That was the last time they saw Janet.

PART IV

Reactions from Family and Friends
Who Were Left Behind

26

Impact of Suicide

Neil's Reaction

Although he had an opportunity to share his thoughts with his mother prior to her death, Neil believes that the way in which she chose to exit did not allow him proper closure. The night before his mom died, she called and said goodbye. The next day, he received a call from his dad informing him that his mother was dead. He later told his dad, "What the hell? This is not normal. This is crazy. This does not make sense. How am I to explain to people that on Sunday I got a call from my mother, and on Monday she was dead? How am I to explain that it was premeditated? It really screws with my head."

When the family was invited as guests on a New York talk show, Neil deliberately declined because he didn't want to add to the controversy by voicing his disapproval of his mother's suicide. However, he did join his dad, along with his two brothers, for an interview with Ken Shram, on Town Meeting, in Seattle, Washington on July 29, 1990. Uncertain of his feelings, the intense disapproval of his mother's decision wasn't clear to him at that time. On television, he defended her position, stating that she had always been a fighter. He told the audience that when she initially talked about what she intended to do it was very hard because she wasn't fighting the disease; she was succumbing to it. But eventually she fought it and won in a different way. She was a very determined woman. The thing he admired most about her was that she loved life and lived every day to the fullest. She had beat him at tennis the weekend before her death. The only regret his mother had was that she wasn't going to be around to see the French Open. When Ken Shram asked him if he agreed with the decision his mother made, Neil answered, "It was her life and her decision. It was one person's decision, my mother's." When asked if he would make the same choice for himself, he responded, "I don't know what I would do." Unsure of his position, he remained silent for many years following his mother's death. With a delayed reaction, his true feelings were expressed when he spoke with passion against the Oregon Initiative on doctor-assisted dying. He called several television stations in Portland and voiced his opinion on the issue. "It is my belief that the individuals who sponsored the right to die movement don't understand that one person's wrongful death can impact a huge group of people for the rest of their lives whether they know it or not. The person dying is trying to ease their pain, but what they don't realize is what it does to the remaining family. When my mother died, our family disintegrated. We all went our separate ways and we didn't talk to each other. Was that my mother's intent? No, but that is what happened. People need to realize the impact that suicide has on the family members. I want it known that I disagree with my mother's decision. I feel that Oregon's law should be repealed because it encourages other people to commit suicide. I believe that if we give people an easy exit they will use it."

Neil believes that the circumstances surrounding his mother's death have interrupted the natural grieving process. He won't go to a sad movie because he's afraid he might start crying and won't be able to stop. He is grieving as much today, as he did the day Janet died. He has gone to two treatment centers, one in Arizona and one in Washington, for a week at a time, trying to grieve the death of his mother. He has participated in many ritualistic ceremonies to release the grieving, including writing a letter to Janet and burning it at the site where a tree had been planted in her memory. He has made a collage of photos of his mother and framed her picture. He often reminds his dad that his mother still has control over him today. Neil still meets with a therapist, and the core issue always goes back to his mother and the fact that she still holds a vital part of his life. He believes that if she had chosen to live with Alzheimer's, she most certainly would have lost her mind. He also knows that she would have ended up a patient in a nursing home. But at least he would have been able to take his children to visit their grandmother and place them on her lap. His young daughter often asks him, "Where is Grandma Janet, Daddy?" Explaining the situation to his innocent daughter is really hard for him. It is sad, but he believes that Janet has robbed his children of that experience. He bitterly regrets that he was not given the opportunity to go through the deterioration of his mother's health. He believes that if he had been given the chance to take those steps with her there would have been some closure in her death.

With doctor-assisted suicide and the interruption of the natural cause of death, Neil believes that people are not aware of what it does to the next generation. "It is like a curse. It doesn't leave me," he often reminds his dad. "Even my therapists are baffled by this strange phenomenon. I don't know if the family will be able to let it go within this generation, and that scares me. I have been trying my damnedest to get rid of it. I want my life and I don't want to be driven by my mother."

Neil still carries anger toward his father for not stopping Janet. He believes that her death drove a wedge between their family members. Being around his family just reminds him of his mother and all the fun times they used to have together. He is dealing with his anger and resentment to the point that the pain is just too much to share as a family.

If you, or someone you love, are considering doctor-assisted suicide, Neil would like you to consider his message before making your decision:

If people want to kill themselves, they need to be aware of the fact that their family may split apart and never talk to each other for years to come. Is this what my mother wanted? I don't think so.

27

Mom's Law

Norman's Reaction

Norman met his dad at the airport on Ron's return from Michigan. When Ron stepped off the airplane without Janet, Norman knew she was gone. His dad had been drinking, which was how he was coping with the tragic event that had just taken place. Reporters were everywhere fighting for the story. His dad became the spokesperson for the family, making it known that there was no foul play and that Janet was competent when she made the decision to end her life.

When Norman learned that his mother had given her wedding rings to his dad and told him to have a wonderful life, he marveled at the courage and strength his mother had to face her impending death. He could not imagine what it would be like to possess that type of conviction.

Norman wishes that his mother were alive today to share in the ups and downs of his life. He made his first million dollars at age thirty-five, which was one of his goals. He purchased a home security business when the market was good. When the market turned down, he tried to change with the times but didn't make the change fast enough and lost all his investment to payroll and bad decisions. When the business was going well, he thought of taking some time off and going back to school. Although that didn't work out, he still holds the dream of furthering his education.

Norman is in support of his mother's decision to end her life. He believes that the Oregon initiative that has passed is really Janet's law, *'his mom's law.'* He realizes that it takes time for change, and he believes that the rules need to be broadened, and will be, when people can prove they are responsible as a society.

When he learned that Dr. Kevorkian had been charged with second-degree murder in the case of Thomas Youk, a fifty-two- year-old man suffering from amyotrophic lateral sclerosis, known better as ALS or Lou Gehrig's Disease, whom Kevorkian assisted in dying by providing a lethal injection himself, Norman defended Dr. Kevorkian with passion.

Norman was quoted in the *New York Post* online edition:

These prosecutors are zealots. It is absolutely outrageous that Dr. Kevorkian has been charged with murder for simply helping a man who was terminally ill die with dignity. Kevorkian is a crusader who must be allowed to continue with his assisted suicides. Helping my mother end her misery was truly noble and it brought great comfort to my family.

Norman is conscious of the fact that his trials and tribulations of early life are part of the fabric of who he is today. He is happy to be alive and to have survived the crazy days of his young adult life.

If Janet were here today, she most likely would say, "I proved my point. Genes are everything."

28

Unconditional Love

Ronald's Reaction

Ronald viewed his mother as the strength of the family. She was the one who brought the family together for holidays, birthdays, and family functions. She was the glue that kept the family together. He believes that her death put distance between the siblings. He's not sure if it was sibling rivalry among the brothers or that they just needed time to sort things out. Maybe it was part of the process in dealing with their mother's death. They each needed their own space to deal with what had happened. But ten years later, the rift between them has not healed.

Ronald believes that his mother was well aware of the impact that her death would have on the media. In an odd sort of way, he thinks it was her style of protecting the family from dealing with their loss. It was her way of helping the family she left behind, especially his dad, who has had a difficult time dealing with the loss of his wife and life-mate. The media was involved within twenty-four hours, and the family was distracted from the grieving process. In some respect, it made it easier for the family to deal with their loss.

If the pain of losing Janet wasn't enough, the pain was intensified with the disappearance of Ronald's precious son, Bryan. The month prior to Janet's death, his ex-girlfriend had shown up with Bryan stating they needed a temporary place to stay. Following Janet's death, she and Bryan disappeared without a trace. To make matters worse, she walked off with the entire $5,000 insurance money that

Janet had left for Ronald. He later discovered that she purchased herself a car and went on a vacation to Disneyland prior to settling in Arizona.

A painful time and feeling as though his life had no meaning, Ronald was naive in believing that a relationship would fill the empty crater that had been created by the loss of his mother and his son. He became infatuated with an eighteen-year-old girl who worked for his brother, Neil, in Seattle. Their short-term infatuation resulted in marriage.

In the continuous search for Bryan, Ronald followed their tracks through the postal service by using a method he had learned from the postman. He was instructed to send a letter to Bryan's previous address and label it Do Not Forward. The letter was eventually returned to him with a new address. Encouraged by his new bride, he made the long drive to Arizona to bring Bryan home. With a court order in hand and police at their side, they rescued Bryan from a filthy environment and eventually gained full custody. "Why are you crying, Daddy," Bryan inquired on the long drive home.

"I'm just glad to see you, son," Ronald replied.

Now that his family was complete, he felt he had been given another chance to create happiness and fulfillment. But he was not about to get a break from the trials and tribulations of life. He had barely enough time to come up for air before he was hit by another pounding wave that sent him reeling to the depth of the sea. Just six months into his marriage, he was devastated when he discovered that his wife was having an affair. Worn down and tired with life, no matter how hard he tried to keep it together, he found it just couldn't be done. Buried in betrayal and deceit, the marriage ended.

But love was not lost forever. Life changed for Ronald when Angelina, a dark-haired beauty, full of spark and spunk, came on the scene. Co-workers at the same brokerage firm, they soon discovered they had much in common. Taking their breaks together, their time was spent sharing stories about their lives. Their most startling discovery was in learning that they were both grieving from common losses. At the age of thirteen, Angelina had lost her father to drug and alcohol abuse. It was odd that she did not consider her father's death comparable to what Ronald had gone through with his mother, as the death of her father during her teenage years must have been a very difficult tragedy for her to deal with. But, for the two of them, they were blessed with the ability to find solace in each other, and the gift to empathize and understand what the other was going through.

They both began to understand that if they learned to love themselves unconditionally, then what the other person did didn't matter. If they were strong in themselves, all else would fall into place. Ronald started to believe that he could love again, even though devastating things had happened in his life. One thing that Janet taught him is that there are many levels of love. Love is opening up and being vulnerable.

Ronald had the opportunity to meet Dr. Kevorkian when he was in Seattle for a talk show. They went out for coffee, and Ronald was able to see a different side of the man who had been portrayed so unjustly by the media. He experienced a sharp, intelligent individual who was empathetic in his cause to help people. "I believe that Dr. Kevorkian's intent has been to shake up society and make them recognize that the plight of the terminally ill and the suffering are real problems that society needs to face. He is not a killer," stated Ronald.

Ronald still grieves the loss of his mother even after all these years. He's just not sure what he's supposed to feel because he hasn't lost a lot of people in his life. "I guess people just go through life, and they all have a different way of dealing with things when they come up.

Grieving takes as long as it takes and is different for everyone. The things that affect us negatively have a way of staying hidden until we are able to deal with them. We don't know when the train carrying old baggage is coming down the track or when something will trigger those memories and they will come jumping out like a jack-in-a-box. Grieving is one of those unexplainable mysteries of the universe.

29

Judge's Chambers

Carroll's Reaction to Janet's Choice

At the time of Janet's death, Carroll was working for a Seattle Judge. When she returned from Michigan and went back to work, she immediately walked into the judge's chambers to confess her part in Janet's death. The judge was reading the newspaper and on the front page was a picture of Janet and the story about her death.

"There is something I need to share with you," she told the Judge. "Janet was my friend, and I was in Detroit with her. I hope it won't cause a problem for you in your position and for us here in the Superior Court."

The Judge was extremely sympathetic and understanding. In that moment he became Carroll's angel. "It won't cause a problem here," the judge replied. "But are you all right?"

"I'm angry at Janet's decision to end her life," Carroll stated with emotion in her voice. "I'm angry at the way I lost my best friend and the fact that Janet chose a method that shut everyone out. Part of the anger is in thinking that Janet didn't trust her loved ones enough to go the distance with her. I would have liked the choice of going through the last stages with my friend."

∞

Carroll's Journal

Soon four months will be gone since Michigan. Who are we now? Who am I now? Different, for certain. It was Janet's birthday on September 10th. I wonder if I will ever forget that. She would have been 55, just like the speed limit. October is when we met thirty-four years ago in France (43 years now). No babies yet. We were babies still. France smelled so good and so very bad, both at once. Our hearts ached and sang. We were the adults with no parents around, nor any older generations, so we were free in ways most people never are. Did we have to get to be 50 to realize that? Or were we wise enough at the tender age of 20 or 21 (she was older, somebody has to be) to revel in the freedom, to tenderly explore ways of thinking that were only ours, or so we thought. We must have, (did we?) in 1956, laid the groundwork, planted the seeds for the last journey we made together to Michigan. Did the opening of my mind in those France years give way to the eventual acceptance of, and the ability to move with Janet through our last great adventure? William Blake said that death was like moving from one room into another. Janet, thought she hated the circumstances that forced her to move sooner rather than later into that room, moved with great good courage and amazing love and grace. Was she always destined to be the one?

Carroll's opinion of Dr. Kevorkian is one of respect. She believes he is an intelligent and compassionate man who recognizes people's suffering and wants to help. Although she is angry about the loss of her friend, she believes that individuals who are dying should have the option to choose which way they want to go. It may not necessarily be the option she would choose for herself, but she does believe that people should have the choice.

For eight years following Janet's death, Carroll and Ron had gotten together every year on the anniversary of Janet's death. Carroll deliberately missed the ninth anniversary. She believes that Janet would want there to come a time when the focus was not on the day she decided to end her life but on the day of her birth, who she was, and what she stood for.

30

Pulling the Plug

Relatives' Reactions

Eunice, Janet's aunt, and her husband, John, learned about Janet's death when they received a call from Neil.

"Mom is gone. Would you please come down and tell Grandma and be with her?"

Living in Canada, they made the long drive to Portland, Oregon, and informed Janet's mother, Vi, of her daughter's death. They all knew that Janet intended to take her life, but they had not been informed of the date.

Janet had frequently told her mother, "I think I will pull the plug pretty soon."

On the weekend that they had been in Detroit, Vi had thought they were vacationing in California. Had Vi had her television set on that day, she would have learned about her daughter's death in a most distasteful way. When the family broke the news, as could be expected, Vi fell to pieces at the loss of her only daughter.

Janet's letter to her mother was of little condolence, and Vi never fully recovered from the dreadful shock that day.

∞

Janet's Letter to her Mother

Dear, Dear Mama,
You have been a wonderful mama, a funny mama, and a loving mama. You have always made me feel important! I hope I have done that for my sons. I feel lucky that I had you in my life for a long time. Thank you for all the many, many things that you've done for me and the many, many things you've done for the boys. You have been a wonderful part of our lives.

Remember that life is for the living and if I could, I would want so much to keep living. You must keep living as long as people need you. You have wonderful sisters and brothers. You have a great sense of humor and you always make people laugh. I love you so much.

For John, a police officer, notifying survivors had always been the hardest part in his line of work. There was a time that he had to break the news to parents on a Sunday afternoon that their son had drowned. When the mother opened the door and saw John standing there in his uniform, she knew it was about her son. Her husband came around the corner just in time to catch her as she keeled over. It still bothered him, and he was uncomfortable breaking the news to Janet's mother, Vi. Although Vi had always known about Janet's choice, she had no idea that her daughter had set the date.

The news of her daughter's death was a severe blow to Vi, as she had already lost her first child, Janet's brother, to a tragic death. Some years back, she had reunited with her firstborn son, Ralph. He initially came to visit with his wife and two children. After his divorce from his wife, Ralph came to live with Vi in Portland. One day he mysteriously disappeared without a trace. A year later, the family was informed that Ralph's body had been discovered buried in the basement of a house in Portland. He had been shot by one of the men who worked for him. It was Janet who identified the body of her half-brother at the morgue.

Another ironic twist is that Ralph was murdered at age fifty-four, the same age Janet was when she died. Ralph was also born on June 4th, the date Janet died. It hadn't been planned that way; it just happened to be the date that Dr. Kevorkian was available. Vi survived her only children who both died at age fifty-four. Two major events in Vi's life were both on June 4th, the birth of her only son and the death of her only daughter. Now Vi was plagued by two tragic deaths of her children that would continue to haunt her the remainder of her days.

"If Eunice had made the same choice as Janet, I would not have allowed her to go through with it," John stated. "If I had to, I would have carried her kicking and screaming off the plane. I have been able to forgive Ron and the boys, but I don't agree with them, never did agree with them, and probably never will agree with them."

John has dealt with cancer and open-heart surgery. "I would never think of taking my own life, as it is against my belief system," he stated. "I have no use for Dr. Kevorkian. I believe that Dr. Kevorkian loves the spotlight and is just in it for the publicity. He has violated his Hippocratic Oath and belongs in the same camp as the Nazis."

Although Eunice supported Janet's decision, she is not fond of Dr. Kevorkian. "There is something about Dr. Kevorkian that doesn't sit right with me personally," she stated. "It is almost like he is shady. I can't explain it. I agree with what Janet did, but there is something unsettling about Dr. Kevorkian, and I can't put my finger on it. My concern is with him and not with the issue."

To this day, whenever John and Eunice discuss Janet, it always ends the same. John's not changing his mind, and Eunice is not changing her mind. Eunice really does agree with Janet's decision, but it still breaks her heart.

31

National News Report

Helen and Betty's Reactions

Helen, Janet's childhood friend, learned about Janet's death from her mother, Betty, who had heard about it on the national news. They had no idea that Janet had Alzheimer's. Betty had commented to Helen that they hadn't received a Christmas card from Janet for the past several years. "That isn't at all like Janet," she said. "Janet has always made it a point to keep in touch." Now they understood the reason for her withdrawal. Looking back, Helen recalled a time when she and Janet visited Janet's paternal grandfather. When they arrived, he was sitting in his chair with a vacant stare. Not appearing to recognize anyone, he was labeled as senile. Did he have Alzheimer's?

Helen and Betty were shocked by the news of Janet's death. It was strange for them to see the Adkins family on television talk shows. Everything they needed to know about Janet was presented on the news. Because they had lost contact with the Adkins family, they had no idea how to reach Vi or Ron to send their condolences. Although shocked and saddened by Janet's death, Helen wasn't surprised by the method Janet chose.

"It would be just like Janet to make that decision," Helen stated. "She was very principled. When she said something, she meant it. She wasn't just talk. I was shocked by her death, but the way she did it didn't surprise me. Janet would be the type of person who could do it."

"I am in favor of doctor assisted dying," Helen stated.

She doesn't believe that people should be made to suffer if they are terminally ill. She also recognizes the rising cost of medical care that can deplete any assets that a person might want to leave for their family. While working for the State of Washington she heard experts speak to the staff about death and dying. In that seminar she learned that some doctors do enable patients to die by prescribing medication. But she didn't know of any doctor, other than Dr. Kevorkian, who provided such a dramatic exit.

Helen eventually retired from the State of Washington as a social worker supervisor. She is no longer able to play a musical instrument because of arthritis in her fingers. Her father, Bill, died in 1984, and her mother, Betty, died in 2000 at the age of ninety. She still grieves the loss of her loved ones, especially her son, Johnny, and her childhood friend, Janet.

"Grief of my loved ones is something I will carry forever," Helen stated. "Mentally ill patients suffer a real anguish. For all the money that is spent on arms buildup and space, it would make a difference if a tenth of that money could be directed into mental health research."

In 1999, Helen was diagnosed with bile-duct cancer and given six months to live. Fortunately, her condition was operable, and her life expectancy was extended. Since then, Helen has passed on and joined Janet on the other side.

32

Judgment by Friends

Judy and Friends' Reactions

When Judy learned of Janet's death, she never thought for a moment that Janet would have used her return ticket. Janet had convinced her that she was happy with the solution to her problem and that she had no plan of turning back. Judy's only regret was that it could not have been done in more pleasant surroundings. But she knew that the surroundings made no difference to Janet. When she heard that Janet's final words were *'Thank you! Thank you! Thank you!'* she wasn't a bit surprised. She knew that is exactly what Janet would have said.

Judy was hard hit by Janet's death. She was shocked to see the amount of publicity generated by her dear friend's choice to take her life. To Judy, having the press invade Janet's private memorial service felt offensive, and she wondered what Janet would have thought about all that. Knowing Janet, she was probably looking down on all of them right at that very moment amused by all that had taken place.

After the memorial, Judy received an unsettling call from Ron. He advised Judy that she might be hearing from the authorities that were investigating Janet's death. When the call came, a detective informed her that she was required to write a statement about Janet's death.

For the next year, Judy was keenly aware that Ron's life was in turmoil. She was concerned that he might run off and get married to pacify his grief. He was caught up in the middle of an enormous whirlwind of interviews, one right after the other. Judy told him that everyone in their circle of friends was impressed by the professional way in which he handled himself on television talk shows. They all agreed that the subject needed to be discussed and was something that society needed to face. Because numerous medical and ethical questions needed to be addressed, Ron hoped that someone from the medical profession would step forward to defend Dr. Kevorkian's position and perform a similar service.

"It's too bad there isn't a more personable representative," he told Judy. "Dr. Kevorkian has been depicted as an oddball by the media. He's way out there at times and turns a lot of people off."

Judy thought it was too bad that Dr. Kevorkian had the audacity to say, "I'm not going away, and I'll keep pushing this issue until people stand up and take notice."

Many people wanted to talk with Judy about Janet's death. Some of Janet's close friends totally disagreed with her decision and did not believe that she should have taken her own life. Judy was upset by the comments she heard from people in their circle of friends: "She wasn't that bad off. She could have had a lot more months with her family at home. I heard she played tennis the week before she died."

Judy gallantly defended Janet's position. "You've missed the whole point here. Our society does not allow her the courtesy of making that decision. Janet may have had many more months with her family, but she couldn't take the chance of slipping over the edge without any warning. She had to do it herself and make the choice while she was still mentally competent."

Judy misses having Janet in her life because she was a wonderful friend and an uplifting person whom Judy benefited from greatly. She helped Judy better herself spiritually and intellectually. She knows that Janet would never have wanted it to be difficult for Ron, and she knows how difficult it has been for him over the years.

Judy still has a difficult time dealing with Janet's death. "I cry often when talking about our friendship and the circumstances surrounding Janet's decision to end her life. I have been unable to resolve my grief in a way that feels complete. Even to this day it stays with me. I can't put my finger on it, but something bothers me about Janet's death. It haunts me to this day. It must be very subconscious because I can't get at it. I have agreed with her decision from the very first moment, so I don't think it is an ethical thing. I'm just sad that the situation couldn't have been more pleasant. When deep feelings of sorrow bubble to the surface, Judy recalls Janet's words, 'Judy, I want you to be happy for me.'"

In response Judy looks to the heavens and softly whispers, "Be Bamboo."

33

Double-Edged Sword

Shirley and Dell's Reactions

Janet's death became the topic of conversation among their friends for months following her death. "What were they thinking? Why did they do it? How is this good? How is this bad?" Some of their friends were angry and adamantly against Janet's actions. Although they understood the devastation of Alzheimer's, they thought Janet went much too early. For Shirley and Dell, understanding Janet's decision was difficult, especially because they had not been prepared. Later years, when one of their friends was faced with death, Dell was able to understand Janet's decision and reversed his opinion.

Shirley viewed Janet as a strong person, and her opinion was that a strong person would not have needed assistance. A strong person would just have shot herself or taken a dose of poison. In Shirley's mind, that Janet had flown to Detroit and got some stranger to help her die was a far-fetched option. After thinking about it, Shirley realized that Janet would not have been able to make that decision if she had waited.

Shirley recalled Ron telling her about friends who were remodeling an old house to be used in their bed and breakfast business. Janet thought it would be fun to come back and haunt their house as their resident ghost. They all laughed about it, and they said, "Sure we'd love to have you there." Janet was making light of her death right up until the end.

Dell can understand why Janet made the choice she did, but he feels certain that she went too soon. Shirley has some concerns about doctor-assisted dying, and she sees it as a real dilemma. "Although people should be able to do what they want with their own bodies, it is a double-edged sword. We are the role models for the next generation. If we take the easy way out, we are not being good role models for people to fight, exist and survive. That is the only downside I can see. Sometimes when I am really low, and I think I should end it all, I don't because of my children, grandchildren and other people I am close to. It would just make life tougher for them if I were to give up. I just have that survival instinct. So it is kind of a dilemma."

34

Reincarnation

Bob and Peggy's Reactions

Bob and Peggy viewed Janet as a person who liked to create drama but they didn't believe that she had any idea of the impact her death would have on the world stage. Observing the chaos that was generated, as a result of Janet's death, was difficult for them to watch and absorb.

Peggy shared her feelings of the past. "I remember hearing Ron complain that Janet was calling him at the office all the time because she was lost and didn't know where to go. I think Janet's calls were interfering with his business, and I certainly understand how he would have felt. After Janet was gone, he was so devastated. I suspected he probably felt a little guilty. I knew that once the disease progressed Janet would not be able to dress herself or go anyplace without constant supervision. I knew that Janet had saved Ron from a lot of grief."

Peggy admired Ron for his mission once he was pulled into the spotlight by the press. She knew that he felt strongly about doctor-assisted dying and needed to do his part to help promote Janet's cause. But after a while, Peggy began to believe that his constant involvement was unhealthy as it was only intensifying his grief. She wished that he could have gotten on with his life and stopped thinking about Janet all the time after she died.

Peggy was sure Janet never envisioned Ron getting involved in her cause or ever realized the issue would be so important. "Janet didn't like publicity. Ron was always the one who could get out in front of people and was never concerned about making a fool out of himself," Peggy stated.

"Janet was very easygoing and very strong. When they went to see Dr. Kevorkian, she told Ron not to tell anybody. She was concerned that Dr. Kevorkian might get arrested and put in jail, but at least she would be on her way. Everyone thought that Janet's death would be just an investigation and that would be the end of it. But somehow or another, it got leaked to the press, and the whole situation exploded."

Ron told Peggy that he never felt any guilt after Janet's death. He just felt that God had played a bad joke on them and life wasn't fair. He was supposed to die first, and Janet was going to live and take the kids to France.

Peggy thinks that the biggest problem was that Ron was very dependent on Janet. She was like a mother to him because his mother died when he was so young. Peggy believed that Janet was the power in their family, and that Ron leaned on her a lot.

Several years after Janet's death, Bob developed cancer. He knew his days were numbered and that he would eventually reach the point of wanting to end his life. He admired Janet for her decision, and he thought of her as a role model. He often told Peggy that he hoped he would be as brave as Janet was when it was his time to die. He felt that Janet's solution was a far better alternative than the .38 caliber he kept in the basement. Bob died from cancer on August 12, 1999. Although Bob was strongly in favor of assisted suicide, he did not take his own life, partly, because his doctor was not committed to helping him.

Janet believed in reincarnation. Janet and Bob have likely already formed their own FART club in the sky. Prior to her departure, Janet joyously exclaimed, "I will be sure to reserve tennis courts up there for all of us."

35

Cave of the Heart

Ron's Reaction

When Ron returned from Michigan without Janet, relatives surrounded him to provide support. Hounded by the press, Ron was faced with the grim realization that his privacy had been ripped away, leaving him in a very vulnerable position.

Reality set in after everyone went home, and he was left alone to face his grief. He was exhausted and hoped to escape his inner turmoil through sleep. But he could not be consoled. Night after endless night he was plagued with the memories of Janet and the loss of his precious love. The continuous dreams of Janet left him drenched with sweat as he desperately sought shelter from the fury of the storm that was taking place within him. The crackling sounds of thunder pierced his very soul, as fierce gusts of wind reached out to grab anything in their path. Bolts of lightning lit up the midnight sky as he scrambled to find safety among the strange terrain. The warmth of his clothing did little to comfort him from the chills that traversed his spine. Nourishment went unnoticed as the gnawing feeling of unrest churned in the pit of his stomach. His loss of control and feelings of despair were enough to invoke a panic attack in the most undignified manner. As if stalked by a predator, he had no safe place to hide. Afraid of tangling with his fears, he became paralyzed and shut down. His stream of consciousness wreaked havoc with his mind like music out of tune. The hard rain beat on him relentlessly as he realized that he had no idea where he was or how he had gotten there. He was numb, and he could not make sense of his thoughts. He was in another place, another time, another dimension, and all of it was unfamiliar territory. He had retreated into the dark cave of his heart.

Sometimes he would awaken during the night and cry out to God, "Why did you take my Jannie?" Why didn't you take me instead?" It was clear that his inner being was not in harmony with the outside world. Memories that were buried deep in his subconscious mind oozed from the cracks of his foundation. He began to spiral down with the darkness spinning around him. Suspended in a black hole in space, he eventually lost his sense of self.

"I miss you so terribly," he sobbed. "I'm so lonely and afraid. How can I possibly go on without you?"

Then his anguish would be released through a river of salty tears. In his darkest hour, a ray of light would peek out from the depths of the blackness. Just when his strength began to return to his frail body, he would be the recipient of another grief attack, leaving him no time to shield against the onslaught.

That's what grief did to him. It stripped him of reality and forced him into the cave of his heart. He begged for his strength to return and the courage to venture out into the light of the day.

A song kept running through his mind:

∞

**Played at Janet's Memorial Service—
A. Hammond and C. Bayer-Sayer,
"When I Need You"**

*When I need you,
I just close my eyes and I'm with you,
and all that I've so longed to give you,
it's only a heartbeat away.*[1]

---

[1] "When I Need You," written by Albert Hammond and Carole Bayer Sager, performed by Leo Sayer, *Endless Flight* (Warner Brothers, 1978).

Several months after Janet's death, Ron decided to make a fresh start and find new living quarters. He moved to the Portland Center Apartments and took a unit on the twentieth floor with a view of downtown Portland. Choosing a decorating theme that represented his mood, he chose a décor of black and white to represent the duality of extremes. He developed a love of zebras and used that motif throughout his home. He selected a bedspread with black-and-white zebra stripes and found many interesting zebra pieces for his collection: zebra pillows, zebra towels, and zebra dishes, among others.

The apartment was a welcome change, but he still felt wounded and alone. In the evening hours, he escaped from his solitude and took a walk downtown. He visited restaurants that he and Janet used to frequent. Sitting alone with his cocktail before ordering his meal, he took notice of all the couples, especially the lovers. He felt how different it was now with only the memory of Janet in the chair across from him. When the waiter brought the menu and asked if he would like another cocktail, he nodded. He would order some of the things he remembered ordering when he had dined with Janet. When he finished, he would usually visit the places he and Janet had gone to for an after-dinner drink: The Heathman, Brasserie Montmarte, or Huber's.

When he entered a restaurant, he sat at the bar and waited for the waiter to bring him his drink. All the waiters knew his favorite drink (Absolut on the rocks with a twist). Many nights he tried to drown his sorrow with drink, but his grief always seemed to float to the surface. Being around all the people in the restaurants did not help to diminish his feelings of sadness and aloneness. He ended the evening by walking home, often too intoxicated to hold any conscious fear of the emptiness in his apartment and his life without his beloved Janet.

36

Great Expectations

Ron and Sharon

With the encouragement of his therapist, Ron enrolled in Great Expectations, a well-respected dating service. He took out a membership in Seattle, Portland, and San Francisco. Coincidentally, the first woman he dated was named Janet. She was an artist, piano player, and owned her own business. She was attractive and talented but lacked the excitement that he had shared with his wife. He dated an attractive doctor but decided not to take it any further. She had young children, and he was most definitely past the child-rearing days. He was surprised to find that a number of young attractive women were open to having a relationship with a man of his age. That gave him the encouragement he needed to keep searching for his future mate.

His first serious relationship was with a woman from Portland. She was an attractive and fashionable woman who traveled in the wealthy and blueblood circles in Portland. She had been a debutante in her younger years and had married into money. Her style was much different from Ron's. She openly shared her feelings and informed him that she had fallen in love with him right from the first date. Of course, he found that very flattering. Much of his time was taken up with television shows, radio talk shows, and interviews with the press. As the relationship developed, as could be expected, she became resentful of the media. She wanted Ron to put a stop to the publicity and get on with their lives.

The first New Year's Eve after Janet's death, Ron and his lady friend attended a party. As they were dancing, Ron recalled the year before when he had held Janet in his arms. As the clock struck twelve and the band played "Auld Lang Syne," he started weeping when he realized that the woman in his arms was not Janet. His lady friend was furious with having to compete with a ghost for the last dance of the night. Angry with his date for her lack of compassion and understanding, the evening ended with an exchange of harsh words between them.

Ten months later, with her hope of winning Ron's heart, his lady friend put on a tea party that was attended by two hundred guests at an elite country club in the West Hills of Portland. The party was a first-class, catered event with a five-piece band. The impressive display of his lady friend's affection for him led his friends to speculate that this was an engagement party. Whispering went on behind the scenes for the entire evening as the guests waited for the announcement that never came. Ron was certain in his own mind that he clearly wasn't ready for marriage. He was doubtful if he would ever again be ready to make that level of commitment in this lifetime. After the party, his lady friend enticed him to take a romantic trip to Europe. He agreed to go, and they had a marvelous time. However, when they returned to the States it was evident to Ron, that he needed to end the relationship.

Ron and Sharon met a year and a half after Janet's death through Great Expectations dating service. She had read Ron's bio and had selected him from a group of prospective men. Sharon was searching for a man that was intelligent, open-minded, and enjoyed travel and exploration. But most important, she sought a partner who understood the Unitarian philosophy, which values the worth and dignity of every human being. It was imperative for Sharon's well-being that she find a partner who would enjoy her free spirit and appreciate her wonderment for life while respecting her active search for truths.

Astonished and stunned by his immediate attraction to Sharon, Ron stared into her eyes and stated, "You don't know who I am. Do you?"

He proceeded to share his story about Janet while she listened intently with great admiration for the way in which he had supported his wife. Although she was very familiar with Janet's case, she had not made the connection when they first met. In a few short hours, they had developed a sense of understanding and oneness between them that went far deeper than the surface.

Eager to start their relationship, they soon discovered they had much more in common than had been revealed through Great Expectations.

Similar to Ron and Janet's life, Sharon's life was laced with tragedy: terminal illness and death of her loved ones. Her mother died at the age of sixty-nine from uterine cancer, and fifteen years later, Sharon contracted the same disease. Determined not to repeat the same cycle, she recovered from a hysterectomy.

After the death of her mother, she faced yet another tragic event, which was the turning point in her life. Her adopted son, Eric, was just twenty-nine years old when he was incorrectly diagnosed with hepatitis. After several months of debilitating abdominal pain, cancer was discovered during exploratory surgery. By that time, it had progressed to such a state that when the doctors opened him up, they took one look and immediately sewed him back together. With Eric's death sentence of six months, Sharon vowed to herself that she would devote those remaining months to helping her son in any way possible. The bond between them grew to such proportions that she was willing to respect whatever choice he made for his final days. Together they planned the memorial service, which was held in 1987, just a few years before Janet's death. Like Janet had done with Ron, Eric encouraged Sharon to go forward in her life.

Unafraid of what lay ahead, and in full acceptance of his circumstances, Eric encouraged Sharon to take an out-of-town business trip for a few days. While she was gone, he died a natural death in a nursing home, content in knowing that she would be at peace with his departure.

∞

Janet's Journal—Carl Jung, quoted in *Out on a Limb* by Shirley MacLaine,

What happens after death is so unspeakably glorious that our imagination and our feelings do not suffice to form even an approximate conception of it.

For Sharon, Ron's kindness and openness was a refreshing change from the other men that she had dated. To her, Ron seemed genuinely honest without any hidden agenda. Filled with the realization that their meeting was no accident, Sharon felt that Janet had brought them together. She was certain that she wanted a relationship with Ron, and she believed she was fully capable of supporting him emotionally through his grieving process. It was also an opportunity for the two of them to experience a partnership on a whole new level.

Ron found Sharon to be accepting of his personal situation that allowed him to openly grieve the loss of Janet in his own way in his own time. She didn't put pressure on him, and she knew that he wasn't ready to make a commitment. Because of her acceptance, the relationship flourished.

As the relationship grew between Sharon and Ron, they decided to bring their families together for special events. Getting to know the Adkins family for the first time, Sharon attended a Christmas dinner party at Neil and Heidi's house. Heidi put on an elaborate and delicious meal; the decorations were stylish and beautiful, with introductions warm and inviting. Norman and Tami Jo arrived after a three-hour drive. Tami Jo was expecting their first baby, Lance, and she glowed like an angel in anticipation of a miracle. Ronald and his fiancée arrived with Ronald's son, Bryan, and Sharon marveled at the obvious love between them. In the evening, after the festivities, the Adkins men gathered around the table to play cards. When the final game of winner-take-all was played, Norman, Ronald, and their families left for the long drive home. On several other occasions, Sharon's sons joined with the Adkins family in their celebrations.

As Sharon grew closer to Ron, she became aware of the challenges that lay ahead. It became evident to her that his grief was no ordinary grief that would pass with time. The grieving seemed to go so much deeper than that. Ron was unable to relax the tight fibers of his being, and his invisible scars quickly exposed themselves whenever she accidentally touched a tender spot that had not completely healed. She knew intuitively how to caress those wounds with compassion, but much deeper wounds remained hidden far beneath the surface. The wounds were entangled in such a way that it was difficult to distinguish one from the other. Unbeknownst to Ron, he was grieving not only the loss of his wife but also the loss of his childhood. Even he could not possibly know the depth of his sorrow that was well disguised behind the mask of a jokester.

Since Janet's diagnosis, Ron had found making a living exceedingly difficult. Having been a highly successful stockbroker, he had found it nearly impossible to concentrate on his career when Janet became sick. His mind was not on his work and it only got worse after her death. Propelled into the limelight, he had become an advocate for Janet's cause, but an advocate without an income does not pay the bills. When he and Sharon had first met, he was drawing a modest salary by working for one of his sons. But he was phased out when his son decided that his staff needed to be active in the Christian faith.

Most of the responsibility of financial support fell on Sharon's shoulders; however, she was more than willing to accommodate Ron until he got through his grieving. As time went on, it became evident that he was suffering from severe chronic depression. At times, he would stay out in the bars late into the evening and then break down sobbing when he got home. Sharon would embrace him and listen to him talk, but it was apparent that his situation was getting worse. With the stress of financial pressure, and the inability to earn a steady income, he plummeted into darkness, threatening suicide on more than one occasion. His cries for help to relieve his anguish resulted in an intervention by family members. He was presented with the option to attend a grieving center in Arizona that carried a hidden agenda for alcohol treatment. He agreed to attend the three-week program, and Sharon supported him through the process.

While he was in the program, his sons made the decision to limit their communication with him. Neil and Norman eventually had a change of heart and visited one day during family support week. Neil levied an ultimatum to his dad, stating that if he didn't quit drinking, he would not be allowed to see him or his family, including his grandchildren. Neil followed through with his ultimatum for the following year. Ron completed the three-week program and never talked about suicide again.

The day after Neil's ultimatum, Norman called Sharon to check on his dad's well-being and give his support. "You are a gutsy gal," Norman stated.

Sharon views the Adkins family as a group of four men struggling with their grief. "Some of them have no idea how to go about it. They had a wonderful mother and wife, and the loss of Janet will be felt the rest of their lives. It is my opinion that Janet's death was not responsible for splitting the family apart. I believe that the problems between the boys existed prior to Janet's death and resulted over a business dealing that created competition between Neil and Norman. Once Janet wasn't there to hold things together, the problems surfaced with their own timing. It was Janet's philosophy that problems could be solved in an open setting, but to me it seems that no one is willing to discuss the problems."

Sharon had an opportunity to meet Dr. Kevorkian when they were invited to a picnic in Dowagiac, Michigan. The surviving families of Dr. Kevorkian's patients attended the gathering. They had come together in support of one another and to honor their loved ones who had passed. Ironically, the site for the picnic was only a few miles from where Ronald's wedding to his first wife had taken place only a day earlier.

The picnic was done in first-class style. Large party tents were set up on the grounds, one of which encased a variety of tasty midwestern foods. Life magazine had obtained exclusive coverage on the picnic, and they were busy interviewing the families and taking pictures. Because of the controversy surrounding doctor-assisted dying, they later chose not to publish the story. Sharon observed Dr. Kevorkian playing ball games with the guests and talking with others. She finally met Dr. Kevorkian and was able to form her own opinion of him that was not tainted by the news media. Dr. Kevorkian approached her, and they immediately struck up a conversation. Sharon felt a kindred spirit with the doctor after discovering that they had music, art, and other topics in common. He seemed relaxed and truly interested in hearing what she had to say. She also met with Dr. Kevorkian's sister, Margo, and developed a warm relationship. Margo vowed that they would continue their friendship, but unfortunately, she died of a heart attack before they could meet again.

The similarities between Sharon and Janet are remarkable, allowing a smooth transition into the Adkins family. Sharon and Ron have eighteen grandchildren between them. Norman and Tami Jo's son, Lance, was born on the same day as Sharon's birthday, with just a three-minute difference. Sharon delights in the fact that most of the grandchildren call her "Grandma." They both make an effort to share "Grandma Janet's" rich heritage with all the grandchildren.

There Are No Wrong Roads

Ron's Conversation with Janet's Spirit

The essence of Janet was representative of a teacher. She was a woman who had the ability to awaken the mental and spiritual aspects of those who were drawn to her. Her teachings were neither boastful nor patronizing, springing instead from a heartfelt love of learning and curiosity.

Janet embraced her choice to die before Alzheimer's stripped her of her dignity. She was at peace with her decision and excited about the unknown journey that lay ahead. Indeed, she was a woman of great courage. She loved life, but she also believed in an afterlife and reincarnation. She had always been curious to know what was on the other side of the thin veil that separated her from the unknown. To journey there alone did not frighten Janet. She saw death as an adventure like climbing to the top of a mountain. To Janet it was a journey of discovery and wonderment.

She was a child with new eyes, anxious to see new horizons. Janet was never stopped by an impasse. She would always discover a detour or a bridge to get to where she wanted to go. She often used the phrase *'There are no wrong roads.'* She was willing to go where others feared to tread. Such was the journey for Janet in life and in death.

Janet was a role model for women, as demonstrated by the way in which she lived her life. She was a strong, intelligent, compassionate, and independent person. Janet's excitement for a life of independent choice is to be celebrated. Her letters and journals are evidence of the love she shared with her family and friends. With Ron's loving support, Janet pursued a life where she had no regrets. She explored mountain paths and ocean depths. She read and examined many philosophies. Having no limits to what new concept or experience she would explore next, she often discussed with others her findings and lovingly nurtured her friends in their growth. Janet had no idea of the impact her decision would make on the world stage. She had no desire to be a trailblazer, but that is what history has made her. She has accomplished this status not because she followed any specific belief or dogma but because she developed her own. She walked through life and death with her eyes wide open. Her intelligence commanded her to read and contemplate the aspects of both. Like a traveler preparing for her departure to a foreign land, she meticulously planned the intricate details of her trip. When she was ready to depart, she lovingly and compassionately handed her family and closest friends the keys to a well-lived life.

Knowing that Janet believed in an afterlife, and sensing that she had been actively participating in the writing of this book from its conception, Ron decided to make contact with his beloved. He believed that Janet would be eager to enlighten the readers with insights from her journey.

∞

A Dialogue Between Janet and Ron

My beloved Janet, are you at peace?
You know I was at peace with my life on earth. So too, I have been at peace with my afterlife. I am so excited about being on this side. It is not necessary to be concerned about how I feel or how I am. The feeling is good. There is no future; there is no past; it's all one. My spirit, my essence will always be. If anything, I shall grow larger in my spirit from the exciting aspects of being a part of all—all that is, all that has been and all that will be. I am not separate. I'm a part of everyone that is; every breath that you

take, I am that breath. Every light that comes from the stars, the sun, I am a part of it. It is as though I've been let out of the cage by crossing over.

Janet, I was so in love with you. I thought you loved me less. Was this true?

Now you are asking me about your perceptions. I know you believed that early in our relationship. We had a normal relationship with each of us having different needs and different growth patterns. Our life together was filled at times with an abundance of love. Other times one would love while the other was disappointed in the other person. So it goes back and forth like a pendulum on a clock. It's the moment that you try to evaluate who loves whom the most that you stop the clock. The depths of love cannot be shattered by momentary problems and conflicts. The underlying theme is like the swells and the currents of the ocean. Powerful, severe, the wind can blow across the ocean and create whitecaps, but that's not all that is there. The power underneath the ocean is there and it's solid. At the end of our physical life, as a partnership, we truly exemplified unconditional love. I could feel your love for me as you supported me in my choice. I truly loved you dearly—so dearly that I released you to find love on the physical plane once again. I have no regrets.

Janet, has your perception changed about your diagnosis of Alzheimer's disease?

Disgusting! You know, Ron, I was terribly upset. I hate the word Alzheimer's. I could not believe it! I could not believe it! God had played a terrible joke on me. I could not imagine my mind, my strength, all this taken away. It's a death sentence to my intellect. I told you I would have preferred cancer, as I could have fought it. I could not understand how it came about. It was a disease, which interfered with my life, but we must do what we have to do. We must face issues as they come in life. I am proud of my choice to leave before my sickness got too bad. I was hurt by having to cut my life short, but the decision, I feel, was made for me by the master planner and I was ready to move on. All of the people I left behind have to take charge of their lives and fulfill their destiny. There are no shoulds, no blames to be put on anyone. They are responsible for their lives, as I was responsible for mine. We live with our decisions. One must make decisions that one can live with even in death. I was so concerned that you wouldn't be able to go on. I'm still concerned. I know that you long to be with me. Go on with your life. Go on with the children and the grandchildren. Be there for them so my life will be fulfilled through you.

Janet, your childhood remains much of a mystery. Can you help the reader understand your early years and the role it played in our marriage?

You have heard from my relatives and my family about my life as a child. There are things in my childhood that not many people know, as there are always things in a life that we keep to ourselves. The growing up with my parents and their problem with alcohol had many ramifications. There are things and times I don't want to think about and have pushed to the back of my being. It is not necessary to know all those things. I dealt with them in the best way I could. They did influence me as a mother and as a wife. I coped with these as positively as I could. We cannot help our past. All we can do is make our future better than our past. To be concerned and to dwell on the things that have influenced us takes time away from the expectations and the joy of what lies ahead. Much like the anchor that holds the boat in place from going forward, so does our past. The future and new destinations are what our dwelling should be on.

Ron, you know we were both doing the best we could. It is my belief that we grew tremendously in our marriage. When we started out we played old scripts from our childhoods. Together we grew into true partners. The old scripts made me want to control the people around me. I had a childhood where I could not rely on satisfaction of physical needs and affection. As a child I wanted to please the adults around me. I worked hard and was studious. I learned to rely on myself early in life, and to me, that was one of my greatest gifts. I know that my parents loved me so much in the best way they could. They were stuck in old scripts and didn't have the inclination to move on. I have been hurt by their actions many times, but there were so many gifts to me from their actions. The one gift I rejoice in is that I have found happiness and peace with myself.

Janet, there have been many accounts reported of communication between the spirit world. Why are there so many variations?

The spirit world is in our own consciousness. I have read so many books about *'out of body' and 'near- death experiences.'* I always wondered why many of the people were met by Jesus after they followed the light and very few were met by others. It all depends on your individual belief system. I have been met by great thinkers, my family, and friends. It is such a relief not to be encumbered with the physical body. Ideas circulate up here as they do on the physical plane. It is much easier to comprehend Camas, Emerson, Thoreau, and all the other great thinkers. I am enjoying this so very much. This is still very much who I am. Variations are part of life. All life and all the things in life, that are alive, are all variations on life. So as there are variations throughout life there are variations in the afterlife. We record and we respond and we speak of all things in different ways. The goodness of this variation is that we can select the variation that is true to us. As long as we are honest and true to ourselves then we can receive from the other side in honesty. To be with your truth, and to be honest with yourself, is the only way to live and the only way to die.

It is apparent that many of those you left behind have not resolved their grieving. Some of them have expressed that they feel "haunted" by your departure. Can you explain?

The media has interrupted both my family and friends' grieving. Now is the time to grieve. Do it and keep grieving until you get through it. You still have a life before you with so much love in it. Grief must be honored as joy must be honored. Both are necessary for the dance of life. Don't try to talk anyone out of it; don't interfere with their grief. Their grieving is a personal matter that they must work with and through. Grief must be dealt with on an individual basis. In a sense, the grieving is not for me. They're grieving the eventual grief that they are facing by not being accepting of the continuum of life and death. They're stuck holding on to the past memories of me. They're frightened of the future. They want to stay where they are. They want things to be as they were. Things are the way they are. Each new moment brings a new life. By holding on to the past and grieving of a loss, they cannot move forward in their lives. They're being held captive by the fear of the future. The future must be taken as an exciting journey with goodness ahead. The fear of not knowing plays upon them to stay where they are in the grief mode. I have shared Elisabeth Kubler-Ross's books with you. In both of her books *On Death and Dying* and *On Life after Death,* she illustrates the process of grief and how it heals one's life after a loss. Elisabeth Kubler-Ross even gives you the steps for grieving. In grieving these steps do not necessarily come in order but after you process anger you are well on your way to more joy in your life. I also suggest *The Tibetan Book of the Dead*. I hope these books help you to grieve.

Once my story is complete, I think my friends and my family will be at peace because they can then move on in their lives knowing that the last chapter has been written and the pages of the book have been closed. They will always have a place they can go to recall past memories. But more importantly, they can spend more time in living their lives more completely without being held back by the past. Regardless of how they view my decision, each person must make their own decision for each moment of their lives and face the next moment with excitement and expectation of goodness as I have done in my life, as I did in my death, and as I am doing now. The book itself is a page in the life of a family. As books are kept in libraries, this book shall be kept on a shelf for people who want to remember. For those people who want to look back, this will be a rearview mirror.

∞

Message from Ron's Dream

Near the completion of the book, Ron had a dream that Janet came to him dressed in a full-length black evening gown. She was wearing a silver leaf broach on her neckline. The place in which she stood was surrounded by makeshift tents, which indicated that she was with many people who were in a temporary holding place. Researching the meaning of the silver leaf broach, Ron was pleasantly surprised to discover that leaves in general can be a pun on leaving or departing. Dead leaves represent old memories from another time, which need to be cleared and cleansed on a physical, mental, or emotional level. Ron believes it was Janet's way of letting him and her loved ones know that the time has come to release the past, step through the temporary holding pattern, and move on with their lives. After all, there are *'no wrong roads.'*

38

Where Are They in 2019?

Ron Adkins Today

Ron spent many years fighting Janet's cause and dealing with the controversy surrounding her choice to die. It was a tough battle, one that eventually took over his everyday life and his ability to find peace and resolve his grief. Having survived two heart surgeries for a faulty heart valve, at the age of eighty-six, he is retired from the public view, and he intends to keep it that way. He has no desire to be a spokesperson for assisted dying and is more than happy and relieved to pass the torch to the author, Susan. Unfortunately, he lost his ability to play an instrument or sing in the choir, but he has his sense of humor, and he can still tell a good joke. Ron enjoys his solitude and his everyday life with his current partner, Maggie, who he loves dearly, and his family and grandchildren. When asked if his grief has lessened over the years, his response is, "It never leaves me."

Because Ron loved Janet so deeply, it has been impossible for him to stop loving her just because she died. He has not been successful in making those feelings disappear with the push of a button. It was hard to lose Janet and it is still hard to this very day for him to deal with the loss of his beloved wife. He still thinks of his Jannie every day, as he has since her death. He is still as connected to her as he was the day they married. Janet will always be a part of him, and a part of his ability to love. He doesn't want that to ever go away. He did go along with what Janet wanted in her life. He helped her and was there for her. He wouldn't change any of that. After Janet's death, he could have gone on with his life and ignored the issue. However, he felt he had an obligation to help those people who are suffering today. He can help them by sharing Janet's story so that they can make an informed choice if they are facing a terminal illness.

He would like to take a cruise, go to Europe, and spend some time in Paris, Spain, and the Rivera for six months. He'd like to renew himself in a fresh new environment where he can enjoy the sun and the lifestyle.

He encourages everyone to live in the moment. "Don't put off what you would like to do till later. Do it now even though it might not make sense with your job or your economic situation. You will either have your job or you won't have your job. You will either have money or you won't have money. You never will for sure have this moment again. Be true to this moment and go for it. There will be additional pain if you look back and say I wish I would have. As long as you are alive and well, and have your health, that is the time to do the traveling, the silly, crazy things. There will come a time when you are old and gray, and your feet won't work, your back hurts, your eyes are bad, and you are not comfortable with leaving your house. Then you can't do anything. It is all lost. It is gone. I encourage you to live in the moment."

To My Love, Ron—From Jannie— *I Prithee Send Back My Heart,* by John Suckling

I prithee send me back my heart,
since I cannot have thine.
For if from yours you will not part,
why then shouldst thou have mine?[1]

---

[1] John Suckling, IV. Wooing and Winning, "I Prithee Send Me Back My Heart," accessed July 29, 2019, https://www.bartleby.com/360/2/161.html.

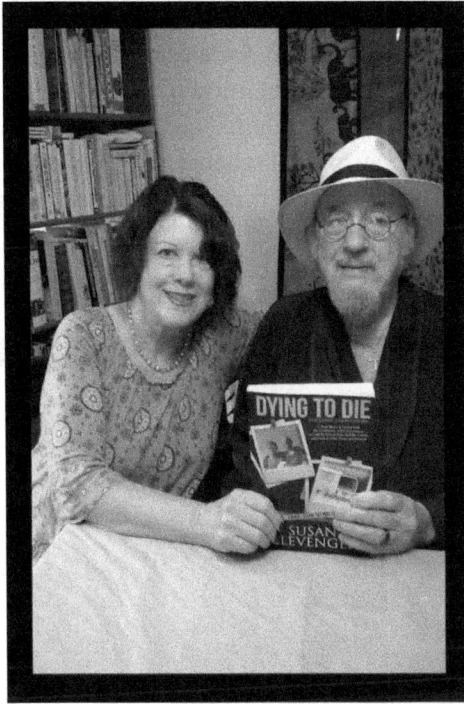

Susan and Ron

On September 15, 2019, the author personally delivered the first print of the book, *Dying to Die* to Ron for his eighty-seventh birthday that he would celebrate with his family the following weekend. Because Susan and Ron hadn't kept in touch for the past twenty-years, it was a tearful reunion. She was delighted to meet Maggie, and witness the deep love between them. It was not surprising to Susan that Janet's photos were on display in every room of the house, and that Maggie was accepting of Janet's Spirit being a part of their everyday lives.

While Ron, Maggie, and Susan dined at their favorite restaurant in town, the night was filled with excitement as numerous townspeople walked by the restaurant window, waved to Ron and Maggie, and came into the restaurant for a personal hug.

Because Ron is well known by the people of the town for his musical talents and entertainment, they are sure to be surprised when *Dying to Die* is released and they read about the special uniqueness and intimate details of their *'Music Man'* and his loving support for Janet's choice to die.

**Ron Adkins, the *'Music Man'*
Photo by Larry DeBord**

Neil Adkins Today

Neil is happily married to his Vietnamese wife. They have six children, two stepchildren and four adult children, along with two grandchildren by his son Justin. Neil enjoys business, traveling, playing tennis, running, hiking spending quality time with his family, and attending a Christian church together. Neil and his wife planted a tree in the arboretum in Portland in remembrance of Janet. He still thinks of his mom often and will never forget the amazing person that she was. He is very happy in life now but will always remember the choice that his mother made that changed the course of their lives.

Norman Adkins Today

Norman's life today is one that is rich in relationships with family and business colleagues. Sadly, Norman lost his wife, Tami Jo, very suddenly in 2010 due to a rare lung disease (usual interstitial pneumonia, or UIP). Eventually he finished raising his three boys and, like Neil, found love again with his Vietnamese wife. Norman co-owns a green business with his older brother, Neil, and is looking forward to retiring in a few years. He is healthy and happy and enjoys spending time traveling and sharing love with his wife and family. Norman greatly misses his mom and makes it a point to do something special every year on her birthday. Going back in time, he recalls that the media circus was really hard on his family, especially his dad. Norman is grateful that his dad eventually found peace and love. He speaks with his father every day and visits him whenever he can.

∞

Ronald Adkins Today

Ronald's journey led him to explore spiritual growth that introduced him to a new career path and brought him closer to family and fatherhood with his biological son, Bryan. After his divorce, he traveled for a while, which allowed him the much needed solitude to contemplate his past, present, and future. During his travels, he received many insights and was fortunate for the opportunity to meet the love of his life and to marry again. Like his two brothers, Ronald also married a Vietnamese woman. Together, they share their faith with God as their center and have joined their families as one. Ronald is truly grateful for his spiritual journey from exploring Buddhism with contemplative meditation to now being called to be a Catholic. In his career, he is part of a management team within a palliative health care organization. This career has allowed him to bring forward the difficult, but much-needed, family conversations around end-of-life care. Ronald is grateful for his father who nurtures him from afar and quietly watches over him as his life continues to unfold. He feels blessed to have had a mother who was never a follower of society's social norms but one who always questioned and chose her own path. He would like readers to know that he has never once questioned his mother's choice, as he believes that each person has his or her own journey to follow. He is grateful for this life that his father and mother gave to him and considers himself blessed.

∞

Dr. Jack Kevorkian—Deceased

After Janet's death in 1990, Dr. Jack Kevorkian continued to rebel against the authorities and went on to assist a total of 130 terminally ill patients in their deaths from 1990 to 1998. After his final arrest, the author spoke with Dr. Kevorkian by phone. She was informed that he was under a gag order and could not speak about Janet's case, but he was confident that the people would never bring a conviction against him. He was eventually brought to trial and convicted of second-degree murder in the euthanasia death of a man with Lou Gehrig's disease. In 1999, Dr. Kevorkian was sentenced to ten to twenty-five years in a maximum-security prison. He received an early release on June 1, 2007, for good behavior after assuring the authorities that he would never conduct another assisted suicide. A crusader for his cause, he continued to speak out about doctor-assisted suicide until his death in 2011. He died in Beaumont Hospital in Royal Oak, Michigan, on June 3, 2011, at the age of eighty-three, after being hospitalized for kidney and heart problems. Today, as a result of his crusade, eight states and the District of Columbia, have legalized doctor-assisted dying and many more are considering passing the law.

PART V

Town Hall Debate

39

A Villain or a Hero?

Dr. Kevorkian was considered a hero by the patients he helped and by many of those patients' families. To others, he was viewed as a villain who defied the laws of society. It is the nature of duality. Everything has its opposite, the yin and the yang. We cannot have light without darkness. Could it be that Dr. Kevorkian was a modern-day hero who represented justice and humanitarian service? Or was he a renegade who opposed the church and political control? One thing Dr. Kevorkian was not was a marionette dancing to the strings of society. He did not covertly hide his agenda behind a mask of deceit. He did not lurk in the shadows. He blatantly demonstrated his cause to the world. Some found that offensive while others hailed his courage.

Haven't human beings always had to take up the sword from the beginning of time as a catalyst for change? How many heroes were burned at the stake, beheaded, or put to death unfairly for their truth? How many gave their lives for the sake of humanity? Was Dr. Kevorkian any different from those who came before him? From the beginning of time, human beings have fought for their freedom and for a cause they believe in.

Within weeks of Janet's death, the question about the right to die with dignity became a heated debate nationally and internationally.

The following transcript is from the Town Hall show on Channel 2, KATU, a Fischer Broadcasting Company, in Portland, Oregon, from July 8, 1990, titled "Death with

Dignity." This is a good example of the public's opinion on doctor- assisted dying in 1990:

The views expressed on Town Hall are not necessarily the views of KATU, or Fischer Broadcasting Company "Death with Dignity."

Jack Faust (Moderator): In early June the nation was shocked when Portlander, Janet Adkins, killed herself with the help of a doctor and his homemade suicide machine.

Ron Adkins (Janet's husband): She didn't want to be just a shell of Janet. She wanted to exit while she was still rational and able to do so. I respected her wishes. She was an intelligent person and she thought this thing through.

(Coming across the TV screen: "Was her act illegal, immoral or sensible? Do people have the right to decide when and how to die? Death with Dignity.")

Jack Faust: It's been said that life imitates art. Two months ago the Portland Opera premiered a new opera called *Lucy's Lapses*, the story of a woman who has Alzheimer's disease and decides to end it by committing suicide. One month later, one month ago, Janet Adkins of Portland, as you all know, imitated that art by doing exactly that for the same reasons. Only she did it with the assistance of a medical doctor. This sounded a note that was heard around the world. People everywhere are asking, 'Is that right? When someone wants to get out of this life should medical doctors help them along?' That is our question on Town Hall tonight." Ron Adkins is introduced.

Ron Adkins: [Ron tells the viewers his story of how Janet died and why she chose Dr. Kevorkian to assist her.]

Jack Faust: [Carroll Rehmke is introduced.]

Carroll Rehmke (Janet's friend): I was the friend who accompanied Ron and Janet to Michigan.

Jack Faust: Describe for us how Janet committed suicide?

Carroll Rehmke: Janet committed suicide by pushing a button that allowed solutions to enter her system. She fell asleep, and within five minutes her heart stopped. It was all very painless.

Jack Faust: [Derek Humphry is introduced.] Derek, would you tell the viewers who you are?

Derek Humphry (President and Founder of the National Hemlock Society): I'm Derek Humphry, the head of the Hemlock Society.

Jack Faust: What is the Hemlock Society?

Derek Humphry: It is the right to choose to die organization.

Jack Faust: This is a national organization.

Derek Humphry: Janet was a member of our organization.

Jack Faust: I'm going to ask you, Mr. Humphry— Did Dr. Kevorkian, a medical doctor who helped her end her life, did he do the right thing?

Derek Humphry: Yes, he did.

Jack Faust: Why?

Derek Humphry: Because other doctors did not have the courage to do what he did.

Jack Faust: Why was it right to do what he did?

Derek Humphry: It was morally right to do what he did.

Jack Faust: Why?

Derek Humphry: Because we live in a nation of free choice. This was an intelligent woman making a rational decision. If we are a free people then we must respect what Janet Adkins did. Other doctors turned her down, I understand. She sought out Dr. Kevorkian, and he had the courage to do it. This is the tip of the iceberg. This happens a lot, covertly. This is just a case that has come out in the public. As the head of the Hemlock Society, I know from what doctors tell me, and patients tell me, and survivors tell me, this is going on extensively, secretively and not satisfactorily.

Jack Faust: In your view are they doing the right thing?

Derek Humphry: Yes, but it would be better if it was open and lawful.

Jack Faust: [Jack addresses a woman from the audience.] What is your condition?

Toni Carson (woman coping with cancer): I have been living with cancer for the past five years. I was diagnosed with breast cancer, which has since metastasized to my bones, my lungs, my brain, and now most recently my spinal fluid, which gives me symptoms like multiple sclerosis, deterioration of nerve damage.

Jack Faust: You have, in a sense, the same choice that faced Janet. What is your decision?

Toni Carson: I would never do that.

Jack Faust: Why not?

Toni Carson: Because of my faith in God, I am a stronger person for having gone through this. I choose to stay alive so I can be a part of my family. I have two children and a husband. Hopefully, I can give other people hope.

Jack Faust: What is your feeling in a situation where someone like Janet makes a contrary decision from yours? Should a doctor help her along?

Toni Carson: I don't believe that is right. I don't believe we have the authority to take our own life.

Jack Faust: Let's take a couple of views from the medical profession on that, at this moment. The first is from Dr. Kevorkian himself. He couldn't come out for the program. Eliza MacQuade, one of our producers, interviewed him by satellite. The first question is to Dr. Kevorkian, the doctor involved in this case: "Why did you help Janet Adkins kill herself?"

Dr. Jack Kevorkian, MD (by satellite from Detroit, Michigan): Janet Adkins represented a very good case to do. She was one of the best patients I could have run across. Her disease offered just a small-time span in which she could make a decision mentally. A person has to be mentally competent to be a candidate for what I am doing. The disease is also terminal but it is not a quick terminal. It is a long termination and is probably one of the most horrendous terminations that one can have in life. Therefore, with her brief time span, and with her adamant wish, firm, she never flinched, with the full support of her family, and having gone through a drug treatment that didn't work, I decided that this was a case where I had to act, and act fairly fast.

Eliza McQuade (producer for Town Hall): Dr. Kevorkian, did you try to talk her out of it?

Dr. Jack Kevorkian: Oh, yes. I think the whole family did, and I did too. All along we kept saying that she could change her mind anytime, and no one would be offended. I said it right up to the last minute in the van. She was very adamant. She wouldn't even consider that. She wanted it done and without delay.

Eliza McQuade: Would you use the machine to assist another suicide?

Dr. Jack Kevorkian: There is a great need for this. There always was. Sure I'll use it. But you see, I want to make a point. With this device a doctor isn't necessary. I suppose my being a doctor makes it a little more sensational and exciting. What this device does, in essence, it removes euthanasia for conscious patients from medical ethics. A doctor need not do it. If the doctors don't want to do this, then just have them pull away. But somebody, some group, has to get together and make this available to patients, and maybe outside of the medical profession.

Jack Faust: We have just heard from Dr. Kevorkian who did it here. Let's meet another doctor. [Paul Stull, MD, is introduced.] "What do you think about what you just heard? What would you do if the same request were made to you?

Paul Stull, MD (Director for the Lower Columbia Hospice): "I would have to deny that."

Jack Faust: Why would you have to deny that?

Paul Stull: Because I gave an oath when I became a physician to help patients, not to terminate life.

Jack Faust: Your view is that it is wrong in every instance, even if the patient feels that's the help they want?

Paul Stull: Absolutely.

Jack Faust: Why?

Paul Stull: Because it is morally wrong. As physicians, our traditional role has been one of a caregiver, a protector, to support life with dignity. For physicians to become involved with assisted suicide, we jeopardize our traditional values. I feel as a hospice physician, we have some moral and ethical solutions that are alternatives to this type of care.

Dr. Jack Kevorkian: The medical professionals that are stonewalling this would like it to go away and sweep it under the rug. So do the theologians and the judicial officials. The people don't. The need is there. Those who have stared death in the face, and the families who have seen the suffering, know there is a need for this. The others who are healthy merely pontificate with some abstraction they have in their mind, which they want to force on somebody else. That's immoral.

Jack Faust: Dr. Kevokian has noted right there that there is opposition to his philosophy. Opposition to the kind of choice we are talking about tonight. [Bob Castagna is introduced.] Bob, in the paper you were quoted as saying when you heard of Janet Adkins's case that you felt like you had been hit by a ton of bricks. Why?

Bob Castagna: (General Council and Executive Director of the Oregon Catholic Conference, Public Policy Office for the Catholic Church in Oregon): Because of the implications for society.

Jack Faust: What are those?

Bob Castagna: While being moved with profound sorrow for the killing and the taking of Janet Adkins's life, I am even more greatly moved for the implications for society. If we head down a road, which permits killing of the terminally ill, as a solution to terminal illness, we open Pandora's Box. In the Netherlands where this activity is tolerated, despite the fact that it is not legal, the testimony is now starting to come out that what started as voluntary euthanasia is crossing into involuntary euthanasia. My concern is, once we head down this quality of life philosophy and analysis, the mentally retarded are at risk, the developmentally disabled are at risk. People who have been traditionally discriminated against in society are at risk, once somebody else starts determining the quality of life one must have to continue to live. I'm also troubled as we look at the media attention to suicide. Since the Janet Adkins situation, we have had three prominent media cases in Portland, the last one being teenagers. I'm concerned that once adults start modeling this behavior, and once we move our baseline of what conduct is acceptable in society, we model that behavior for young people to be replicated. Suicide is not healthy for society. Personal autonomy and choice have limits. We recognize that in our daily lives. Whether it is putting a seatbelt on, not smoking in a building, whatever society imposes as a speed limit, for example. Choice and personal autonomy do have limits for the interest of society. The courts have traditionally recognized in this country that the preservation of life, the prevention of suicide, maintaining the ethical integrity of the medical community, and the protection of innocent third parties such as children, are legitimate state interests which cross any religious or philosophical bounds, but are there for the protection of society.

Jack Faust: You said this, and this is, of course, the central theme; you said there are limits on the right of personal choice. Is this where the limit should be, audience?

Robert M. Brown (man with Parkinson's disease): Your argument doesn't hold water with me because it is easy to pass laws to protect the innocent. In my case, I'm eight-two years old and have Parkinson's, bad. I've led a wonderful life. I love my work always, and I love my family. I have four children, eight grandchildren and three great grandchildren and a bunch of in-laws. They are all behind me in what I would like to do.

Jack Faust: What is it that you would like to do?

Robert M. Brown: I would like to just get me a good book or a magazine, and lay back and go to sleep, and be able to turn the light off, and push the door shut. That is the way I feel. My whole family is with me. They all love me and I love them. I want them to remember me as an energetic, busy guy, not as a pitiful corpse. I think I should have that right and I feel that anyone who tries to butt into that should be ashamed of themselves. [Loud applause]

Jack Faust: Is there someone here who is not ashamed of themselves and wants to disagree with that?

Vickie Maurseth (past President of the Oregon's Right to Life): Two thousand years ago, Hippocrates raised the medical profession out of what was considered a witchdoctor stage by saying, "You are not going to be an instrument of death." I think by turning to the medical profession and saying, "You are now going to be an instrument of death, again," we are not elevating that profession at all, but we are downgrading it. We are turning back in time.

Jack Faust: Is this nothing more than a matter of professionalism? Or is it more than that?

Barbara Peters (Attorney for Vancouver): I have a personal firsthand experience in watching someone with a chronic illness die. My mother died of lung cancer and emphysema. I was with her most of that time. You talk about death with dignity. I think it takes tremendous courage and dignity to endure a chronic illness day to day, and to put up with all the suffering it entails. I am here to say that I believe there is tremendous redemptive value, not just for the dying person, but for those around them when you talk about suffering. I had an incredible opportunity to love my mother and show compassion to her. I know that we deeply believe in God, and we believe there is a spiritual side to suffering, too, that will come back to benefit us. I believe that when I look up I see order in the universe. and see how in order the universe is. It's so incredible. How could you not believe that there is someone in control? If that is the case, then who are we to say when life ends?

Jack Faust: You mentioned your love and compassion for her. Supposing she said to you, "If you love me, if you have any compassion for me, you will help me to end this." What would you have thought then?

Barbara Peters: I wouldn't talk too much. I would pray. I would pray, pray, pray for her to be enlightened.

Jack Faust: Would you change your course of action?

Barbara Peters: No, I don't think so. I would pray because I believe God is in control of that. It is a black and white deal. God is either there, he is both all-powerful and knowing, or he isn't.

Beverly Ickes (daughter of the man who has Parkinson's disease): There are many people, as this man just said, that want their life to end. This is my father. I love this man and I am devoted to him. I don't want his life to end, but I support, completely, his right to end his life at the point where he chooses not to live anymore. [Anger in her voice] I wonder why this woman thinks she has any business, any business, interfering with his right. We would like to have a humane, absolute sure way, cleanly, that he could end his life, as Mrs. Adkins did. I don't understand why this productive, generous, humorous, loving man, should be told by someone totally uninvolved in the situation how he should continue his life. He does not believe in God. This has no relevance to him. This is a complete dichotomy for me, why anyone thinks their belief in God should judge the way he conducts his life or chooses not to.

Ron Adkins: Janet, of course, and myself, included, believe that the individual has the right to take the most precious thing they have, which is their life, and to do with it as they feel right. If the dignity they have has gone away, they have the right to exit in a dignified and humane way. Janet thought that, and she did that. As you are aware, we have in Oregon, a Humane Society for animals to make sure animals die in a humane way. We need a humane society for humans to make sure that humans die in a humane way. [Loud applause]

Rosalma St. Lawrence (woman coping with cancer): I've had cancer three times, and I almost committed suicide eleven years ago. I know what it is to suffer. I can't see why they hold the doctor responsible, because he didn't push the button. That was up to Janet, and she chose. If I had had a humane way eleven years ago, I probably would have done the same thing.

Jack Faust: The point is sounded again about the right of individual freedom. The person who owns the life, being right.

Helen Donovan (woman from the audience): We have to think about Western civilization and two thousand years of it where the citizen was protected. We took care of each other, and we protected each other and the society with laws, and all kinds of structures. To see this intrusion of someone choosing their own time to die, is just the opposite of what we have developed our society on for two thousand years: citizenship, helping each other, not doing each other in.

Elizabeth Rae Clumpner (woman from the audience): I have studied theology for fifty years; I have studied Western civilization. What you are overlooking, my dear, is the fact that in many societies and cultures throughout the world, when someone was ill and there was no hope, they did the gracious thing for their family and they went off into the hills. It is part of certain cultures. We have to dignify life. I disagree with Dr. Stull. I know the hospice. I have dealt with the Alzheimer's patients as a psychiatric social worker. I have had them in my family. I was married to a man who turned from loving to cruel, who tried to kill me. He would say, 'Stop me, don't stop me.' In his quiet times he was the man he was. But when he went into a rage his mind went out of control. I know what it is like to love someone and have to step away. I think we have to look at the tragedy of extending life that is not viable.

John Cantwell Kiley, MD: I am a physician and a philosopher. I think that part of what is lacking in Dr. Kevorkian is precisely the understanding of how things come to be when you think them. In Janet's case she wasn't so much in flight from Alzheimer's or from death but from the thought of it. One of the administrations that Dr. Kevorkian could have ideally afforded this woman, rather than trying to talk her out of it, was to try to explain to her that her morbidity was self-produced and that she didn't produce it in any given amount. It simply wasn't there, and she would not be in flight from it. That is one point. The other point I want to make is this; The Hemlock Society has been challenging us for atmospheric reasons. Actually, Socrates did not commit suicide. He was forced to execute himself. For that reason, I think that using him as a symbol—I think rather the symbol that could be possibly used for the Hemlock Society would be that afforded by that religious group within the Hindu society who worshiped the god of destruction, Kali. They have given us a word in their language and the word is Sagi. These people use a strangling cord to put people to death.

Jack Faust: I don't believe they are consenting victims.

Derek Humphry: We use the word hemlock in the Hemlock Society because it was the plant that was used in ancient Greece in the Roman society. Socrates was the main user of it.

Jack Faust: The pointed issue that he is making is that this is the termination of life in the nature of a murder.

Derek Humphry: No it's not. That is semantics. It is death by request. We have to realize that in today's society where people are more autonomous, where the churches do not dominate us like they used to do in history, death by request is what a lot of people want. What Dr. Kevorkian is demonstrating should be there. To murder someone is to take the life of someone who doesn't want to die.

Bob Castagna: The Hemlock Society initiative spoke about it when they introduced it to the Secretary of State's office last June of decriminalizing homicide and assisted suicide. We are talking about actively killing people. We have to be very clear. We are not talking about withholding and withdrawing life-sustaining treatment. We are talking about taking active measures to kill people. The Hemlock Society, as measured by its own terms, says that this does not constitute a homicide or a suicide. They attempted to decriminalize what currently is a class B felony in the state of Oregon. To be clear about what we are talking about, we are talking about physician homicide and physician-assisted suicide. That is not a matter to be taken lightly. In fact, it is unprecedented, both from our research and, as far as we can determine from their writing, that there is no legislation anywhere in the world that would permit this activity. Nowhere in the world, and I don't think that Oregon or the State of Washington wants to be the first in the world to introduce this into legislation. [Applause]

Carol Helm (husband committed suicide): My husband died in 1974 from cystic fibrosis. He was thirty years old, and he suffered for thirty years. He lived fifteen years beyond his life expectancy. For the last year and a half of his life, he was confined to the house on oxygen. When this man went to the hospital for the last time, he refused to take any medication to prolong his life. They told him that if he survived this visit that he would go into a nursing home. This man was thirty years old, and he had suffered for thirty years. He did not want to suffer anymore. They said he was incompetent. He was not. He was in his right mind, and he knew what he was doing. I said, "I want you as long as I can have you, but you can go anytime you want."

Jack Faust: How did he go?

Carol Helm: I've been toying with this myself. I think I helped him to die. He refused to take the medication, so the mucus built up in his lungs. I forced him to lie down in bed, and he died two hours later. This was his choice. He refused the medication.

Jack Faust: A suicide, class B felony, a voluntary leaving of life? Whatever it is, it is going on. What is going on today behind closed doors?

Dr. Jack Kevorkian: I don't think God brings us into this world, does he? I think an obstetrician does. An obstetrician is a doctor, and I am a doctor. Even though I am a pathologist, I am a doctor. I think if an obstetrician is justified in helping a baby come into this world by a caesarian section, which is playing God, I'd say, then I think I am justified in helping a patient who wants to exit, exit the best way possible.

Jack Faust: Dr. Kevorkian says he is justified in helping a patient exit. [Paul Smith, MD, is introduced] How often are doctors making that kind of a choice today, in reality, and helping people along? How much is that going on?

Paul Smith, MD (Surgeon from Salem, Oregon): It depends on your definition for help. The organization I work for was one of the first organizations to push hospice. At that time, some of these same arguments surfaced that we were helping people die, that we shouldn't leave them at home, and they should come into the hospital. Now everybody accepts that hospitals are a terrible place to live, and they are an abomination to die in. It happens all the time. There is what is called long term intravenous lines that are put in for terminal and cancer patients that are left in forever. For people with severe pain problems, their relatives are taught how to give them narcotic shots. Who knows if they get a little bit extra overdose?

Jack Faust: Do you just look the other way? Doctors are doing that?

Paul Smith: It happens via home nursing. The patient goes home, and the home nurse will come out and teach the family how to use the equipment. Who knows what happens at home? That is one of the advantages of hospice. It restores the individual to the choice instead of putting them in the hospital where the doctor makes the choice, and he's afraid because Cousin George is going to come from Minnesota and sue him if they don't do everything, and there are twenty lawyers looking over his shoulder. We subject these people to this incredible dehumanizing, undignified existence. I get emotional about this because I went through this with my mother.

Jack Faust: How often do you think that the physicians in the hospitals are actually helping the people along with their exits?

Paul Smith: Helping in terms of withholding medication? Not with an overdose, it is too hard to hide. In a hospital you can't do that.

Jack Faust: But taking away hydration and nutrition, of course, is an everyday affair.

Paul Smith: Not in a hospital, generally speaking. The goal is to get them out of the hospital. My goal as a surgeon, when I have a terminal patient, is to get them out of the hospital into a hospice situation, educate the family, and then it is their decision, basically, to make.

Jack Faust: [Bob Shoemaker is introduced.] My question to you, for our viewers is. In Oregon what's legal? We have the patient. The patient is comatose, the patient is judged as having no chance of recovery. What is legal? What can be done in the hospital?

Bob Shoemaker (Attorney, State Senator, and Chair of the Senate Committee on Health Insurance and Bioethics for Oregon): I think you are getting into the death with dignity area, Jack, which is a little different. Let me come to that second.

Jack Faust: I want to talk mostly about the withdrawal of life support. We have some new laws here.

Bob Shoemaker: We do have some new laws here. If you execute a power of attorney for health care, or if you have executed a Directive to Physicians, then the physician should follow that. It is legal to follow that, which includes withdrawing respirators, dialysis, and antibiotics, whatever. It does not include actively assisting in the death. It includes withdrawing life support and allowing death to occur naturally.

Jack Faust: It is also proper, and with the proper power of attorney, to withdraw nutrition and hydration.

Bob Shoemaker: Yes that is correct. There is a legal presumption that an adult would consent to artificial feeding.

Jack Faust: And it can be done by a power of attorney?

Bob Shoemaker: It can. You can specifically state that you do not want nutrition and hydration. That means you have not consented. And then, it is not only proper to withdraw it, but it would be improper to provide it.

Paul Smith: Can I provide a clarification? This is something new in Oregon and probably the best law in the country right now. A power of attorney basically means that if my father were to become ill, he could sign a power of attorney giving me basically the rights to do whatever I want.

Jack Faust: Not just because you are a doctor?

Paul Smith: Not because I am a doctor, but for anyone. He says, "You act in my stead if I am incompetent." If I think it should stop, and he's incompetent to decide, I can do that.

Jack Faust: If I have one of those, and it is my father, I can stop the hydration, I can stop the nutrition, and I can stop the food and water?

Paul Smith: This is a much more powerful tool than the so-called living will. It is much more efficient.

Bob Shoemaker: You have to be clear and specific about it. If the Cruzan case were to occur here, Nancy Cruzan, who did not execute a power of attorney, had talked about not wanting to live like a vegetable but had not said, "I don't want feeding tubes," if she were in Oregon, she would be stuck.

Jack Faust: My question for you, Bob Castagna, is this: If it is legal for me to have a power of attorney where I can say for my father, "Stop the food, stop the water," and he is going to die, how much difference is there then in that case, where we are condemning him to death in effect by my decision, which he has empowered me to make? How much difference is there then, in just making it quicker by doing what was done with Janet Adkins?

Bob Castagna: There is a world of difference, Jack. And I think the world of difference revolves around the dignity and sanctity of that individual human person's life. Life is not to be equated to animals. We have heard the expression "We have a humane society for animals. We should have a humane society for people." We have hospitals, we have hospice cares, and we have families for people who can be surrounded by care, compassion and love. That is our mission. Our mission is not to become killers and terminators of life. When we do that, we show fundamental disrespect for the dignity and sanctity of that human person. There is a world of difference between withholding and withdrawing, and allowing death to occur naturally, as a natural process of life, than actually killing someone. That is the activity we are talking about.

Mary Jo Kahler (Human Life of Washington): Dignity isn't something that you or I give to another person. Each one of us has dignity by reason of our existence. When we fail to recognize that dignity, that's when we say something about ourselves and about our society that is really a condemnation of who we are, not of the person whose dignity is not recognized.

Jack Faust: What is your point?

Mary Jo Kahler: My point is, we don't give dignity to people because they already have it. If we fail to recognize it, that's our problem. They still possess a dignity. I saw dignity in the most moving example in my life, and I relate to it personally. My aunt lived for eleven years with Alzheimer's. It's a very significant part of my family history on my mother's side. I fully expect that may be a factor in my life in the very near future, because early onset is significant in my mom's family. When I look at that, I would hope that my family, and I know they will, in recognizing my dignity as a person, will care for me when I have to take from them, and I can't give back. When they will surround me with compassion, and care, and with real dignity, recognizing that as a human being, I possess it. It is to their advantage, and to my community's advantage to acknowledge that, and care for me. [Applause]

Jack Faust: [A question is asked of Beverly Ickes] You are supportive of your father's right to make the same choice as Janet. Your question was why someone else could tell him not to. The answer we are getting is that there is a superior, transcendent, value to human life. Even though this may be a free choice of your father's, it is cheapening the value of human life. How do you respond to that?

Beverly Ickes (daughter of man who has Parkinson's disease): I recognize the inherent value in this man's life. He has been a wonderful father and a businessman. He built an enormously valuable business. At the age of seventy-two, he learned how to use computers and practically writes his own programs. He doesn't need me to tell him he has value and dignity in his life. Nevertheless, all of my life, I have known that he did not want to live out his life in some nonfunctioning, noncontributory way. I support his right.

Jack Faust: Let me make the point. You are focusing, as you have and as Ron has, on the decision being made by the person involved. The counter is that they are saying there are greater rights by society at large. How do you answer that to the impact on society?

Beverly Ickes: I think, perhaps, at a very young age, society has a vested interest in preventing suicide among young people, twenty-years-old, to forty-years-old. A man of eighty-two who has contributed to society all his life, taking care of himself and his family, has an absolute right, in my opinion, to decide not to live any longer. [Applause]

Unidentified man from the audience: I think that it is ludicrous to say that a disease confers some kind of a constitutional right on somebody. If the right is there, it is there for everybody. It is not just there for the sick. And that is one of the reasons why I object to this whole thing, because it will become panoramic. We will begin killing off people who are not consenting, and we are already doing that. [Noticeable disagreement by the audience over that statement.] We are killing off people who are in vegetative states. We are asking for the death of Nancy Cruzan. It goes all the way to the Supreme Court for the right to kill their daughter who never said she wanted to die. [Disagreement from the audience]

Jack Faust: Derek, you are the President of the Hemlock Society. I would think the point he made there, he says why should it just be disease? How would your organization feel about somebody who suffered an enormous financial loss, and they decide they want to end it because of that?

Derek Humphry: They should not be helped. They should be helped to live to get through their particular problem. The Hemlock Society is against suicide for emotional reasons. Let me make the point: we live in a civilization and we live under the rule of law. We must draw laws, which say certain conditions of illnesses can have euthanasia, other people can't. People who are mentally handicapped, and have drawbacks in their life, they will not, under the laws proposed by the Hemlock movement, be able to get help in dying. [Concern for the welfare of the disabled from those opposed to euthanasia] The Hemlock Society would oppose any euthanasia for mentally ill people, handicapped people. We would fight it tooth and nail, and I hope society would join us.

Paul Smith: Jack, what they are saying in essence, is that some people have to suffer so we don't have to feel guilty. [Loud applause]

Christi Sifri-Steele, RN (Critical Care Nurse): I think what we need to focus on is not the extremes, but rather what is going on now, especially with Oregon Health decisions. And this new senate bill that was passed, and what is capable with it, as far as withdrawing life support. And, who can withdraw life support, and at what time. Take the Nancy Cruzan's case, where you are a vegetable, and you have a feeding tube, and you have signed this. Unless you are there, and you see that going on, and you are in there daily with those doctors trying to save a person that is not going to be saved, and they have this directive, and we don't follow that, that is a shame.

Sharon Caldwell (woman from the audience): I lobbied in the last two sessions with the legislature against euthanasia bills. First of all, I am very offended. I have heard the term used twice. I am very offended by the term, vegetable. I think if there is any word demeaning a human being, it is that one. Secondly, I agree with Thomas Wolf who said recently, "That because our society is so affluent, that we now feel cocky and confident enough to begin gestating all of our traditional values." Basically we have turned our country into a coast to coast carnival. Of course, this happened in Germany in the 1920s. They instituted the German euthanasia program, which ultimately turned into the Holocaust. I believe that this is happening again now. Basically, this is just another sideshow.

Jack Faust: I'll put that back to you, Ron. Your wife made a statement with her death. You have heard what was said here. What is your response?

Ron Adkins: We are a twentieth-century society. You remember that in the old days, horses used to be frightened by cars. Atomic energy is dangerous. But we have intellect, and we can make laws, and devise systems and means whereby people can exit with dignity, for those people who want to. For those that don't want to, that's fine. I might also add that Janet was a religious person. She believed in God. Before she pushed the button, Dr. Kevorkian's sister read the twenty-third Psalm. She had faith. She also wanted to die with dignity, and felt that she believed in a "Good God."

Thelma Lofquist, PhD (woman from the audience): I deal with families and caregivers of Alzheimer's every day. We are having a crisis. You are talking about dignity. Our nursing homes are full. We do not have enough Alzheimer's units. If you are very wealthy and have Alzheimer's, you can find a place. The poorer you are, the less options there are. Families can't take that daily grind of being up all night. Day cares don't work. You can't take your mother to a day care, pick her up at night, have her up all night, and have her on weekends. There is no time. It grinds out good memories. I know that I would do exactly what Janet did, because I have seen it. Alzheimer's is not dignified. It is a cruel disease. [Loud applause]

Ralph Crawshaw, MD (Project Director for Oregon Health Decisions): Jack, we have three questions here: (1) A question of personal autonomy. (2) A question of ethics of the media in what's going on. (3) A question of ethics of the medical profession. Physicians are trained to be healers. We are not for euthanasia; that is not what we are for. We are healers in the sense of doing what the patient wishes to be done. We are servants of the patient. Therefore, it is really important for the public now, to know that they should be informing their physicians of what they wish. How it works out from that point on is a very private doctor–patient relationship. [Loud applause]

Jack Brown (man from the audience): To the doctor from the hospice, I would like to say that I would never suggest that any doctor should take an action that is against his conscience. But at the same time, I think that any doctor who feels justified in carrying out a patient's wish certainly ought to be able to do that under law, and under medical ethics. Second, my father would like to see a show of hands of everyone in this room that is over sixty-five who is in favor of medically assisted suicide.

Jack Faust: Let's see a show of hands. How about over sixty-five and opposed to it? It looks like we have a balance.

Unidentified woman from the audience: Two of my three children are disabled. I guess I am right in the middle. I am concerned about the issue of other people making judgments on who has the right to live and the quality of life. Yet on the other hand, we have a son who is terminally ill with a metabolic disorder. We have gotten the paperwork all together that he is not to be put on life support. We want to help the process of dying for him. I'm caught right in the middle, and it is real interesting.

Unidentified woman from the audience: I have a sister who has Alzheimer's and a niece who has terminal cancer. My first husband died of a heart attack. I have been with many people as they have died. I want to ask, "What about the life hereafter?" Nobody has addressed this. Peggy Lee sang a song, "Is This All There Is to Life?"

Jack Faust: Maybe that will be another program.

Minister from the audience: I work daily with dying people. I would simply like to say that many people approach this subject looking forward to death because of their religious belief. Secondly, I know many physicians who have assisted dying patients to die, and I can tell you that the families of those patients are very grateful for what those physicians did.

Jack Faust: Ron, that was your statement about Janet's decision. That part of her decision was prompted by the idea that she had religious faith.

Ron Adkins: Janet was not frightened of death. She looked forward to moving on. She was so thankful for the doctor helping her.

C. Budie Gary (man from the audience): Who's to say the real signal isn't to our medical profession. If they can actually create a picture that is so dreary that someone would actually lose their God given faith to live in the first place shows there has to be some kind of upgrading with regards to following through with the Hippocratic oath.

Pediatrician–Physician from the audience: I would like to respond with another question because I know time is short. I would just like to ask for a show of hands from anybody in this room who has a life without pain or suffering.

Unidentified woman from the audience: Rather than opening the door to death, if I get ill, I would rather see society working out its own problems to open up if I am poor, and I have a disabling disease, and I can't afford health care. Now I find out that all the nursing homes are full, and social security is falling apart. Please don't open the door to death. Keep it closed. Open the door instead to other alternatives. If you open the door to death, I know society will not help me. We are not going to be forced to confront this problem and solve it.

Mickey Clay (Director of Evangelical Lutheran Church of American Lutheran Public Policy): That is my point also. When we talk about death with dignity, let's begin right now preventing illness, preventing it in the young. Let's take care of our elderly. I just put my mother into a care home. I know what the situation is. Let's take care of those people and provide the resources for them.

Unidentified woman from the audience: One point that hasn't been made here tonight is about the mystery of life. Life is a mystery. Death is a part of that mystery. Socrates himself praised the mysteries of life. This is one of the greatest.

Don Heberling (man from the audience): Why involve physicians. Thirty thousand people do it each year without physicians, most of them. The choice is there. It is not a matter of individual choice. If we involve physicians, it gives suicide a legitimacy that will then spread throughout society to the teenagers and to those who are emotionally distraught.

Jack Faust: You have heard Janet Adkins's answer to that, which was that she wanted to be sure that the death would be peaceful by having a physician involved.

Elaine Thompson: I see over, and over and over again undignified death in the hospital. I really do believe in pro-choice. You need to let your family know ahead of time, and you need to get the legal documents, because if you don't, we will try to save you. You may die with a ventilator in and restrained so you can't move. That is not very dignified.

Jack Faust: That is an important point that has been made again. That doesn't have to happen, does it? Under Oregon law, the new law?

Father Evan Ash (Director of The Good Samaritan Pastoral Services): I think everyone is here tonight because they are compassionate people. I think we all probably would like to believe that we are not afraid of death. I would like to suggest that maybe we also not be too afraid of life. Life today often becomes very one-dimensional. When that dimension of our life, that we seem to hang our life on, becomes threatened, somehow, we think life itself is gone. There are many issues and experiences in life, which open up new dimensions in our life that we can't know about.

Jack Faust: [A question is addressed to Bob Castagna] If you could sum it up for our viewers. If someone is making a decision to take their life alone, why should the rest of us care? Why should we try to prevent that with laws?

Bob Castagna: Life is precious. It is sacred. We have a body of laws to provide a standard of conduct in society. If we lower that standard of conduct to allow either physician homicide or physician-assisted suicide, we open Pandora's Box. We have heard references to the poor. If this becomes a societal option, the pressure in society will be on the poor to avail themselves of that option to save society money. The pressure will be on senior citizens to take this route to save their family's money and their own guilt of having to spend money on medical care, on nursing home care, etc. The road we are going down is one of taking the lives of terminally ill people.

Jack Faust: [Derek Humphry is asked to respond.] The argument is, if we allow this, we go down the slippery slope.

Derek Humphry: We draw up a careful law, and it is time to put it to the electorate to vote on this matter.

Jack Faust: What would that law be?

Derek Humphry: Under careful conditions, a dying person could request their physician to help them to die. [Loud applause]

Jack Faust: Would you sum it up briefly. Why should we vote "yes" on that?

Derek Humphry: Because we are a free people.

Jack Faust: You have heard it right here, just now. Again, we have all these choices between the right of an individual to make a decision and the right of society. You may say there is no right of society here. You may say there is no right of the individual. But this is the way the argument is phrased. "I have my right to determine my life," and the others say, "No you don't because society has larger rights."

(**Coming across the TV screen: "According to a USA poll, 2/3 of people say that the terminally ill should be able to choose when to die and medical facilities should help them commit suicide."**)

Six-months after Janet's death, on December 3, 1990, Dr. Kevorkian was charged with her murder. After all the evidence was presented against Dr. Kevorkian, the judge could not find that a crime had been committed. No law in the State of Michigan made it illegal to assist in the death of a patient. When Judge McNally dismissed the criminal charges against Dr. Kevorkian, Prosecutor Thompson appealed. "The courts would love to burn me at the stake, and the prosecutor is trying to light the fire," an angry Dr. Kevorkian stated.[1] "Society is making me Dr. Death. Why can't they see I'm Dr. Life?"[2]

---

[1] UPI, "Suicide Doctor Might Disobey Court Order," October 4, 1990, accessed June 26, 2019, https://www.upi.com/Archives/1990/10/04/Suicide-doctor-might-disobey-court-order/7797655012800/.

[2] Pamela Warrick, "Suicide's Partner: Is Jack Kevorkian an Angle of Mercy, or Is He a Killer, as Some Critics Charge?," Los Angeles Times, December 6, 1992, accessed June 26, 2019, https://www.latimes.com/archives/la-xpm-1992-12- 06-vw-3171-story.html.

Dr. Jack Kevorkian's *'Suicide Machine'*

'The Mercitron'

The Author's Conclusion

It has been a privilege and a humbling experience to write Janet's story. I honor each and every person who contributed to this book and applaud their courage for providing intimate details of their interactions with Janet and for sharing the many ways in which she enriched their lives.

When I started this project, I was naïve in my understanding of the subject. I knew nothing about Janet's cause and very little about Dr. Kevorkian. Personally, Janet has opened my eyes to the plight of the terminally ill and the needless suffering that goes on in the world. As a person with great compassion, I am sensitive to people of all walks of life, and I support dignity and quality of life. After twenty years of gestating on this issue, I am proud to say that what I have learned from Janet is I must take a stand for what I believe. I have recently moved off the sidelines and support individual choice.

I have great admiration for Ron and the many years he spent fighting for Janet's cause. He deserves to find some peace in his final days, knowing he made a difference in the world by bringing Janet's story to the forefront of society.

The following quote best describes the essence of who Janet was:

Here Comes There Goes You Know Who,
by William Saroyan

You betray honor, you betray yourself,
and you betray the human race
when you believe the way to truth is
the way taken by the mob.
When you agree because it's convenient,
when you accept, when you conform,

***when you don't go after the truth
as if it had never before been seized.***

Her philosophy was a great match with Dr. Kevorkian, which made her the perfect candidate to take his cause to the world. It has been nearly thirty years since Janet rang a bell that was heard around the world. Although we have made progress with death with dignity laws in a small number of states, we as a society have a long way to go.

My journey has exposed me to many terminally ill patients who are suffering needlessly because the laws are not broad enough to include their disease. With the requirement of a six-month window till death, sadly, Alzheimer's is one of those diseases that does not qualify because a doctor cannot determine how long these patients have to live.

It is my hope that this true-life story will create open, honest, and transparent conversations between family members and friends of all ages, so that anyone can make an informed decision on end-of-life choices. Would you be willing to ask yourself, "What do I want," or "What would I do?"

- ➢ How would you feel if a loved one who is terminally ill wanted to end their suffering by ending their life, in accordance with the right to die movement?
- ➢ Could you or would you support them?
- ➢ If you were terminally ill, would you like assistance to end your life, or would you prefer to die naturally when you take your final breath of life?
- ➢ Would you consider taking the next step and making your final wishes written down in your Advance Health Care Directive?
- ➢ Do you want to die at home?
- ➢ Do you want to die in a hospital?
- ➢ Do you want people to mourn your death, or celebrate your life?

➢ Do you have your final affairs in order? (Health Care Directive, POLST—Physician Orders for Life Sustaining Treatment [this replaces DNR—Do Not Resuscitate]; Durable Power of Attorney for Finances; Will; Living Will; Trust; and final arrangements?) If not, why not?

Like birth, death is part of the natural cycle of life. Will you allow yourself permission to choose and take charge of your death?

In remembrance of Janet's final words,

"Thank you! Thank you! Thank you!"

APPENDICES

Appendix A

List of People Mentioned in This Book

Adolph and Magdelena—Janet's grandparents
Bill and Betty—Helen's parents
Cal—Ron's Best Man—Died by suicide
Carroll—Janet's lifelong friend who accompanied her to Detroit
Del Adkins—Ron's dad—died in a fatal car accident
Dr. Kevorkian—Assisted Janet in dying
Einar—Janet's dad—died on the street from alcohol
Emily Adkins—Ron's mother—died from Multiple Sclerosis
Eunice and John—Janet's aunt and husband
Grandfather Oxley—Ron's grandfather—died by suicide
Grandmother Oxley—Raised Ron
Helen—Janet's childhood friend and bridesmaid
Janet Adkins—Died by Dr. Kevorkian's suicide machine
Johnny—Helen's son—died by suicide
Judy—Janet's life-long friend
Myriam Coppens—Family Counsellor
Neil, Heidi and Justin Adkins—First son and family
Norman and Tami Jo Adkins—Second son and wife
Opal Adkins—Ron's stepmother
Peggy and Bob—Janet and Ron's life-long friends
Ralph—Janet's brother-murdered
Ron Adkins—Janet's husband
Ronald, Angelina, Bryan Adkins—Third son and family
Sharon—Ron's partner
Shirley and Dell—Janet and Ron's friends
Vi—Janet's mother

Appendix B

Current Death with Dignity Laws

Oregon: Oregon Death with Dignity Act; 1994/1997.

Washington: Washington Death with Dignity Act; 2008.

Vermont: Patient Choice and Control at the End of Life Act; 2013.

California: End of Life Option Act; 2015, in effect 2016.

Colorado: End of Life Options Act; 2016.

District of Columbia: D.C. Death with Dignity Act; 2016/2017.

Hawaii: Our Care, Our Choice Act; 2018/2019.

New Jersey: Aid in Dying for the Terminally Ill Act; 2019.

Maine: Death with Dignity Act; 2019.

For updates on the current laws and states

under consideration go to:

https://www.deathwithdignity.org.

Appendix C

List of Ron's Media Interviews

Television/Videos

➢ *Sally Jessy Raphael Show*, Universal Television Enterprises, 1990—Interview with the Adkins' family and Dr. Kevorkian.

➢ *Larry King*, CNN, 1990—Interview with Ron Adkins.

➢ *Nightline*, ABC News, 1990—Ted Kopple interview with Ron Adkins.

➢ *Town Meeting*, 1990—Interview with the Adkins family.

➢ *Town Hall*, 1990—Ron Adkins and Dr. Kevorkian, ethics debate.

➢ *Good Morning America*, ABC, 1990—Interview with Ron Adkins and Dr. Kevorkian.

➢ *The Journal*, 1990—Coverage of Janet Adkins's death.

➢ Medical Consultation with Dr. Kevorkian, 1990—Janet's interview with Dr. Kevorkian.

➢ *The Dini Petty Show*, Baton Broadcasting System (Canada), 1991—Interview with Ron Adkins.

➢ Japanese Television, 1990—Special coverage of Janet Adkins's death.

➢ Spanish Television, 1990—Special coverage of Janet Adkins's death.

➢ Canadian Television, Toronto, 1991—Interview with Ron Adkins.

➢ *The Rolanda Watts Show*, 1991—Interview with Ron Adkins, ethics debate.

> "Alzheimer's Special," CNN, 1991—Coverage of Janet Adkins's death.

> "The Health Quarterly," *Frontline*, PBS, 1991—Coverage of Janet Adkins's death.

> *Larry King*, CNN, 1991—Interview with Dr. Kevorkian and coverage of Janet Adkins's death.

> "The Kevorkian File," *Frontline*, PBS, 1991—Interview with Dr. Kevorkian and the coverage of Janet Adkins's death.

> *Inside Edition*, King World, 1991—Special coverage of Janet Adkins's death.

> "Help Me Die," KGW Television (Portland, OR), 1991—Coverage of Janet Adkins's death.

> *The Maury Povich Show*, Paramount Domestic Productions, 1991—Interview with Ron Adkins, ethics debate.

> *The Donahue Show*, NBC, 1992—Interview with Dr. Kevorkian demonstrating the death machine used by Janet Adkins.

Magazine Articles (chronological)

> Newsweek Staff. 1990. "The Doctor's Suicide Van." *Newsweek Magazine* (June 18): 46–48.

> Newsweek Staff. 1990. "Testing for Alzheimer's." *Newsweek Magazine* (June 18): 49.

> Gibbs, Nancy. 1990. "Ethics: Dr. Death's Suicide Machine: An Ailing Teacher's Last Decision Inflames the Euthanasia Debate." *Time Magazine* 135, no. 25 (June 18): 69–70.

> Gibbs, Nancy. 1990. "New Hope for Alzheimer's Victims." *Time Magazine* 135, no. 25 (June 18): 70.

> Johnson, Bonnie. 1990. "A Vital Woman Chooses Death." *People* (June 25): 40–43.

> "Donahue Show Taught Suicide Machine Mom How to End All." 1990. *Star Magazine* (June 26): 10.

> Carr, William H. A. 1995. "A Right to Die." *The Saturday Evening Post* (September/October): 50–51, 70–73.

> Webb, Marilyn. 1997. "A Matter of Life or Death." *The Ladies Home Journal* (January 1997): 106–09, 142.

Newspaper Articles (chronological)

> Smith, James L. "She Pulled A Switch and Died." *The Seattle Times*, June 5.

> Meehan, Brian T., and Sura Rubenstein. 1990. "Suicide Machine Takes Life." *The Oregonian*, June 6.

> Meehan, Brian T., and Sura Rubenstein. 1990. "Portland Woman Uses Suicide Machine." *The Oregonian* (AM Sunrise Edition), June 6.

> Belkin, Lisa. 1990. "Doctor Tells of First Death Using His Suicide Device." *New York Times*, June 6.

> Wilkerson, Isabel. 1990. "Physician Fulfills A Goal: Aiding a Person in Suicide." *New York Times*, June 6.

> Egan, Timothy. 1990. "As Memory and Music Faded Alzheimer Patient Met Death." *New York Times*, June 7.

> Angier, Natalie. 1990. "Diagnosis of Alzheimer's Is No Matter of Certainty." *New York Times*, June 7.

> Mauro, Tony. 1990. "The Life-and-Death Issue. 'Justice to Join National Debate.'" *USA Today*, June 8.

> Walmer, Tracy, and Bonnie DeSimone. 1990. "She Believed in a Dignified Death." *USA Today*, June 8.

> Haj, Georg. 1990. "Poll: Suicide Option up to Terminally Ill." *USA Today*, June 8.

➤ Meehan, Brian T. 1990. "Janet Adkins' Suicide Brings Euthanasia Issue into Spotlight." *The Oregonian*, June 10.

➤ Goetze, Janet. 1990. "Friends Recall Student of Life." *The Oregonian*, June 11.

➤ Altman, Lawrence K. 1990. "Use of Suicide Device Setsin Motion Debate on a Disturbing Issue." *New York Times*, June 12.

➤ "Janet Adkins' Controversial Assisted Suicide." 1990. Letters to the Editor, *The Los Angeles Times*, June 16.

➤ McCarthy, Dennis. 1990. "Ronald Adkins Says His Wife Died Honorably in Her Suicide." *The Oregonian*, July 4.

➤ Beck, Joan. 1990. "Assisted Suicide and Fear of Waiting too Long." *Chicago Tribune*.

➤ Johnson, Malcolm. 1991. "Action Delayed on Suicide Bill." *Kalamazoo Gazette*, February 27.

➤ Associated Press. 1991. "Pathologist Says Poll Shows Majority Back Doctor-Aided Suicide." *Kalamazoo Gazette*, May 6.

➤ Meehan, Brian. 1991. "Living after Death." *The Oregonian*, June 4.

➤ Lesko, Ron. 1991. "Death No Downer, Widower Says." *Kalamazoo Gazette*, June 11.

➤ McCall, William. 1994. "Adkins' Husband Fights for Right-To-Die Cause." *The Oregonian*, May 29.

➤ Orstein, Charles. 1998. "Oregon And Michigan - A Studyin Contrasts on Assisted Suicide," *Dallas Morning News*, March 30.

Speaking Engagements

➤ Managing Mortality, "Assisted Suicide and Euthanasia," Bloomington, Minnesota, December 3–5, 1992.

➤ Annual Conference of the National Society for Patient Representation and Consumer Affairs of the American Hospital

Association, "Physician Assisted Dying," San Diego, California,
October 25–28, 1993.

Radio Talk Shows

➢ Portland Radio Talk Shows, 1990.

➢ Minneapolis Radio Talk Shows, 1992.

➢ Australia Radio Talk Shows, 1994.

➢ Oliver North Show, 1997.

www.ingramcontent.com/pod-product-compliance
Lightning Source LLC
Chambersburg PA
CBHW060244100426
42742CB00011B/1638